Spiritual Astrology

– Course 7 –

Spiritual Astrology

The Origins of Astro-Mythology
and Stellar Religion

C. C. Zain

The Church of Light
Los Angeles

Published in the United States in 1997 by
The Church of Light
2341 Coral Street, Los Angeles, California 90031-2916

©1997 by The Church of Light. All rights reserved

Individual chapters originally copyrighted in 1935 by
Elbert Benjamine.

Library of Congress Cataloging-in-Publication Data
Zain, C.C. (Elbert Benjamine), 1882-1951.
  Spiritual Astrology : the origins of astro-mythology and stellar
religion / C.C. Zain. —Rev. 2nd ed.
        P.   cm.   — (The Brotherhood of Light : course 7)
  Originally published: [S.7.] : E. Benjamine, 1935
  Includes index.
  ISBN 0-87887-377-5 (alk. paper) : $16.95
  1. Astrology. 2. Spiritual life miscellanea. 3. Occultism I. Title.
II. Series
BF1729.S64Z35 1997   96-12680
133.5—dc20   CIP

Spiritual Astrology may be obtained through your local bookstore
or you may order it from The Church of Light, 2341 Coral Street,
Los Angeles, CA 90031-2916, (213)226-0453.

Portions of this book not exceeding a total of 2,000 words may be
freely quoted or reprinted without permission, provided credit is given in the
following form:

Reprinted from *Spiritual Astrology* by C.C. Zain, copyright 1997,
The Church of Light.

(∞)   Printed on long-lasting acid-free paper.

Contents

List of Constellations   *vii*

1 Our Spiritual Legacy   1
2 The Fountain of Youth   23
3 Knights of King Arthur   45
4 Story of the Three Bears   67
5 The Ladder to Heaven   89
6 Is There A Santa Claus   111
7 Why Eve Was Tempted   133
8 The Marriage in Heaven   155
9 The Scorpion and the Eagle   177
10 The Bow of Bright Promise   199
11 News From the Summerland   221
12 In the Reign of Aquarius   243
13 The Tree of Life   265

Study Questions   283
Index   301
Other Brotherhood of Light Books   311

List of Constellations

Aries	19
1st Decanate—Triangulum	20
2nd Decanate—Eridanus	21
3rd Decanate—Perseus	22
Taurus	41
1st Decanate—Lepus	42
2nd Decanate—Orion	43
3rd Decanate—Auriga	44
Gemini	63
1st Decanate—Ursa Minor	64
2nd Decanate—Canis Major	65
3rd Decanate—Ursa Major	66
Cancer	85
1st Decanate—Canis Minor	86
2nd Decanate—Hydra	87
3rd Decanate—Argo	88
Leo	107
1st Decanate—Crater	108
2nd Decanate—Centaurus	109
3rd Decanate—Corvus	110
Virgo	129
1st Decanate—Bootes	130

2nd Decanate—Hercules	131
3rd Decanate—Corona Borealis	132
Libra	151
1st Decanate—Serpens	152
2nd Decanate—Draco	153
3rd Decanate—Lupus	154
Scorpio	173
1st Decanate—Ophiuchus	174
2nd Decanate—Ara	175
3rd Decanate—Corona Australis	176
Sagittarius	195
1st Decanate—Lyra	196
2nd Decanate—Aquila	197
3rd Decanate—Sagitta	198
Capricorn	217
1st Decanate—Cygnus	218
2nd Decanate—Delphinus	219
3rd Decanate—Pisces Australis	220
Aquarius	239
1st Decanate—Equuleus	240
2nd Decanate—Pegasus	241
3rd Decanate—Cetus	242
Pisces	261
1st Decanate—Cepheus	262
2nd Decanate—Andromeda	263
3rd Decanate—Cassiopeia	264

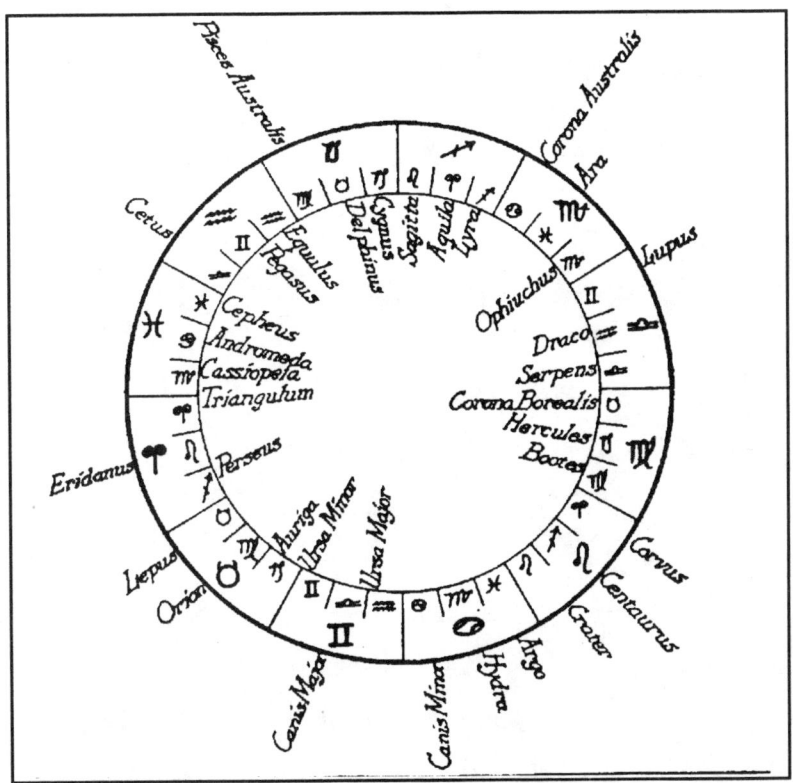

Correct relation of each constellation as picturing the influence of one section of the zodiac.

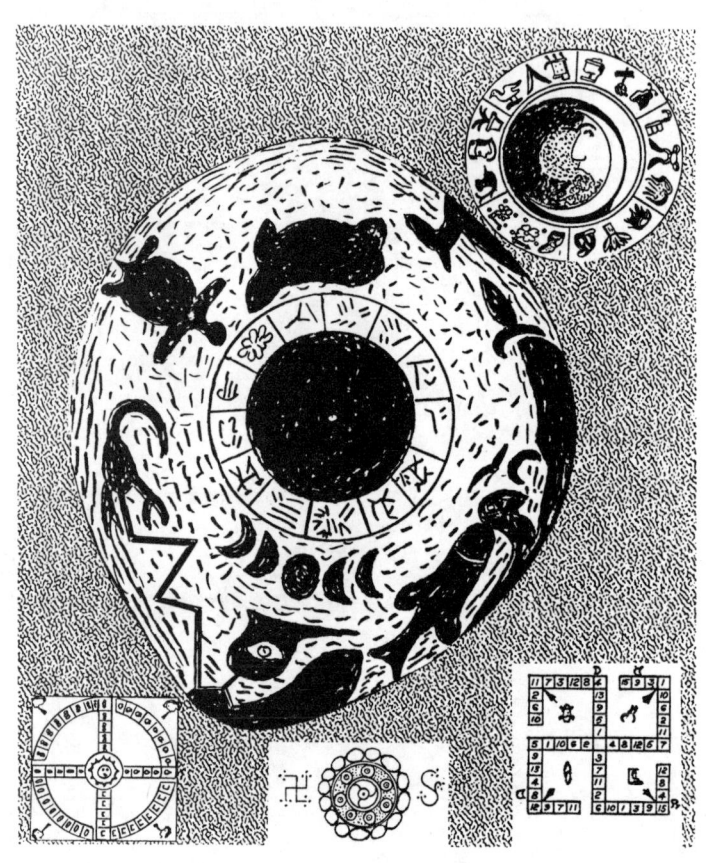

Chapter 1

Our Spiritual Legacy

A LEGACY of untold value has been left by spiritual and intellectual giants who labored in the dim and misty past. It is the purpose of these lessons to transmit this priceless heritage to the people of the present day, to whom now rightfully it belongs.

We of the present have specialized in material science, and as a result of that specialization have possessed ourselves of mechanical contrivances and an industrial achievement far superior to those of any people in the past. Yet in that past there were specialists also; the equal of any on earth today. But instead of devoting their energies to material things, their field was that of spiritual research. And they were as far in advance of our material scientists in their chosen field, as the material scientists of today are in advance of their ancient knowledge of the physical properties of things.

We are where we are today in matters of physical science because men of vast understanding like Sir Isaac Newton and Albert Einstein have labored in research and recorded their findings for other men to read. Were it not for the records left by those of unusual ability, ours would be a sorry world of muddled thought.

Such records give not merely the details of information, to which other men left to devices of their own might seldom attain, but by revealing the correct method of ascertaining the fact they eliminate wasted effort on the part of those who otherwise would follow many a blind trail before finding the one leading to it. Yet because these men, who themselves have stood upon the intellectual shoulders of other geniuses who preceded them, have left to us their findings, there is no implication of blind belief.

Not only are their findings included in the records, but the experiments which led to these findings also. And it was understood by them, and is so understood by us, that all and sundry are to have full liberty to repeat these experiments, or if they can, to devise better experiments of their own, to test the accuracy of this recorded knowledge.

Likewise, far in the past other men of exceptional talent, generation after generation, labored under conditions of exceptional advantage to acquire a knowledge, not of the chemical and mechanical properties of matter, but of the nature and possibilities, here and hereafter, of the human soul.

To them that which was of supreme interest was the character of man. Other knowledge was valuable only to the extent it could be made to contribute something which would enable the soul to reach a higher, fuller destiny.

These men also, standing on the shoulders of other inspired geniuses who preceded them, acquired vast knowledge in their chosen field; and of this knowledge they left a careful record.

In here setting forth this record, and something of the methods they employed in reaching these facts, there is no implication that anyone should accept their findings in the spirit of blind belief. No more so than that he should thus accept the findings of our chemists that each molecule of water contains one atom of oxygen and two atoms of hydrogen.

It would require more than one lifetime to perform every experiment recorded in the chemical treatise to be found in our libraries. Nevertheless, they have been performed by others, and anyone is at liberty to perform such of them as he chooses, again and again to his own satisfaction.

The laboratory of Nature is always open. Whether it be a problem in Euclid, the law of falling bodies, the influence of the planets on human life, or the survival of the personality in the spheres of the beyond, he who is willing to perform the requisite amount of labor need take no statement of fact on faith. Nor was it the desire of the ancient masters of spiritual science that he should do so.

The Language Employed In Recording the Legacy

These records left by the wisest men of a very ancient time could not, of course, have been written in the English language. Even the writing used by the Maya, a race yet surviving, and conquered by the Spaniards only about 400 years ago, can but be deciphered now sufficiently to reveal dates and their astronomical learning. The meaning of the more conventionalized characters is quite unknown.

The most ancient form of writing is the pictograph, in which the thought to be conveyed is actually, although perhaps roughly, pictured. Until modern schools were introduced the American Indian often made use of such writing. To represent good hunting, for instance, he merely painted or carved on a rock the picture of deer and other game.

The scope of true pictographs, however, is too narrow to recommend their exclusive use among a people of advanced ideas. But this scope was vastly widened through using them, not solely to picture a condition as it actually exists, but to represent other things with which the pictured object most commonly is mentally associated.

To indicate in our desert region, that there was a water-hole in a certain direction, the American Indian traced on a rock a line in that direction. Where the line ends is the water-hole; for every Indian trail, in such a region, ends only at a water-hole.

In such writing he has gone beyond simple pictograph and employed universal symbolism. He has not felt the need of picturing the water or the waterhole. He knows that the end of a trail in every Indian's mind is associated with a water-hole. When he pictures where the trail ends, he thus conveys to any other Indian the information that there water can be found. Such picture writing can be found from Mexico to Canada throughout the arid region.

We say, "The pen is mightier than the sword," to convey the idea that the written thought is superior to warfare. This also is universal symbolism, even though it be not pictured by a broken sword lying beneath an arrogant pen.

Thus in addition to that which can be recorded as a picture there is also that which can be recorded orally. The myths and legends and folklore of the various peoples of the world often are very interesting as stories. But in addition to their entertainment value, which is given to them to insure that they shall be perpetuated, they also, quite as much as a picture drawn on a rock, convey ideas of more serious import.

Either pictures or stories may have a certain attractiveness of form; but pictures are not drawn, nor stories perpetuated, by primitive peoples except as they are employed to give expression through pictograph or universal symbolism to important thoughts which there is a desire to convey to other minds.

And because the attributes of objects are fairly constant, as are also their common associations, thought conveyed in such a manner remains clear and understandable across intervening centuries and regardless of race or clime. It is in such language as this, whose meaning does not pass away, nor changed by time nor place, that the sages of old recorded their ineffable wisdom.

Source of the Legacy

Few details persist of the civilizations that once existed on the land area over which now rolls the waters of the Pacific. This land, called Mu by some of the peoples deriving from it, and termed Lemuria by those of the present day who find evidence that the lemurs had their origin there, probably was inhabited by several races in varying stages of culture.

That it actually existed there is abundant geological, biological and ethnological evidence to prove. Such proof, however, belongs more properly to Course 12, *Evolution of Life*, where the origins of life-forms and human cultures, and there spread from centers of dispersal, are considered in some detail. But as a lot of nonsense has found its way into print about this Pacific land area it may not be amiss to indicate that *The problem of Lemuria*, by Lewis Spence, is a book based upon scientific findings and is consequently free from the wild speculations written as fact that too frequently are outstanding features of other books on the subject.

There is even more abundant evidence that Atlantis once occupied some portion of what is now the Atlantic Ocean. Atlantis, by Ignatius Donelly was written many years ago, but is still a good book. *The History of Atlantis*, by Lewis Spence, brings the findings down to date, and is authoritative. But, as in the case of Lemuria (Mu), what we know about the inhabitants of this ancient land rests wholly on tradition.

That somewhere on the earth there was a people of intelligence and prowess superior to the Neanderthal Man who inhabited Europe during glacial times is not tradition, but positive knowledge. When the last ice sheet receded sufficiently to make the climate of Europe a little more attractive, the Cro-Magnon race invaded that area and exterminated its more primitive inhabitants. The indications are that they came out of the west. In cranial capacity and physique, as shown by their abundant remains, they were the equal of any race on earth today.

Also in America, as soon as the great ice sheet had receded, a people arrived from somewhere. They were not Indians, and apparently their culture extended to the Atlantic seaboard. Their flint points were first turned up in 1925 near Folsom, New Mexico, along with a type of bison now extinct. After the place where first discovered, they are called the Folsom people.

Equally certain it is that there existed some people in the distant past who knew vastly more about the unseen world, about spiritual laws, and about the influence of astrological energies upon human life than does the modern scientist. This is just as certain, and for the same reason, as that there were Cro-Magnons and Folsom people. Portions of this knowledge persist, and are being uncovered from time to time, in various areas of the world where long ago they took lodgment.

Just where the Stellar Wisdom first was practiced, and from whence it spread, there is as yet no conclusive evidence to enable us to decide. That in forms which are but modifications of an identical original it was present at the very beginning of the seven ancient centers of civilization—Egypt, India, Crete, Peru, Mexico, China and Chaldea—it is easy to demonstrate. And experience proves that wherever a particular biological form, or a culture having many complex yet identical interrelating factors, is present in different areas of the world, it had its origin in a single region of dispersal.

Atlantis and Mu certainly existed, and it is quite probable that each was inhabited by several races, some member of one of which perhaps rose to great heights in spiritual knowledge. But as a naturalist, and a student of the development and dispersal of new life-forms on earth, I find no evidence on which to base the popular conception that the inhabitants of these ancient lands were skilled in the construction or use of machinery. Nor do I believe they were the equal of present-day astronomers in making precise calculations.

In the Great Pyramid of Egypt, and in some of the embankment mounds of the Mississippi Valley of America which seem to employ the same formulas, astronomical proportions and cosmic knowledge are included which have a vast range. We do not know just how vast, because as scientists of the present day make new discoveries regarding the structure of our universe, it is revealed that such also are included in these monuments to the wisdom of the past.

On the whole, however, in so far as there is any evidence to indicate, in the work the ancients contemplated they had no need for, and did not use, the minute precision which marks the work of present day laboratory scientists. Their knowledge of astronomical ratios and cosmic relations was derived from applying the Law of Correspondences with the aid of their highly developed psychic faculties, rather than through the use of refined mechanical contrivances such as are employed today.

They were interested in the various factors, seen and unseen, with which the universe abounds, as they relate to human life and destiny, here and hereafter. And it is to their everlasting credit that they worked out a mathematics, and formulated methods of procedure, which were adequate to meet these practical requirements.

Origin of the Constellations

Without setting the date when the method as we know it, and as it has passed down to us through the Chaldeans and the Greeks was perfected, nor attempting to decide how much and when it may have been modified in its passing, we can trace the road traveled by these ancients who left to us our spiritual legacy.

We can do this with great confidence because we know that the purpose for which they studied astronomy was to be able to chart astrological influences as they affect human life, and to correlate spiritual truths with these observed influences. All the more positive can we be in thus following their steps because most of the methods they used are still similarly employed in some portion of the world today.

We know, for instance, it was desirable in that ancient time, as it is desirable today, that some point be fixed upon from which to reckon the days in the year, and from which to indicate the east-and-west position of the objects to be seen in the heavens. One cannot, very well, refer to the place of an object along a circle—either a circle of days or a circle in the sky—unless there is some established point to reckon from.

The ancient astrologers of almost every land, as far back as we can trace them, seem to have recognized the earth to be round.

Aristotle, who dominated scholasticism from the fourth century B.C. until after the time of Copernicus in the sixteenth century A.D., held and taught this view. Eratosthenes, the librarian at Alexandria, who died 196 B.C., measured the size of the earth's globe; and Hipparchus, born 160 B.C., working from the accepted idea of the Chaldean astrologers that the earth is a globe, and from his observations that the Sun varies in the speed of its orbital progress, demonstrated that the earth does not lie at the center of the Sun's (we now know apparent) orbit.

It was Christian dogma, misinterpreting, certain biblical passages, which forced its followers in many localities—although Aristotle was still considered the better authority by many scholars—on pain of punishment to accept a flat earth with four corners.

Because a conspicuous star is so easily located such may at first have been chosen, to mark the line extending southward from the apparently immovable Pole Star, from which the positions eastward of the other stars could be located. The conjunction of the Sun with this star also could have been used to start the year. But in time it was found that some stars have a motion relative to others, and that the position of the Sun on the longest and shortest days of the year was shifting westward among the stars.

It became apparent, therefore, that the best point from which to locate stars and planets in reference to east-and-west, and from which also to commence the year, is the place in the heavens occupied by the Sun when the days and nights are equal. And as the spring is looked forward to with such eagerness by people who have felt the oppressive weight of winter, the Vernal Equinox was the one chosen.

Because it is the best starting point, it is still so used by astronomers; both the timing and east-and-west positions of the stellar bodies being stated by them as so far from the Vernal Equinox, or first point of Aries.

They draw a line from the Pole Star directly south through the point on the equator where the Sun crosses it. This line, called the Prime Meridian, cuts off the old year and the old circle of stars. It is 0 hours of Sidereal Time, 0 degrees of Right Ascension, and 0 degrees of Zodiacal Longitude where it cuts the celestial equator. It is thus the point both where and when a new cycle starts.

It had been observed that people born within 30 days after this chosen starting point, that is, from March 21 to April 21, were aggressive, used their heads when taking the offensive, and were given to leadership and to "butting in" on the affairs of others. In selecting a symbolical pictograph to represent these Aries qualities nothing seemed so appropriate as the Ram.

When it was found that people born in the following 30 days, from April 21 to May 21, were slow to anger, but violent and headstrong when once aroused, that they did not turn aside from obstacles, but stubbornly crushed their way through them by force and perseverance, the Bull was selected as best representing these Taurus traits.

The pictures thus selected to convey the outstanding qualities of those born under each 30 degree section of the path of the Sun were traced in the sky as stellar constellations. These constellated pictures are not each 30 degrees in extent, as are the signs which they describe. Some are more and some are less than 30 degrees. Yet a pictograph system must portray the first major division of the zodiac with the first constellation, and the second major division with the second constellation in the circle, wherever these may have shifted in the precessional cycle.

It was also anciently found, and made constant use of by the Chaldeans, that each of these twelve signs could be divided into three sections, and each of these sections, which were called decanates, had a distinct influence of its own; only less pronounced than that of the sign itself.

Therefore, to express in pictograph writing the influence of these 36 sections of the zodiac, embracing 10 degrees each, the ancients traced the 36 ultra-zodiacal constellations in the sky.

And in placing these symbolical pictographs of the influence of the 36 decanates of the zodiac in the heavens, they used the same system as they did when they traced the pictures of the 12 signs. That is, the first ultra-zodiacal constellation pictured the first 10 degrees of the zodiac, the second ultra-zodiacal constellation pictured the second 10 degrees of the zodiac, and so on.

Modern maps of the sky have many more than 48 constellations, because with the study of modern astronomy, kings and notables desired something placed in the heavens to remember them by, and the astronomers were accommodating. But the Greeks visited Chaldea and brought home the celestial sphere of the Chaldeans. And these old Greek sources show only the 48 constellations given in the illustration on page x in the front matter of this book.

To form 48 distinct pictures, both north and south hemispheres of the heavens were used. To place pictures covering much of the two hemispheres on a single plane surface in their true relation to their distance from the commencement of the zodiac, causes pictures of one hemisphere greatly to overlap and obliterate the outlines of pictures of the other hemisphere. Hence, if the pictures of all 48 constellations are given on a single page, their true positions must be distorted.

The illustration on page x thus gives the ancient picture of each of the 48 constellations in correct detail, and proper proportion as to size; but moved sufficiently from its true place in the zodiac that the complete picture can be shown. The relation to the particular section of the zodiac which each ultra-zodiacal constellation represents in pictograph, is here denoted by the symbol of the sign to which the decanate belongs, and by a number showing whether it relates to the first, second, or third decanate of this sign. The diagram on page ix shows this relationship fully.

The System Used to Denote the Zodiacal Relationship of Each Constellation

Modern astronomers, because their work largely relates to observation, find it more convenient to locate positions in the heavens east from the Prime Meridian. Thus the east-west positions of the planets and stars are given in the Nautical Almanac for each day of the year in terms of Right Ascension.

But a vast amount of observation both ancient and modern—the Anu Enlil Series of the Chaldeans, which recorded both the positions in the heavens and the coincident events which happened on the earth, alone extending unbroken for over a thousand years—has made it clear that it is the position of a planet along the path of the Sun, and not its distance eastward from the Prime Meridian, which determines its influence upon human life.

Not only the signs of the zodiac and their decanates are measured along the path of the Sun, called the ecliptic, but the aspects that are formed between the planets, both in a birth-chart and by progression, are calculated along this path. The same point which is cut by the Prime Meridian is used as a starting place, that is, the first point of Aries; but the line of reference instead of extending south from the Pole Star through this point, extends south through it from the Pole of the Ecliptic. The distance from the Vernal Equinox, and from this line of reference, along the path of the Sun, or ecliptic, which a star or constellation is, is called its Zodiacal Longitude.

Because it is the Zodiacal Longitude of a heavenly body, instead of its Right Ascension, which determines its influence over human life, astrologers do not use the positions of the heavenly bodies as they are given in the *Nautical Almanac* in erecting and progressing birth-charts. Instead, they use an astronomical ephemeris, in which the ephemeris maker has conveniently, and by means of a simple formula, converted the Right Ascension positions of the Nautical Almanac into the Zodiacal Longitude which is required in all astrological work.

Now as astrologers of every age have used the Zodiacal Longitude positions of the heavenly bodies in their work—the star tables of both Hipparchus and Ptolemy including such zodiacal longitudes—it is apparent that if they wished to indicate the order of sequence of pictures drawn in the sky they would use Zodiacal Longitude to indicate it. And that is just what we find they did.

The outlines of these pictures are not suggested by the contour of lines of stars. The pictures are imposed over star groups where their sequence would correspond to the same sequence of the sections of the zodiac which they were drawn to explain. The boundaries of the constellated figures, consequently, are quite arbitrary.

Modern astronomers, in ignorance of their true purport, have expanded some of the constellations to embrace adjacent areas, and contracted others to allow for the inclusion of new ones not recognized in ancient times. Thus in the matter of their size and sequence no reliance can be placed upon modern astronomical atlases.

Fortunately, about 1820, Alexander Jamieson published in a school atlas the pictured constellations of the ancients, with Longitude, Declination, Right Ascension, and Latitude of each correctly mapped for that year. Jamieson obtained these from some large, highly emblazoned, foreign monkish charts, which were reduced according to scale. Whence Jamieson obtained these old celestial maps, no one appears to know. But they are the most authentic maps of the ancient heavens we now possess, and are to be found reproduced in Henry Melville's *Veritas*, published in London in 1874, which only recently has gone out of print.

We are under no obligation to accept the Ram as the proper picture of the influence of the first 30 degrees of the zodiac; or that the Sea Goat, able to swim in water, travel on the land, and scale the mountain heights, correctly portrays the diplomatic qualities and vaunting ambition of our Capricorn friends, over whom the tenth 30 degree section of the zodiac holds particular sway. Yet our everyday astrological observations convince us that these pictographs have been given their proper allocations.

Nor do we need to rest on any arbitrary method of sequence to convince ourselves that the pictured constellation corresponding to any decanate of the zodiac really portrays the significant quality over which that 10 degree section has special influence. Thousands of astrologers are using these decanate influences in their work. They have found that the picture and its Keyword accurately describe the influence of each.

Thus when we trace the manner in which they were given their proper place in the sky, we find it was after the system most direct and easily understood:

Starting after the first constellation which was to picture the first 10 degree section of the zodiac, no matter how far north or south the following ones were placed, the first point of their pictured outlines touched by Zodiacal Longitude determined their order of sequence. According to this simplest of methods the second constellation, picturing the second decanate of the zodiac, was placed so that the portion of its outline nearest 0 degrees Aries was second in Zodiacal Longitude. The tenth ultra-zodiacal constellation, picturing the tenth decanate of the zodiac, in that portion of its outline nearest to 0 degrees Aries, was tenth in Zodiacal Longitude. And the thirty-sixth ultra-zodiacal constellation, Cassiopeia, picturing the last decanate in the zodiac, was farthest removed in the Zodiacal Longitude of that portion of its outline nearest 0 degrees Aries, following eastward around the circle.

The proper order of sequence, both according to the Zodiacal

Longitude of the most westward point in the outline of each ultra-zodiacal constellation and according to the findings of research in natal astrology, is given in picture and in diagram on pages ix and x.

The Method Used to Perpetuate the Spiritual Teachings

The objects sought by the ancients in these pictures, however, were not merely to portray the influence of a section of the zodiac over human life, but also to set forth the particular spiritual teaching which was equally related to the same zodiacal section.

Each position in the sky that had an influence over human conduct, to them implied that there should be a definite teaching which revealed how the individual could overcome the threatened danger, or how he could take fullest advantage of the spiritual opportunity offered.

Natal astrology was not ignored. It was used as an avenue by which to make life on earth more successful, to the advantage of the individual and of society as a whole. But it was never lost sight of that the soul existed before incarnation in human form, and that it would continue to exist and function after the dissolution of the physical body. Therefore, they deemed it of even greater importance to know the spiritual trends associated with each astrological position than it was merely to know its influence as affecting the material fortune.

It was these spiritual teachings which defined the relation of the soul to other entities and to the cosmic whole, as revealed by the influence of the various sections of the zodiac, that the wise ones of old most earnestly desired to perpetuate, and to pass on to coming generations as the most valuable of all possible bequests. Yet the amount of information which could be conveyed by a single symbolical pictograph was narrowly restricted to the ability of others coming later to interpret it.

There is, however, also an oral form of universal symbolism commonly employed by primitive people. It conveys information through the avenue of a story. Therefore, to make correct interpretation of the pictographs drawn in the sky more certain, and to give details that were difficult to incorporate in such pictures, those who traced the constellations wove about each a symbolic story.

These stories, modified by time and custom though they are, still

Spiritual Astrology

clearly reveal their correct stellar relationship. Some of the constellations and some of the stories, like those relating to Halloween and the destruction of the world, to May Day and the May Pole Dance, and to the Great Bear that circles the northern pole, are to be found among the people of every continent. Others are now less universally known; yet still are to be found as the cherished myths of certain peoples.

Thus it is that the sacred literature and the sacred customs retained by various peoples, when collected and interpreted according to the universal symbolism employed by those who gave them origin, afford a clear exposition of the Stellar Wisdom of the past. Racial memory, even though their meaning has long been lost, still feels their sacredness, still feels that they have spiritual import, and still preserves them, even as lifeless cloaks from which the vitality they once embraced, and which rightfully they still should clothe, has long since departed.

In each of the twelve lessons to follow, using the same universal symbolism in reference to the zodiac that was employed by those who first traced the constellated pictures, and using the stories about the characters thus pictured that are still retained in myth, legend and sacred custom, I shall indicate the spiritual teachings which originally were attached to one of the zodiacal constellations and the three constellations picturing its decanates.

In each instance I trust to be able not merely to indicate the spiritual doctrine taught by a constellation, but to point out the obvious implications of the universal symbolism employed by those who drew the picture in the sky and told a story to still further explain its purport. And I hope to do this in so clear a manner that the reader can easily discern the process followed by the ancients in thus perpetuating their findings, and that he will be able to recognize in each instance just why they adopted the picture and story employed, and thus to discern how wisely they selected each as best fitted to transmit the idea they wished to convey.

Why Moderns Are So Ignorant of the Stellar Wisdom

Their wisdom in using pictures among the stars which the vandal hand of man has been unable to erase, and stories which have persisted in sacred literature, or like that of Santa Claus, in spite of the accepted sacred literature, is not merely demonstrated by the history of the past, but by events of the present day.

It has been the almost universal custom of those who rose to power, for the purpose of fastening their own pet religious beliefs upon the minds of their followers, as completely as possible to destroy all records and remembrance of every preceding religion. Even the name, as well as the beliefs, of Akhenaten, that most spiritual ruler of Egypt, was chiseled from temple and tomb wherever found.

In the Alexandrian Library, founded by Ptolemy Soter about 300 B.C., had been collected, in so far as vast resources and research could obtain it, the written knowledge of the world, reputed to represent 700,000 volumes. It was over these scientific documents and treasures of literature, in so far as they had been collected, that Eratosthenes had been brought from upper Egypt to act as custodian. No wonder he could measure the globe and lay down precedents for finding latitude on the earth's surface which in principle are still followed by the mariners of our day!

When the Roman emperors adopted Christianity they saw in this great body of scientific knowledge and spiritual tradition a menace to the blind belief they demanded of their subjects. They destroyed the Alexandrian Library, and not content with burning books, they demolished all statuary, wherever found, that would give any inkling of the wisdom of the past. Of the Alexandrian volumes that escaped the ravages of Imperial Rome, the Mohammedans, equally as fanatical in their desire to preserve only the Bible and the Koran, made short work as they invaded westward.

When America was discovered it was rich in astrological wisdom. But the decree went out that every vestige of that knowledge, which was looked upon as diabolical, should be destroyed.

In The Church of Light Quarterly I have published articles—Stellar Religion and Healing of Akhenaten (Egypt); Stellar Religion of Southwest Indians; Astrology of the Aztecs; Posidonius and Chaldea; Itzamna, Great Initiate of the Maya; The Arkansas Astrological Stone, etc. in which has been set forth in considerable detail the Stellar Wisdom of various peoples in so far as it has been uncovered by modern research. These articles are available in the book, *Astrological Lore of All Ages* by Elbert Benjamine.

In this course, therefore, the stellar attainments of particular peoples will receive no consideration. Instead, the attention will be devoted to indicating the spiritual doctrines which in part measure were retained by all, in much larger measure by some and in lesser measure by others, and in full measure probably only by the most enlightened few.

Even the detailed explanation of the Aztec Calendar Stone which forms the lower illustration on page xi must be referred to the article on Aztec Astrology. Suffice it here to say that it is a single season calendar by which not only the day of the year, but the zodiacal position of both Sun and Moon could be ascertained on that day. Too large to destroy, as it is of basaltic porphyry eleven feet, eight inches in diameter, and weighs some twenty-four tons, sometime between 1551 and 1559, after the execution of such Aztecs as were known to possess historical or astrological knowledge, Friar Alonso de Montufar had the stone secretly buried.

No one suspected its existence for over 200 years until in 1790, when some workmen, excavating in the Plaza Mayor, unearthed this huge testimonial of astrological knowledge, and it now rests in the Mexican National Museum.

The picture above it, preserved by Veytia, gives the names of the 13 days in each week, and the 7 weeks in each season, the dots being, of course, the universal symbols for the number of the week or day. It is thus, together with the universal symbolism in its center, merely a less conventionalized reproduction of the same factors sculptured on the Aztec Calendar Stone.

All four seasons of the Aztec Solar-Lunar calendar have been preserved to us by Diego Duran, who paid for his disregard of Spanish orders by being burned alive. The sketch, which was included in his "History of the Indians of New Spain," written earlier than 1588, is reproduced at the lower lefthand corner of the illustration on page xii. The diagram at the lower right-hand corner of the illustration explains just how it was used to find the relation between Sun and Moon on any day, and to find when any given aspect of Moon to Sun recurred throughout the year.

At the upper right-hand corner of the illustration on page xii is the Triskelion Calendar used by the Aztecs, as preserved by Clavigero. By its means the Aztecs and other people who used it, could determine any distance in the future or the past, when an eclipse would occur and where visible, also when New Moons would occur, and which house of the chart they would occupy.

In the lower center of the illustration is a sketch of a date stone found on a Tennessee tomb, which employs both the Triskelion and the Swastika Calendars, after the Aztec manner, to record the time of an important burial. To left and right of it are Triskelion and Swastika symbols as commonly found in Europe.

The main part of the illustration on page xii represents the Arkansas Astrological Stone. It was found a few years ago by a boat builder on the bank of Lake Hamilton, which is formed by damming the water of the Ouachita River near Hot Springs, Arkansas.

This Astrological Stone, although using quite different names for the 13 days in each week, and for the 7 weeks in each of the four seasons of the year, employs the same method, and determines the relation of Sun and Moon on any day of the year in precisely the same way, as does the Aztec Calendar Stone. In addition there are other symbols which relate to the astrological practice and the occult knowledge of the mound builders. These are fully explained in the article.

There is no call, I am sure, to give further instances of the fanatical endeavors which at various times have swept all important lands in the effort to obliterate all knowledge of preceding beliefs and customs; for we can see the process now in operation. Soviet Russia has placed a ban on God and religion; the Scopes trial made it illegal to teach evolution in the schools of Tennessee; and Hitler, dictator of Germany, not content to decide the religion his people must adopt, has made it illegal even to possess any book or literature relating to astrology.

The Religion of the Stars in Stone

Yet in spite of the ease with which, for the most part, the more intricate astrological knowledge could be destroyed, so enthusiastically did the people of late prehistoric times build their monuments to the four chief tenets of THE RELIGION OF THE STARS, that the combined vandalism of subsequent ages has failed appreciably to remove them.

Huge stone monuments commemorating the stellar belief are to be found wherever there is land in a belt extending entirely around the world. Thousands of them, embracing four different types, still stand. In England, in France, in Egypt, in Mesopotamia, in India, in Peru, in Mexico and in the United States, there exist these stupendous stone records of beliefs inherited from a still more ancient people.

Even as the zodiac is divided by solstice and equinox into four quadrants, each represented by an arm of the swastika and presided over by the Bull, the Lion, the Eagle or the Man, so the ancient Stellar Religion had four corresponding outstanding doctrines, which like the quadrants of the swastika (see page xii) united in the complete circle of spirit to express a single all-embracing spiritual doctrine.

Dome-shaped mounds were used for magical ceremonies and for initiation. They are so used today by primitive peoples, the kiva of the Indians of the Southwest being a single example of many that can be cited. These were places where they went to demonstrate the hidden powers of the mind.

The sign Taurus, governing one quadrant, is the exaltation of the Moon, ruler of Mentality and of the feminine in nature. It is an earthy sign, and the dome of earth often was provided with a small entrance to the interior. Here then we have a teaching regarding the gestation of thought, and a record of the belief that man, through the proper exercise of his mentality, can control his own life and destiny, here and hereafter.

Huge, straight shafts of rock, upright like the rays of the midday Sun, symbolize the virile masculine powers which are associated with the sign Leo, which governs another heavenly quadrant. The house Leo naturally occupies in a birth-chart is the one concerned with pleasure, love affairs and children.

The love of husband for wife and of wife for husband is a most holy and sacred thing, and is one of the most constructive forces that man can utilize. The love of parents for their children approaches the deific in its sanctity, and germinates the seed of that unselfish love that alone makes immortality possible. These straight shafts of stone, and the round towers which dot the globe, both record the belief of an ancient people that love is the way to life.

A horizontal slab supported by two or more pillars presents the form of a doorway. These dolmens are more than doorways, for the conspicuous feature of their construction is the flat, table-like surface presented by the slab held thus high above the ground. It strikes the eye at once as a plane, a plane above the earth.

The third quadrant of the heavens is presided over by Scorpio, ruling the house of death in a natural birth-chart. In its higher aspect it is pictured as an eagle. Thus does the slab of stone supported by two pillars indicate that death is the doorway to a higher plane of conscious existence, and that passing through it man ceases to crawl in the dust like a scorpion and soars, like an eagle, to a life of greater power and freedom.

Aquarius, presiding over the fourth quadrant of the zodiac, measures the influence of the stars with one hand, while water running from his urn flows down upon the earth even as do the vibrations of the planets.

Huge concentric circles of stone portray the orbits of the planets. These cromlechs, as they are called, bring to us the same message that is revealed by the constellation of the Man. They attest to the belief of those, who at the cost of tremendous labor erected them, that the planets have an influence over human life and destiny.

When these four ancient doctrines are united, their mutual implications become as obvious as that a circle is formed by the united zodiacal quadrants. The whole, as a logical necessity, then becomes summed up as the spiritual admonition, CONTRIBUTE YOUR UTMOST TO UNIVERSAL WELFARE.

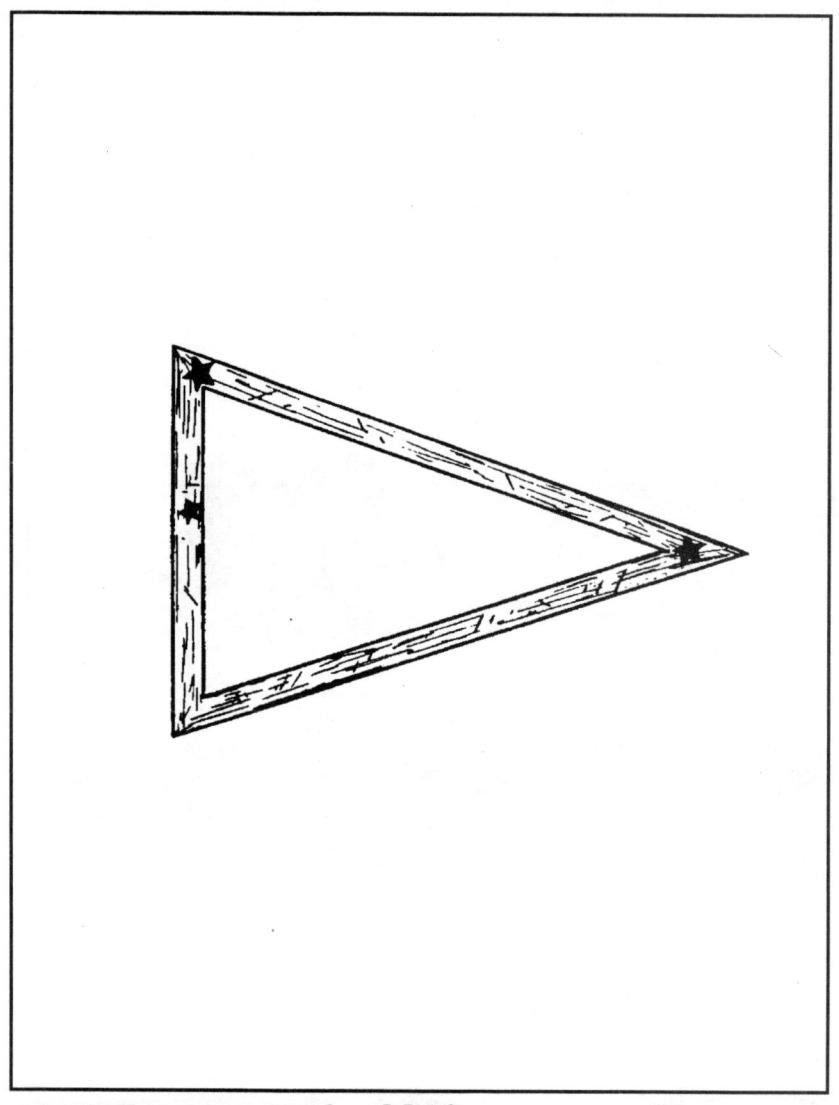

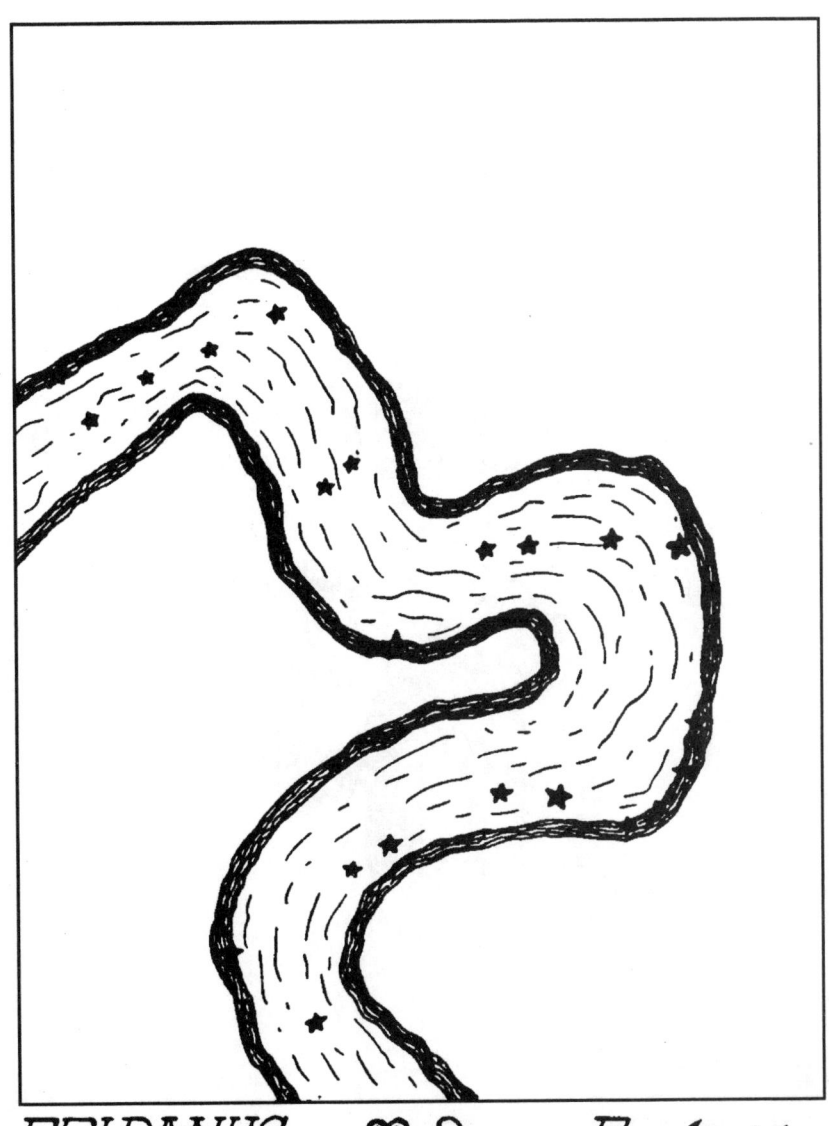

ERIDANUS ♈-♌ Exaltation

Chapter 2

The Fountain of Youth

PASSOVER; Ancient and Modern.
Only in spring occurs that significant astronomical phenomenon which anciently was celebrated by the feast of the passover.

This festival, in its essential elements, although called by different names in other lands, was not unique to the Jews. Nor was its observance confined to the Old World; for we find the American Indians also celebrating in quite as appropriate a fashion the passing of the Sun from darkness into light.

The Hopis, for instance, eagerly watch for the time in spring when the Sun shall rise exactly behind a certain peak of the San Francisco range. For generations they have recognized that when the Sun thus climbs the mountain, to balance a fiery globe atop its lofty spire, that days and nights are equal; and thence forward the day in length will exceed the night.

Because at this time the nights are thus equal to the days, we moderns call it the equinox. It is, in truth, the passing over to the summer half of the year, from the dreary months of winter darkness.

When we think of the privation endured by primitive people, and even by our American pioneers, as their stored supplies became exhausted at the end of the season of snow and cold, we can have no surprise that they universally celebrated the passing of the Sun over the celestial equator from south to north, heralding, as it does, the commencement of the growing period with its new supply of food and its relief from the icy blasts that make demands for special clothes and shelter.

The less provident people of our state of Michigan are wont to say as winter draws to an end that if they can only hold out until the leeks come that their troubles will be over. The leek is an edible plant closely related to the onion. It grows abundantly in the Michigan woods, affords considerable nourishment, and is one of the very first of the "bitter herbs" to show green above the ground.

Why astronomers, both ancient and modern, considered the Vernal Equinox, or 0 degrees Aries, as the best starting point for both time and for measuring the east-west position of a star or planet in the sky, has fully been explained in chapter 1, as also was there set forth the method followed in selecting the pictograph symbols that they traced in the heavens, and about which they told stories and established customs by way of further explanation.

In this language of universal symbols which they employed the winter half of the circle, in which the darkness exceeds the light, is representative of our physical world and its obscuring clouds of misconceptions. The spiritual world, and the spiritual life, are referred to the summer half of the celestial circle.

Even as a week had seven days, one ruled over by each planet, so the life of man had seven corresponding phases of activity. The Sun, of course, was then as now, recognized as the source of virile power.

Among the Jews, who had acquired some of the ancient Stellar Wisdom, it was desired that each boy should be consecrated to a spiritual life of constructive effort. That each planet should have opportunity to impress its influence upon the child before this consecration, and that thus all seven phases of activity should be impressed by the ceremony, seven full days were allowed to elapse after birth.

When the Sun had circled the zodiac and passed over the Vernal Equinox into Aries, a new year began. This to many ancient peoples as well as the Jews, symbolized the transition from the physical world to the spiritual plane of life. To signify that the child, while still on earth, was consecrated to a life of spiritual endeavor, a ceremony was instituted which should represent the circling of the Sun and its annual transition. On the eighth day the boy was circumcised.

As the section of the zodiac pictured by the Ram, into which the Sun moves as it completes its transition, embraces 30 degrees, at its very commencement it could hardly be considered a full grown sheep. Not only among the Jews, but among other ancient people, the first entrance of the Sun into the sign was associated with the beginning of a ram, that is, it was considered to signify a Lamb.

Using the blood of a Lamb as a token that a new and spiritual life had been entered upon was not a custom confined to Christian and Jew; it was part of that universal symbolism employed by all peoples who had inherited traditions based upon stellar correspondences.

The land of Egypt was referred to by the Jews as the land of darkness, corresponding to the dark signs of the zodiac, in which the Sun is prisoner before it passes over into the summer signs. The last of these signs, Pisces, has astrological rule over slavery and imprisonment, and the Israelites were captive in Egypt. The three constellations picturing its decanates are Cepheus, the king of Ethiopia, who sits on a throne; Cassiopeia, the queen of Ethiopia; and Andromeda, their daughter, who is chained to a rock.

The day anciently, as at present, commenced at midnight. When the Sun reaches the Vernal Equinox and first touches the Lamb it requires about six hours after midnight before it rises. Those sections of the zodiac through which it already has passed are of the old order, the old cycle, and are thus among the first born. Also on that day before the Sun appears, and after midnight, there are first born, rising through the house of birth to appear above the horizon ahead of the Sun, Capricorn, the goat; Equuleus, the horse; Pegasus, the winged horse; the king; the queen; and their captive daughter. Yet these all belong to that part of the celestial circle cut off by the passover into Aries. Aries is a militant sign, and thus the Bible relates,

> And it came to pass that at midnight the Lord smote all the first-born in the land of Egypt, from the firstborn of Pharaoh that sat on the throne, unto the first-born of the captive that was in the dungeon; and all the first-born of cattle.

Exodus gives the rules to be observed during the passover ceremonies. No leaven bread was permitted in the house for a period of seven days, leaven being the symbol of impurity and pollution. At the feast the Lamb could not be eaten raw, nor sodden with water, but must be roasted; for Aries is a fiery sign. And it must be eaten with bitter herbs, to indicate the new growth and that the transition from physical life is not without discomfort. To show that the transition should be complete, avoiding earthbound conditions, any that remained in the morning must be cremated.

The Lamb to be used at the passover ceremony must be without blemish, in the first year of its life, and when slain, its blood was to be daubed on the lintel and two side posts of the door to the house. Thousands of doorways, formed of huge stones, where no houses have been, remain in various parts of the world where erected by prehistoric people. On top of two or more upright pillars, there is placed a huge slab of rock to indicate a plane above the earth, that is, a plane of life where people consciously dwell and perform their activities after they have passed through that doorway which commonly we call death.

The feast was to be attended, "with your loins girded, your shoes on your feet, and your staff in your hand; and ye shall eat it in haste." The Jews who attended as thus instructed were plainly prepared to go places and do things. The daubing of the lintels with the blood of a Lamb portrays in universal symbolism the belief of those who originated the ceremony that we enter physical life through a doorway of pain and suffering, and that we take our departure to the next life through another doorway no less difficult. Yet because the blood used is that of the animal by which birth and happier days are represented, it also expresses the conviction that the new life will be an improvement over the one from which the passover has been made.

In a still broader sense the passover of the year has its counterpart in the precessional cycle. But instead of the Sun passing over the Vernal Equinox, the boundary between sections of the stellar circle does the passing. Thus have we now passed over into the Aquarian Age.

Pisces, the sign from which the world is passing, rules not merely imprisonment and restrictions, but crime and its punishment. It gave us a heaven which to most would be nothing more than a prison, and it taught us the doctrine of everlasting torment in hell.

With one hand Aquarius measures the influence of the stars, and with the other pours down his blessings. Right now the world is enduring the pangs of its birth into a heaven of new knowledge. The blood on the doorposts are but the incidents of this passing.

Many truths this new Aquarian Age will unfold. But none,

perhaps, of greater import to the human race that a detailed knowledge of conditions in the after life, of the best training here to fit the individual for his eventual responsibilities there, and the establishment of a non-restricted system of communication between those who live and function on the different planes.

Aries has been given the Key-phrase, I Am, on account of those born under this influence, more than other people, viewing things from the standpoint of Individual survival and expression. Because of this, because they are pioneers who venture into new lands, and because it is here that the transition symbolically takes place, it is eminently fitting that the ancients associated the Ram with their teachings of survival. The text they sought to convey by Aries has been expressed by the poet:

> There is no death! What seems so is transition:
> This life of mortal breath
> Is but a suburb of the life elysian
> Whose portal we call death.

The Drama of the Triangle

If one has ever watched an old ram lead his flock, the use of the Ram to head the procession of constellations will call for no further explanation. The section covered by Aries, however, embraces a full 30 degrees, and is divided into three sub-sections, called decanates, of 10 degrees, each having a distinct influence, which calls for a distinct spiritual teaching, or text, of its own. And until a little thought is given to the matter it is not so obvious why the very first 10 degrees of the zodiac should be represented, not by some heroic figure like Perseus or Hercules, but by something as prosaic and unromantic as the diagram of a triangle.

Yet as each of the other constellations of the 48 was carefully chosen and given its particular place where best it would convey specific information, we must conclude that the placing of a triangle at the beginning of the circle of decanates was not due to lack of more glamorous figures, but was prompted by the necessity of conveying some profound meaning.

Universal symbolism, a language which does not change with

age nor race nor clime, is based upon common human experience. And as human nature in its essentials changes but little with the ages, our first response to the word triangle is probably that of bygone times. The domestic triangle is a favorite plot of stage and story, and a never-ending source of news headlines and neighborhood gossip. But in its more universal application just what does such a triangle imply?

Essentially, even as the green coloring matter in leaves in the presence of sunlight exerts so strong an attraction for the atoms of carbon in the air that they desert the oxygen atoms, with which they have been united as carbon dioxide, to enter a new partnership with atoms of the leafy structure; so does a domestic triangle embrace two forces acting upon a single center, yet pulling in a different direction.

The three sides of the constellated triangle express, better than anything of which I can think, two energies of different polarity, that is, with a different type of motion, united, and the result of that union.

While such a domestic triangle as has been mentioned, suggested by its drama quite as much as by the frequency of its occurrence, is indicated by the starry trine, there is another domestic triangle of still more common occurrence. Father, mother, child, are portrayed in the heavens, have positions of honor on both the tarot and the common playing cards, and represent the means by which nature reproduces and perpetuates the species.

Thus the domestic triangle, suggested by the trine of heaven, upon reflection reveals to us that the interaction of two forces, the diverse pull of polarity, has a potency in either of two directions: It may either build up or tear down, be devoted to creation and construction, or turned into channels which disrupt and destroy.

Although our physical lives are entirely dependent upon such constructive use of carbon taken from the air by leaves, all food coming to us either directly from the vegetable world or indirectly through other animals that have so obtained it, I believe we should seek in antiquity for the reason that the triangle, thus revealed as all-important, should have been placed at the very beginning of the zodiac.

Let us, then, take the story which has come down to us from the remote past which serves as commentary to the first pictograph in the decanate circle. We might well suppose that the start of the starry circle would find explanation at the commencement of some sacred work. Let me, therefore, quote the first three verses of the Bible:

> In the beginning God created the heaven and the earth. And the earth was without form and void; and darkness was upon the face of the deep. And the Spirit of God moved upon the face of the waters. And God said. Let there be light: and there was light.

Great scientific learning is possessed at the present day. But with it all no better nor more scientific description of the bringing into existence of the material universe has ever offered. Out in the infinite spaces, Millikan believes matter is being created, and Jeans believes matter is being destroyed; as revealed by the terrific energy released in the formation of the cosmic ray.

Many scientists hold that stresses in the ether shear out right-hand and left-hand spirals of motion which are positive and negative charges of electricity such as, according to Millikan and Jeans, form the protons and electrons of matter which out in space is being created or destroyed. It is the same kind of matter of which our world is composed.

Substituting the ether of science for heaven, and the matter sheared out of it for the earth, and we possess two sides of the constellated triangle, and a Bible description of the beginning of physical existence which at every point is parallel to that offered by material science.

Until there was the stress of two forces, strains pulling the ether in diverse direction, our men of science say that existence was without form and void; and as light is a particular motion in the ether, there was darkness everywhere.

Cosmic rays, resulting from the creation or destruction of matter, are invisible, as are many other waves in the ether, and thus even when ether and matter, as heaven and earth, were given existence, darkness may still have accompanied these waves; moving upon the face of the deep.

Nevertheless, this interaction, or polarity, generates movement; in fact, no movement, physical, mental or spiritual, ever takes place apart from the union of positive and negative potencies. Thus whether visible or not, when heaven and earth, positive and negative, ether and matter are present, there is action, which, as it is chiefly wave-like and not understood as to its exact nature, is well described as the Spirit of God moving upon the face of the waters; the third side of the universal triangle.

When, however, this energy reaches an intensity that causes the electrons revolving in given orbits about the nucleus of an atom, to make big jumps from their accustomed orbits to other paths, there is a spilling out of energy into the surrounding ether which sets up those wave-frequencies that we see, and call light. Light, therefore, while not the only product of the first interaction of positive and negative forces that divided ether from matter, heaven from earth, was a product that is of paramount importance to human life. As previously indicated, all the food we eat is manufactured by the green leaves of plants, and only in the presence of light.

To trace the universal application of this creative principle would be to encompass the entire realm of science, philosophy and the innumerable relations of life; for the first factor leading to every result is the union of the other two sides of the triangle.

As we are interested in the signs, decanates and constellations, let us consider how they are located and measured; by triangles, of course. Distances along the zodiacal circle from the Vernal Equinox, and distances north and south of the celestial equator, in fact, all distances considered in astrology, are measured and expressed in degrees of arc.

Such an arc is really one side of a triangle, the other two sides being the lines extending from its ends and meeting at the point of observation. The number of degrees east or west, north or south, either in the sky or on the surface of the earth, is merely an expression of the angle between the two lines which extend to the extremities of the third side of the triangle, which is an arc.

The science of spherical geometry and the science of trigonometry were both developed in olden times, and made skilled use of by Hipparchus before the Christian era, to plot the stars and constellations and measure the relations of the planets, each to the other.

The first measurements of time, and also of the positions of the Sun, were made by shadows cast by a stake upon the ground. By such shadows recorded at noon on the longest day and the shortest day of the year, the Chinese, in 1100 B.C. ascertained the inclination of the earth to the ecliptic. The stake and the shadow on the ground formed the sides of a right angled triangle, the hypotenuse being the line from the top of the stake to the end of the shadow. Measuring this angle at the two specified dates, and dividing by two, gave them the angular distance north and south of the equator of the tropic of Cancer and the tropic of Capricorn.

The astrolabe was invented to measure the angular elevation of stars and other bodies which do not cast a shadow which can be measured. And as an astrolabe was a clumsy thing to use aboard a rolling ship, in rather modern times the sextant was developed from it as chief aid to navigation.

Thus it is that triangulation enters now into all surveying on the earth, and all plotting of the heavens; and any mariner who would venture far from land without an instrument by which through the use of triangulation based on his observation of Sun or Moon or stars he can locate his latitude, would be deemed mad.

The measurement of angles—triangulation—is not merely the first step in astronomical knowledge and astrological practice, but the importance of the trinity at the beginning of everything has been recognized by all the great religions of the world: Father, Son and Holy Ghost of Christendom; Brahma, Vishnu and Siva of the Hindus; Osiris, Isis and Horus of ancient Egypt.

Creation involves a trinity, as also does destruction. It is only when the union of contending or divergent factions is properly directed that we attain true progress. Either in our mental conceptions or in our political systems, there must be some destruction of the old, worn tissues, to give place for the sound and new. Yet if the old is destroyed too swiftly and completely, there is insufficient power for recovery.

Those who are born from March 21 to March 31, while the Sun is in the decanate pictured by Triangulum, are distinguished for their Activity. And the starry triangle itself sets forth in its own symbolical language the text: *All Life, Thought and Action Are the Product of the Union of Positive and Negative Potencies.*

The Fountain of Eternal Youth

As the first 30 degrees of the zodiac are pictured by a Ram to denote that they relate to creative energies, we may be sure, as already we have found in relation to the domestic trine, that the other two decanates also have to do with the creative trinity.

We find the Leo-decanate to be pictured by a river; the significance of which, I believe, is clearly set forth in the second verse of the Bible; for as the land can bring forth only when united to water, so in the story of creation, as soon as heaven and earth were manifest, the Spirit of God moved upon the face of the waters. That is, water is used immediately, even while the earth was without form and void, to symbolize the medium, or agent, through which the Spirit of God accomplished His purpose.

Now what is this thing in human life having a wave-like motion which is essential, as water is to parched earth, to its production? The zodiac quickly gives us the clue; for the starry river pictures a decanate having a sub-influence of Leo, which in a natural birth-chart rules pleasures, love-affairs, entertainment and children. Probably, therefore, the river is affected by all of these things.

The most characteristic factor common to enjoyment, love, and the production and care of children is emotion. The Key-word for the watery signs of the zodiac is emotion; and water, from time immemorial, has been used as the universal symbol of those mental states which cause a ripple of the nervous system, as the surface of a pond is stirred by a summer breeze.

Our river Eridanus, however, in which the bestial Cetus dabbles his paws, and on the bank of which brave Orion struggles with the mighty Bull, is a particular kind of water. It is not just any pond, nor is it a raging torrent. It is emotion, but not of the passive, sluggish kind; nor yet is it torrid passion. This river is deep, strong of current, and ample wide. For more details concerning it, let us turn to the rivers of tradition.

Across the black waters of the river Styx, the Greeks were wont to have Charon ferry the souls of their dead; while in Egypt the boat of the Sun transported them to the judgment seat of Osiris. Thus is the river quite definitely associated in one of its functions with the passing over so aptly symbolized by the beginning of Aries.

Just what part this river—picturing the decanate where the Sun, in whose boat the soul is said to depart, has its highest influence—plays in that after life, and how it determines the plane of man's earthly endeavors, sacred literature reveals quite fully in either of two stories; one from the Bible and the other from the Greeks. But as already, with no aid from these, it has become apparent that our river relates to the emotions, let us first consider their chief influence upon human life.

Ponce de Leon might have saved himself much travel in search of this same fountain of eternal youth, so aptly pictured by the river in the sky, had he but known about his endocrine glands, and the varied response of their secretions to the emotions. Minute chemical messengers, secreted into the blood, burn up the life in fits of rage, starve the organs in fear and melancholy, and add youth and vigor at the behests, not of passion, but of unselfish love.

Endocrinology has made it plain just how gross desires and ignoble delights add poison to the system; just how, also, the tender feeling of a mother for her babe, or the compassion which prompts the aid of those in distress, tones up the structure of the physical cells, conferring beauty, strength, and years of life. Here, however, even more than with the welfare of the body, are we intent upon discovering those laws which rule the fortune and the station of the individual, now and hereafter.

That finer body of man, his astral form, the energies of which, as may be proved by progressed aspects and his birth-chart, determine not only his abilities but also each event that comes into his life, is thought-built. His character is composed of thought-cells derived from his experiences, and these thought-cells have been compounded of such grades of four dimensional substance as correspond to the feelings and desires coincident with their formation. They have been compounded also in association with pleasure or pain, and to the extent they feel discord do they attract misfortune into the life, and to the extent they feel pleasure do they work to bring good fortune.

Nor is this Law of Affinity confined in its operation to the physical plane. The thought-built body is the one that persists beyond the tomb. The basic vibratory rate of the character, in that after life, determines the plane, or level, to which it moves. In fact, here or hereafter, it can neither rise above nor go below its basic vibratory level except as some finer emotional state temporarily raises its vibrations, or as through baser inclinations it lowers them to inferior strata.

In that after life, even more than here, the environment to which an individual is attracted is determined by his strong desires. Emotion not only expresses, but nourishes and fattens, kindred inclinations.

Man's etheric body, and the currents which flow over his nerves, as well as his astral form, are receptive to vibratory rates of similar tone coming from without. Thoughts of sufficient potency to engender feeling tune the etheric forces in on planetary energies of similar kind. Thus, not only is man a radio receiving set, but his emotions turn the dial to the program which he receives.

Furthermore, again considering the domestic triangle with which we started on our tour of the decanates, when man and woman are joined in the pure affection of family life, there is a blend of mental and etheric forces, a stream of energy, flowing from each to the other. A complete circuit is formed between them, an invisible river, which transfers without need of speech, the thoughts and inward aspirations.

Those thus united by the astral and etheric flow pictured as Eridanus are said to be in rapport. And their ability to pick up invisible energies of corresponding quality in volume is immeasurably increased. It becomes a potent means, therefore, of lifting them to greater heights, or misused, is equally powerful in their own destruction.

The Greeks relate that Phryxus and Helle were the children of Nephele, queen of Thebes. As the only queen in the sky is Cassiopeia, picturing the last decanate of the emotional sign Pisces, these children must be represented, not by Andromeda chained to a rock, but by two fish. This is further borne out by the ribbon of love uniting them, as the etheric river Eridanus binds together through affectional power.

These children were persecuted by their stepmother Ino, pictured directly across the zodiac as Virgo, the critical woman. To escape her faultfinding and more serious intentions, the queen provided the youngsters with a Ram which was to transport them through the sky to Colchis.

The Ram rose high in the air, bearing on its back, even as can be seen now on any winter evening, the two children; for Pisces rises just above Aries. Phryxus kept his seat and reached his destination in safety. But so high did Aries soar, and so swiftly did he move, that Helle became giddy and fell off, to meet a tragic death in that stream now called the Dardanelles, but renowned in song and story, thus named because of the event just related, as the Hellespont.

The Ram, universal symbol of creative energy, caries those in safety who are level-headed enough not to meddle with rousing the kundalini, or with any one of the abnormal methods by which energies are engendered that once set in motion, more frequently than not, get beyond control. Nor does it offer any menace to those who truly live in chastity. But to those who stimulate and then repress, in monastic life or out of it, desires which normally find expression in founding a family, as there is now a vast psychoanalytic literature to prove, the fate of Helle offers warning.

Of similar purport, and also indicating the survival values in the after-life, of properly cultivated emotions, is a story of passing over the Jordan as retained in the twelfth chapter of the Book of Judges.

There had been a fight, and the Gileadites had taken possession of the river crossings. Survivors of their vanquished foes, the Ephraimites, sought to escape through fording the river; and to do so claimed to be men of their own troops. Whereupon, to determine if this were so, they were required to pronounce the word Shibboleth. This they could not do if they were Ephraimites, as they were unable to sound the H, speaking it Sibboleth.

This H, inability to pronounce which doomed the Ephraimites to be slain, is the second syllable in the divine word, and its omission denoted to those familiar with its significance, that the feminine principle, which constitutes one important factor in the trinity when its action is constructive, was missing. In the language of symbolism it was the lack of the softer, finer, kinder, and sympathetic emotional qualities which betrayed the Ephraimites, and prevented their crossing the river in safety.

In practical astrology it is found that the Sun exerts its finest power from April 1 to April 11, while in the Leo-decanate of Aries, long recognized as the region of its exaltation. And it was to portray that quality in human life which more than any other is able to lift the soul to lofty heights, give youth to the body, and assure immortality in the realms of the beyond, that the ancients sought a fitting symbol.

The Key-word of the decanate is Exaltation; and it would be difficult to find a symbol which so clearly indicates the means to attain this end as does the celestial river. Eridanus, to those who read its purport, sets forth this text: *The Fountain of Immortal Life Springs From Man's Emotional Nature; the Vibrations of Exalted Love Having a*

Rate Sufficiently Frequent to Affect Spiritual Substance and Build a Spiritual Body.

Knight Errant of the Zodiac

Only since the World War, when bureaus were established to create a public opinion favorable to certain ends regardless of their merit, has the term Propaganda, which is the Key-word for the last decanate of Aries, fallen into some disrepute. Its original meaning was that of an organization by which some doctrine or system of principles could be disseminated.

People born from April 11 to April 21 are observed to have a spontaneous enthusiasm for ideas and plans which interest them, and a special ability to impart similar enthusiasm to others. It is not enough for them to believe some doctrine to be worth while; they must also broadcast it to the ends of the earth. And they are as quick to attack falsehood and corruption as they are to strive for world-wide recognition of such truths as they have found.

The ninth house of a birth-chart, over which Sagittarius has natural rule, governs long journeys and air travel; also teaching, lecturing, preaching, publishing, radio broadcasting, and all other means by which opinions are expressed to others. The Sagittarius decanate of Aries, therefore, relates somewhat to such things. Thought, which is thus expressed, is so swift that speeding on the wings of thought has become a current literary phrase, conveying the same idea that the ancients did when they placed wings on the feet of Mercury and Perseus.

In addition to wings on his feet, which Greek legend says were furnished by Mercury, the ruler of thought, Perseus is equipped with a sword, the tip of which is as close to the line which cuts off the old circle and starts the new as it can be and yet follow Triangulum and Eridanus where their outlines are farthest west in longitude. You will remember that David of the Bible had no sword, but that he used one in victory to sever the head—which is ruled by Aries— from the body of the fallen Goliath.

The severed head which constellated Perseus holds is not that of the biblical personification of greed and selfishness, but that of the Gorgon Medusa. In the Bible story it was Goliath who wore the helmet, now seen on the champion of truth and righteousness. Also a famous shield went before Goliath; but in the Greek story is used by heroic Perseus, and is not pictured in the heavens.

To understand these stories of David and Perseus it must be recognized that the ancients knew what modern astrologers grant, that people born with the last Decanate of Aries dominant are natural champions in the cause of truth and ever fighting to destroy greed, licentiousness, and those materialistic trends which fasten shackles on the soul.

In both stories a stone appears, one the smooth white pebble of scientific truth, of material knowledge completely understood, which vanquishes selfishness through the realization that its crystallizing power so narrows the field of accomplishment that its own ends are defeated. The gross, the bestial, the greediness which seeks its own pleasure and welfare only, as typified by Goliath, when seen in the light of careful reflection, are not the way even to the highest material pleasures. Enjoyment of life, even physical enjoyment, is dependent upon appreciation of quality. It is dependent upon a responsiveness to the aspirations of others, and a progress toward refinement, both of which are denied by impervious selfishness.

This aspect of the matter, and that of the influence of licentious thought to coarsen and harden, is made quite plain in the legend of the Medusa, whose hair was serpents, so awful in appearance that whosoever looked upon her was immediately turned to stone.

Perseus, picturing the Jupiter-decanate of Aries, was the favorite of Minerva, a goddess who, as personifying the mental rather than the sporting side of Jupiter's dual sign, sprang without a mother, full armored, from the brow of this Sagittarian ruler.

Minerva is mentioned only because, when Perseus decided to rid the world of the wicked Medusa, she furnished him with a shield so highly polished that he could approach the lascivious monster without actually looking at her. Had he glanced directly at her dread countenance, he, as had so many others, should have been turned to stone. But the shield of Minerva, the mirror of the higher mind, gave him the reflection of this seducer of men, so that, while she slept he was able to make a stealthy approach and sever the terrifying head from her body.

No greater wisdom was ever uttered in reference to character building than is thus dramatically presented. Impure thoughts and unworthy desires not only harden the individual, but they thrive and prosper to the extent attention is paid to them.

There is but one way to destroy them, the way employed by Perseus; and that is to become so interested in something else that the attention is riveted to it—as his gaze was fixed on the mirror of his shield—so persistently that there is no room for the image of the undesirable to find its way into the field of vision.

When we think about a thing we create it in the astral world. Way back in Bible times it was said, that which we fear shall come upon us, and modern psychology is in full agreement with this view. To fear a thing is to keep its image before the mind and, by the accompanying emotion, to nourish it.

But whether the image is vicious or beneficial, destructive or constructive, the energy added to it by whatever emotion is present—fear, anger, hatred, joy, happiness, affection—sets the thought cells within the astral body related to this department of life to working from the four-dimensional plane to attract that thing into the life. If, therefore, the thing be detrimental, find other occupation for the vision of the mind.

This same principle also must be followed if there is to be success in building better habit-systems, if there is to be success in avoiding the inimical thoughts of others, and in combating undesirable psychic forces. The more a habit is thought about, and the greater the emotion felt when so thinking, the more strongly does it become impressed upon the unconscious mind. Bad habits can be cured only through the substitution of beneficial ones which crowd them from the life.

Not all of this Medusa story has been told; only that which relates to mental images and the desires of physical life. She was one of three Gorgon sisters, and when she was slain there was danger of reprisal. Perseus was able to escape them, however, by the use of the helmet shown in the constellation, which made him invisible.

This helmet had been provided by Pluto, ruler of the underworld; the planet now assigned to govern the eighth house of a natural birth-chart, the house which rules all influences from, and relations to, the dead. More than any other planet its influence is such as to enable the individual to tune his vibrations, radio fashion, to influences from the invisible world.

Those who have difficulties of a psychic nature, who have tampered unwisely with the invisible world, are here instructed by the wisdom of the past, as handed down through universal symbolism, in the best method of escaping from these remaining Gorgon sisters.

When through strong desire, we tune ourselves quite completely to one frequency of vibratory rates, this automatically cuts off others. When the dial of a radio set is tuned to pick up the program broadcast by one station, this eliminates the reception of programs which are broadcast over frequencies quite dissimilar. Thus it is, as proved by the experience of many people, that the best way to escape an undesirable psychic influence is not to fight it, which tunes the finer body to receive its rates, but to wear the helmet of Pluto, and become invisible and unaffected by its power, through completely and persistently tuning in on some dissimilar and constructive interest.

True to the Key-word of the pictured decanate, Perseus was a glamorous hero who felt it necessary to help the world along. Escaping from the remaining Gorgon sisters, and triumphantly bearing the severed Medusa's head, he flew high through the air; an aviation exploit which led him to the discovery of a princess in distress.

Like many mothers now Cassiopeia was a slave to pride and station. She wished to be the envy of all the other women in the world. And in her desire to outdo them she boasts of her beauty, claiming to be of greater charm than Juno and the Nereides, nymphs of the sea. This so angers Neptune—who rules the sign in which the decanates pictured by Cassiopeia and Andromeda are found—that he has her daughter, Andromeda, chained to a rock in the sea for the monster Cetus to devour.

But before this fearsome human sacrifice is completed, Perseus, flying high overhead after his conquest of the Medusa, spies the fair maiden in distress, dashes to the rescue, vanquishes the monster of the sea, releases her, and carries her off in happy marriage.

We will not here dwell upon the release of the human soul from the blind beliefs of the Piscean Age through the dissemination of correct information. Nor is it necessary to comment upon the power of undue attachment to any material thing to bind the soul to earth, and prevent its progress, both here and immediately after death.

But again it should be pointed out that the character of the individual is the sum total of his experiences stored in the thought-cells of his finer body. No one can change these for him; no one, therefore, except himself, can slay the beast within nor overcome the noxious influence of creeping slimy thought, nor release the soul from other bondage.

The exploits of Perseus each, in symbolical language, conveys an important message; but most important of all, he accomplished the work himself. The leading text thus portrayed, therefore is: *There is No Vicarious Atonement. Each Soul is a Responsible Being, Working Out its Own Deliverance from the Thralldom Inherited from Ancestry and Forced Upon It by Environment.*

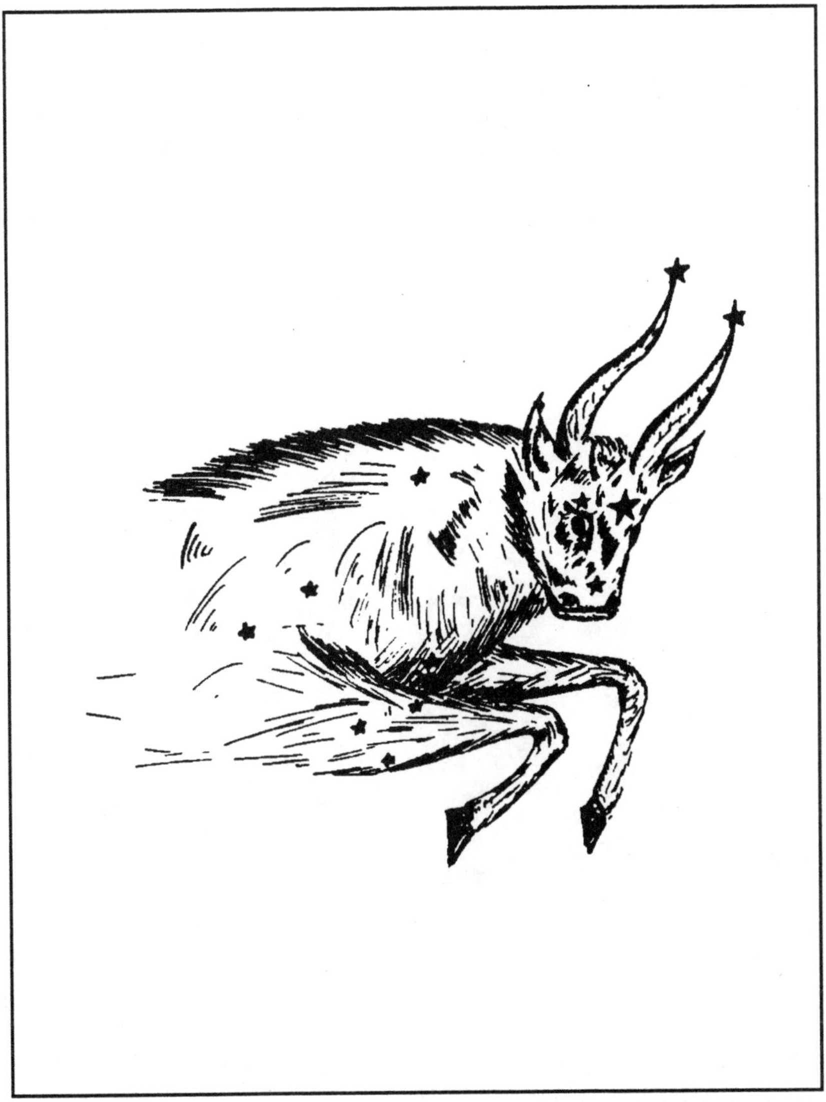

TAURUS ♉ I Have

ORION ☌ ♍ Struggle

Chapter 3

Knights of King Arthur

THE Use of the Golden Calf.
What was the amazement of the first explorers of the mighty Amazon to learn from the Indians that the group of stars comprising Taurus, and picturing the money sign of the zodiac, was known to them as the Jaw of the Ox. Yet when we reflect that the Vedas of India and the Avesta of Persia both make mention of the massive Bull, and the Apis was an object of special veneration in Egypt, it is not so surprising that ideas which doubtless had their origin in Ancient Atlantis and Mu should also have been retained in part by aboriginal South Americans.

The interpreter of Pharaoh's dream reveals himself familiar with astrological practice. Personal possessions are governed by the second house of the birth-chart, over which Taurus has natural rule. When the Egyptian king began to speak of kine coming up out of the river, even as the Bull of heaven appears to be emerging from the river Eridanus, it could refer to but one thing: to wealth. When he told of ears of corn, that also was speaking of a universal symbol long established among the stars. Virgo, the harvest constellation, holds such in her hand.

Joseph revealed his acumen not in his knowledge that the kine meant wealth and the corn meant food, but by his recognition that the seven fat cattle which were devoured by the seven lean cattle, and the seven full ears which were consumed by the seven lean ears, related to future years; and by his ability to so thoroughly convince the monarch of the truth thus revealed that for the seven years of abundance he was willing to set aside one-fifth of all the crops as a reserve against the years of approaching famine.

Picturing the middle decanate of this sign of material possessions there is another hero. The Akkadians called him Sargon, and the Greeks called him Orion, but we are more familiar with him through the Hebrew account. One foot he rests upon the river; for like the far earlier Semitic Sargon, Moses put in his first appearance among the bulrushes.

Yet as here we are interested in the mighty Bull pitching down upon him from the sky, rather than with exploits of valor, he enters our story only to the extent made necessary to reveal the teachings the ancients sought to picture by the Taurus constellation. It all is embraced within the drama of the golden calf.

It will be remembered, or the thirty-second chapter of Exodus can be consulted if the memory has grown dim, that Moses went up Sinai to receive instructions, and came down the mountain with two tablets of testimony, tables of stone, written with the finger of God.

Taurus, the fixed earthy sign of the zodiac, more nearly than any other relates to stone; but this alone does not explain why there had to be two tablets, instead of one. That such was the case is clearly indicated; for after the first set was broken, the laws of God were again written on two tablets, and so survived.

Spirit, being without beginning and without end, has ever been symbolized by a circle, while the earth, as a plane receiving the vertical rays of the Sun, has universally been represented by a square or a cross. As later is to be related, Easter is a festival commemorating the union of Solar and Lunar forces which causes seeds within the earth to germinate; and a feature of Easter custom still retained is the eating of hot cross buns, circular in outline with a cross traced upon their tops.

Removing one of the four arms gives us the Taucross of the Egyptians and some others, from which was derived the Greek letter Tau, the English T, and the common gavel of ancient Masonry. It expresses creative energy moving in the direction indicated by the longer member of the three-armed cross. As this may point either toward heaven or toward earth, by this means was indicated whether the energies of life were being used for gross and physical gratification, or were directed into channels of aspiration by which the spiritual heights might be scaled.

Even as the reversed T was used in various lands to indicate by its upturned point the striving upward of spirit, and by its more commonly down turned point material ambition; so were there also two tablets of stone, one setting forth the laws of physical survival and the other revealing those laws which relate to spiritual realization.

But as Moses tarried on the mountain his people became impatient and induced Aaron to make a molten calf. It was of gold because the Sun rules that metal; and because this orb of day had but reached the commencement of the sign it could not be considered a full grown bull, therefore it was called a calf. It was molten because this section of the constellation is backed against the fire of Aries.

To make this interpretation of the olden story still more certain, Taurus in practical astrology rules not merely material possessions, but also the neck and ears of human anatomy. Repeatedly, in the narrative, those who divested themselves of their earrings, from which to make the golden calf, are called a stiffnecked people. And as the vocal organs also come under the rule of the same zodiacal sign, it was their singing which he heard, as he approached the camp on his return, that first apprised Moses that mischief was afoot.

The constellated hero in the sky is pictured with upraised club in the very act of demolishing this symbol of the greed for gold. On the bank of the river is he in the act of demolishing it. Yet only the story reveals the ultimate fate of the calf so attacked; for strange to say, it was not thrown away, nor again turned into a bauble of adornment.

Instead it was burnt with the fire of spirit, ground to powder in the mortar of compassion, and strewn on the life-giving water from the nearby river of affection. It was neither ignored, nor despised, nor coveted; but was made of spiritual use; for after thus converting this symbol of material possessions into that which no longer could be worshiped, it was given to the children of Israel in their drink.

But before this came to pass, because they had been divested of their earrings, they were seen to be naked. These earrings, as I have endeavored to show, were universal symbols for all the tinsel and display, all the money and its power of purchase, which many men set their hearts exclusively upon. Divest them of this and they have nothing left. Their treasures are purely physical, and they have nothing suitable to clothe their souls in higher realms.

Nothing could be plainer, I think, to one conversant with universal symbolism, that the significance of utilizing, in an affectional way—all the more easily understood because Venus, planet of affection, is the ruler of Taurus—the material things represented by the golden calf. If anyone ever had great provocation completely to destroy, it seems to have been Moses. Nor was it due to a relenting heart that he made use of the material idol when spiritualized, as his orders to the Levites clearly indicate. It was because wealth, station, power, and other physical possessions, all can be converted, as he converted the golden calf, into a means of creating spiritual values.

Some there are, I know, who believe the vow of poverty opens wide the Elysian gates. Others there are who teach withdrawal from the contacts of the world of men, deeming that in solitude the spirit more quickly develops wings. But the story of the golden calf refutes all this.

People come into this world endowed with natural talents of various kinds and diverse degree. Richness of life to human beings comes not from absence of contacts, but through the development of proper appreciations. These imply some freedom from the dulling grind of economic necessity, some surcease from grueling toil. And they depend upon human associations, upon opportunity to learn, and upon material objects through which the senses gain an insight into what is fine and good.

Material things are detrimental when they are worshiped, like the golden calf, for what they bring in selfish gratification. They prevent spiritual growth when they become so insistent in their care that the burden is too heavy. But nothing opens the avenues to spiritual attainment so effectually as being of assistance to others. And often the assistance needed is of a physical nature.

To worship the golden calf of wealth is utmost folly; yet to ignore the power of money when rightly used to advance the welfare of the human race is almost an equal fatuity. Libraries have been built and stocked with books where men may read and free their minds; literature has been published and widely spread by which the spiritual truths have been made accessible; laboratories have been set up for research and clinics established for treatment, that have practically eradicated certain previously prevalent forms of disease; but not without the aid of money.

While we occupy a physical world the body has physical needs, possesses physical functions which if not exercised cause trouble, and must make contacts with physical conditions if we are to gain those experiences which alone fit us properly for a still higher type of life when we have passed on to the next inner plane. A physical body which is neglected detracts from the ability of the individual to do constructive work; hampers his efforts to contribute values to society.

According to the natural abilities, which the birth-chart so surely reveals, is there open to the individual the opportunity to advance himself in the direction of becoming more valuable to others. Whether it is the use of gold, the power to heal the body, ability to teach, inventive genius which contributes a device that, relieving toil, gives time and strength for soul development, or other power to do, it may be turned to spiritual advantage.

Because those born from April 21 to May 21 are found to be so interested in personal possessions the Key-phrase given to Taurus is, I Have. Because the physical is so necessary in developing the spiritual, the ancient text becomes: *Physical Life and Its Opportunities Should Not be Slighted; Neither Should Spiritual Aspirations Be Ignored. Learn, therefore, to "Render Unto Caesar the Things Which be Caesar's and Unto God the Things Which be God's."*

The Good Luck of the Rabbit's Foot

Seeking to discern what the ancients had in mind when they traced the picture of a rabbit in the sky to represent the earthy decanate of the sign of material possessions brings instantly to thought the three outstanding attributes of the hare: fleetness, timidity, and rapidity of reproduction.

Fleetness, as indicated by wings on the feet of Mercury and Perseus, has to do with thought; and as the Moon exerts its strongest power in the Taurus-decanate of Taurus, we perceive the aptness of an association between this section of the zodiac, occupied by the Sun from April 21 to April 30, and the lunar orb, which in a birth-chart rules Mentality.

Easter is a modern adaptation of the old name of the Moon, which by the Chaldeans was called Ishtar, became Astarte to the classical nations, Eoster to the Saxons, and finally was designated by the term now used for her chief annual festival. In this festival her greatest power, as signified by her exaltation in the beginning of

Taurus, is celebrated as chief aid to the function of the Sun. Easter is the Sunday after the Full Moon after the Sun has passed into the summer half of the zodiac.

At this Full Moon, because the Sun is in Aries, where its creative energies are strongest, the Moon must be in Libra, the sign ruling both marriage and eggs. Eggs, consequently, form a persistent factor in that spring festival dedicated to the redemption of the world by united man and woman, even as it is deemed to be rescued from winter through the offices of the united Sun and Moon.

These eggs commonly are colored in various hues to signify diversity in the expected harvest, and they are hidden about, and must be hunted for, even as other seeds are placed in the Sun-warmed dark ground of the beginning of Taurus, where they germinate, and only later thrust green shoots through the surface into the kindly light of day.

Bunnies also are part of the ceremony; for although they do not lay eggs, as children are sometimes led to believe at Easter, they are unusually prolific, and stand symbol of the power of the earth to bring forth.

This decanate where Easter has her strongest power also is associated with the greatest tragedy mankind has ever known. Halloween commemorates the destruction of the world, the fire, the flood, and the sinking of Atlantis. The Sun at that time is in the death-decanate of the death-sign Scorpio, directly across the zodiac from this rabbit-decanate of Taurus. Thus when Ophiuchus, the man in death struggle with a serpent, who pictures the first-decanate of Scorpio, sets in the west, vanquished by the great destruction, Lepus, the hare, rises in the east, and is shown fleeing from the scene of catastrophe as fast as fleet legs will carry him.

Tradition holds that the time when such cataclysms occur may be timed by the position of the Pleiades, a group of stars behind the shoulder of the Bull, in relation to the precessional cycle. As the Bull faces eastward toward the earth as it rises, and as the whole rear half of it has been destroyed in the cataclysm, the Pleiades come up first, as Lepus pictures that section of the Sign Taurus first to rise. Noah quickly left behind his sinful companions when he entered the ark, Lot left Sodom in great haste; and legend says that the wise ones of Atlantis, warned by the position of the Pleiades, went from their doomed land at top speed.

In one of the oldest written accounts in existence, the Gilgamesh Epic of still more ancient Sumeria, the cuneiform tablets of which have been recovered from Assurbanipal's famous library at Ninevah, it is related that after the hero conquers the mighty Bull which has caused seven years of sterility on the earth, that Ishtar places a curse upon him. But Gilgamesh evades the curse, tears the entrails from the Bull, dedicates its crescent horns to the Sun, and washes his hands in the Euphrates, which was the river Eridanus of the Sumerians.

As the earthy-decanate of Taurus may well be taken to represent the more physical section of the sign, so the rear of the Bull, which in rising comes first, is similar in its symbolic implications. It was the materialism and wickedness of the world that made necessary the flood from which Noah fled. It was the turning from God to abominations of the flesh that led to the destruction of Sodom and Gomorrah. And the use of mental powers and psychic forces to enslave the populace is said to have preceded the sinking of Atlantis.

All magic, now more commonly called mental demonstration, new thought, or metaphysical practice, is made possible through the activity of the mind. And this peculiar power resides in greatest measure in those born with the first decanate of Taurus dominant.

Such magic, such healing energy, and such force of mind, can be used in either of two directions. The voodoos of our South follow the example of Ishtar, and place a curse upon their enemies. But others more enlightened follow the example of Gilgamesh, and dedicate this crescent power the horns of the Bull, to spiritual purposes, represented by the Sun.

That the self-seeking, materialistic, or destructive use of this lunar power must never be countenanced was portrayed by the ancients when they failed to picture other than the front portion of the Bull in the sky. Nor will the Jews, preserving the symbolic custom to this day, eat of a beef other than the portion pictured. To those of that orthodox faith the portion omitted from the stellar picture is unclean and may not be served as food; as they say, it is not Kosher.

As the Sun, in practical astrology rules the Individuality, and has its exaltation in the Eridanus decanate, and the Moon rules the Mentality, having its exaltation in the Lepus decanate, when the epic hero of Sumeria dedicated the crescent horns of the Bull to the Sun and washed his hands in the river, in pantomime he was consecrating his Mental powers to their highest, most spiritual, use. And these horns of the Bull, through various avenues have descended to us as a means by which the adverse effect of mental forces can be avoided.

How blind are those who can see no farther than the material plane; who prostitute their souls for the attainment of carnal desire, and whose minds turn only to wickedness and destruction. When Sodom and Gomorrah fell in flames the Bible relates:

> And they smote the men that were at the door of the house with blindness, both small and great, so that they wearied themselves to find the door.

This blindness of devoting the energies solely to the gross, with no thought for the finer experiences of life; and that even more terrible practice of using the psychic powers for the injury of others, is pictured by the star which blots out the eye of the rabbit in the sky. Blindness is also traditionally associated with the Pleiades, the cyclic pointers of cataclysmic destruction.

Ptolemy, compiler of ancient astronomical knowledge, says that when the Moon is with the Pleiades and afflicted by Mars in a chart of birth that the person will go blind. As a matter of astrological research, when the Moon is greatly afflicted by Mars, trouble with the eyes may be expected whether the Pleiades are involved or not. But in this manner has the tradition of loss of sight through evil mental practices come down to us.

And thus it is today, in all regions where prevails the belief in "evil eye," which is supposed to be a curse placed upon one person by another's malignant look, that the attempt is made to ward it off by forming the sign of the Bull's horns. This is done by closing the hand in such a manner that the first and little finger stand out to form a crescent, and then gouging in the direction of the person casting the spell as if to gouge out his eyes.

The rabbit in the sky is pictured fleeing in great haste from all such influences; and as he is moving directly away from the section of the zodiac where the cataclysmic struggle takes place, turning his back on the scene of various iniquities, the legend persists to this day that, like those who fled from Atlantis before it sank, and like Lot who made his escape from Sodom, the rabbit gained safety. It thus acquires an implication of good fortune.

The foot of any creature is the universal symbol of understanding of some kind; and the foot of the rabbit implies an understanding of those things for which the rabbit stands, that is, of mental practices devoted to injury, and how to escape their influence. The negro who carries a rabbit's foot to prevent a "jinx" being placed upon him, and as a talisman of good luck in general, is merely perpetuating, by means of a symbolic ritual, an ancient truth of vast import.

It requires great determination not to look at, or think about, the thing which if permitted to do so would cause fear: and thus those born with the first decanate of Taurus dominant have, as the Keyword clearly indicates. The earthy decanate of the earth's own sign in particular needs to exercise the Determination which it so abundantly possesses to face away from the gross and sensual, and to escape the paralyzing effect of fear.

The hare, although fleet of foot, is a timorous creature that burrows in warrens beneath the ground, like those who, submerged in materialism, live in constant dread of death. Lot escaped from the hail of fire and brimstone, but his wife, unable to resist visualizing the thing which she feared, looked back, and became rooted to the spot. The salt, which ultimately she became, shows the crystallizing power of selfish inclinations.

When we positively desire a thing we flash the image of that which is sought upon the mental screen, and the thought-cells belonging to that department of life work with such energy as they possess to make that condition a reality. But when in fear the image is the opposite of that which we seek, these four-dimensional sparks of consciousness work just as hard to carry out the orders they thus receive, disastrous though the result may be. Even as the rabbit is blind, so fear blinds the eyes to the proper mental picture, accepted as a command by unconscious mind, to get wished-for results. Hence follows the text: *One of Man's Greatest Enemies is Fear.*

Knights of King Arthur

Jason conquered the brazen-footed Bull in one of his adventures while searching for the Golden Fleece, and Sargon of Akkad, fourteen hundred years before the time of Moses, came up out of the bulrushes to deliver his people from their tribulations. But nearer to our own time, and perhaps, therefore, dearer to our hearts, is King Arthur and the famed Knights of his round table.

As is common to traditions when the historical background is dim or lacking, there are variants of the original, but the most authentic version of the story finds twelve knights, bold and strong, seated at a circular and revolving table; ready, like a panel of modern jurymen—twelve men good and true, each to view the matter from the angle of one sign of the zodiac—to pass judgment, and, unlike these later representatives, to fare forth in valiant exploits in the enforcement of their decisions.

The most conspicuous constellation on any yuletide night, while the Candlemas Bull, Taurus, goes sailing overhead, as legend says it must, is Orion, who follows with upraised club. In every land is he recognized as a warrior, and the three stars in his belt are known in every land. In the region where the Tigris and Euphrates flow they are called the Wise Men of the East; but Celtic Druids held them to be three ladies who were present at King Arthur's birth.

Not only is Orion a warrior, but whether as Sargon, Moses, Jason, or the western legendary king, the fight he wages is not merely against oppression from without, but also against the materialistic tendencies and selfish ambitions of his own men. In every legend relating to him, he fights with environmental forces that endanger his plans; and in every struggle some loss is sustained.

Moses, you will remember, when he had vanquished and utilized to more spiritual purposes the golden calf, called upon those who would support him, even as the constellation thus pictures it, every man to put his sword by his side. And legend relates that the round table episode was precipitated by the personal ambitions of Arthur's men.

Each one desired the place of honor at the yuletide feast; each man believed himself entitled to sit near the head of the table. Nor, although so many hundred years have passed on what should have been progressive feet, do we witness much diminution in the ardor for similar social prestige. But on this notable occasion the snubbing of one's neighbor was insufficient to express the fires of jealousy that raged within, and a brawl ensued which resulted in many slain; as a thousand years before a like slaying had occurred over the incident of the golden calf.

And thus, as Moses in the Bible times had been confronted by a serious problem, so was Arthur put to it to prevent a recurrence of such an incident among his men. Nor did he shirk the responsibility thus at hand. After all, ancient or modern, there is always a best way to meet every situation, always an opportunity to make the obstacle less retarding to progress than otherwise it would have been.

The Bull is pictured full tilt, as if enraged and pitching down upon the hero from the sky; who looks up to meet the impact of its charge undaunted, and with club well poised to deliver its most effective blow. As belonging to the earthy-earthy sign, the Bull itself most appropriately typifies the crowding strength of the material environment with which we all must struggle and win if we are not to die.

But in its headlong plunge from the regions of above it also conveys the significance of those forces, invisible but potent, which assail man from the sky; the energies from planets and zodiacal signs, which, though more subtle in their attack, have even more power to shape and mold the destiny of man.

Environmental forces, those from the stars and those from the earth, are ever present, and their impacts call for well considered resistance. We can not escape them, as the timid hare seems to seek to do as it scampers from beneath Orion's feet. When problems are present, which every day they are, be they large or be they small, their issues must be met. And for each such problem there is always a best of all possible ways in which to meet it.

This applies to all of them; and that they should be met with courage and full confidence, as Orion meets the rushing Bull. No situation of life should cause the soul to quail. Whatever physical disaster may come, whatever distasteful thing may be uncovered in the recesses of the unconscious mind, it is always better to face it squarely, to recognize it for what it is, and then to formulate plans by which the situation may best be met.

Those who form the patients of psychiatrists more frequently than not have refused to face something in themselves, or have refused to face some situation of their lives. Freudian literature is filled with cases of illness due to unwillingness to recognize certain facts of people about themselves. And even more serious is the effect of refusal to meet some crisis in the life; for when a condition is present which can not be faced, the mind turns back upon itself, invents unconscious lies to explain behavior, and if the case is extreme enough in its unwillingness, there develops dementia praecox, one of the most prevalent forms of insanity.

We must face the problems of life firmly. And among those problems is that of meeting the impacts from the stars.

The only possible way that the planets in their courses can exert an influence on the life of man is through imparting energy to him. Whether spiritual, mental or physical, whenever work is done, whenever action results, there is always a proportional expenditure of energy. Without consuming energy nothing is accomplished.

Within the body of man at his birth are lines of tenuous substance that act as aerials do on a radio receiving set. And after birth, in response to the progress of the planets, other lines temporarily form that have a similar function. It is these stellar aerials, mapped by aspects, which pick up the energy of the planets, load it with harmony or discordant static, and convey it to the thought-cells of which the finer body is composed. They transmit to man, at times which can previously be ascertained, those forces from above symbolized by the downward pitching Bull.

Man is influenced by heat and cold and wind and rain and sun and innumerable other conditions that comprise his ever-changing environment. But his reaction to the impact of these physical conditions is largely within his own control. He can not change the weather, but he can prepare to meet it, or if favorable, to take advantage of what it has to offer. Neither can he change the motion of the planets in the sky, but he can change his own character, and in so doing receive energies more to his liking.

The permanent lines which extend across his finer body, and act as aerials to gather the programs from the planets, are expressions of his character, expressions of the harmonies and discords that have been organized within himself. And if he changes these, so also will he change the aerials within his finer form, or even construct others not present at birth, which tune in spontaneously to the energy broadcasts of his seeking.

The temporary lines which form in response to the progress of the planets pick up energy corresponding to the rates to which they are attuned. But the harmony or discord of the energy thus acquired may be vastly modified, so that it has a beneficial influence when it reaches the thought-cells.

Not only so, but the dial of man's own consciousness can be turned, if he used the resolution of Orion or King Arthur, to make an

Spiritual Astrology

even more potent radio receiving set of his whole nervous system. He can tune in on the planetary rate desired so completely and persistently that other programs coming from above reach him very little.

Here we see the wisdom of King Arthur. To prevent a recurrence of the discord occasioned by each knight desiring the preferential place, he called to him the most cunning artificers of the land and instructed them to make a round table that would revolve, at which all the knights could sit, and each could thus consider himself at its head.

In the region where fabled Arthur is said to have reigned are still found today cromlechs, concentric circles of stone erected in prehistoric days to portray the orbits of the planets. And in that land, as also among the Maya of Yucatan, the people array themselves in shirts of white on the first day of May, to dance in circles about the symbol of the Sun, the upright Maypole.

The weaving in and out of the dancers, as they hold ribbon strands reaching to the central post, cause these to form, one with another, sextiles and trines, squares and oppositions, and the other aspects by which astrologers ancient and modern plot the harmony or discord reaching the earth from various parts of heaven.

On that day the Sun has just entered the Struggle decanate of Taurus, so-called because the life of those born from May 1 to May 11 is so seldom free from obstacles that must be overcome. It is the decanate pictured by Orion.

We can not doubt, therefore, that the problem of settling the conflict between his knights, with which King Arthur was confronted, was the same problem which confronts each individual at this day; the problem of avoiding the strife of influences coming from the planets as they sit in their seats among the twelve signs, and of winning their harmonious allegiance.

And he solved it as it must be solved today, by devising a method by which the dial of consciousness can be so revolved that any planet in its seat can be considered at the head, can be given temporary prominence, and thus enlisted fully in support of the most cherished endeavor. Thus is derived the text: *The Task of the Soul on Every Plane of Manifestation is to Struggle With and Overcome the Limitations of Its Environment.*

The Mantle of Elijah

Not always are we so fortunate as to have preserved to us, in the stories handed down from remote antiquity which serve as commentaries on the pictographic teachings of the constellations, both the danger to be avoided and the end to be sought. But these are amply set forth in the dramas associated with Auriga, the heavenly charioteer.

Orion, picturing the previous decanate, is shown using the solar fire of the Sun, even as the Maypole about which the dancers revolve reveals its source, as a shield of courage in his battle with the onslaughts of his environment. The lion's skin upon his arm gives him a resistance hard to crumble.

It is quite to be expected, therefore, that the last decanate of Taurus, through which the Sun sheds his influence from May 11 to May 21, should offer further comment on the Bull and on the use of the celestial fire.

It was the duty of Phoebus, according to the Greek account, each day to drive the chariot of the Sun across the heavens. Phoebus had a son, named Phaethon, arrogant with the inexperience of youth, who begged his father constantly to be allowed to drive the prancing steeds. For a long time the father was adamant in his refusal; but at last in a moment of paternal weakness he gave permission to the boy, for one day, to do his work.

But the horses were too hard to hold; they were beyond the strength of the untrained youth, took the bit in their teeth and veered from the accustomed course. To make matters worse, having left the beaten road, they neared the den of the vicious Scorpion, pictured across the zodiac. With upraised tail he struck, burying his sting in a horse's flank. Then they completely ran away.

It had been a sorry day, indeed, on earth, if Jove, from high on his Olympian throne, had not glanced that way. The frightened horses went tearing toward the earth, the heat drying up the lakes and scorching the plains. Something had to be done if the world was not to be consumed in flames. Jove hurled a thunderbolt from where he sat, and as a bird is shot when on the wing, Phaethon was dropped into the adjacent Po, the stream now called Eridanus.

Dangerous, indeed, it is to develop forces which get beyond control. Many methods there are by which energies can be set in motion. Oriental breathing systems which have this for object gain such results. The etheric energies of the body may be increased until they surge in frenzy against the bit. But unless controlling skill is developed at an equal pace there is no proper guiding them.

Thus also is the kundalini power of Oriental fame a source of potential energy; but those who thus incautiously approach the Scorpion's lair more frequently than not receive the venom of its sting.

The bit and reins which Auriga holds in his strong right hand speak in no uncertain terms of careful guidance. Mastership, which is the Keyword of the section of the sky thus pictured, is the very opposite of irresponsible mediumship.

When forces from the invisible realm, whatever may be their pretensions, invade the physical organism of man and take charge of his mental processes, to the extent this is true, is he in danger of the fate of Phaethon.

To invite the control of any intelligence other than one's own, from this plane or from any other, is to play the part of the self-assured son who begged to drive the chariot of his father. When such steeds gather headway, and realize the hand that holds the reins is too weak for their restraint, no one can tell where they will go, or what the result will be.

One rule always holds, whether it be applied to driving a car on a crowded street, to developing the vital etheric flow of life, or to the use of the psychic senses; energy and speed must never exceed the power that guides and directs them. If, therefore, new sources of energy are tapped, a habit-system of more effective control must be inaugurated at an equal pace.

In the time of Elijah a Phaethon-like drought had taken hold on the land. As Ishtar in the long ago had cursed the Sumerian Gilgamesh, so Jezebel had likewise sworn to take the life of the Bible prophet.

The third-decanate of the second sign is pictured by the charioteer. It is the decanate of Mastership; and mastership implies control of the solar fire and a willingness to sacrifice material things, as symbolized by the Bull, for the benefit of others.

The test as to his possession of these qualities came to Elijah during the great drought as related in the eighteenth chapter of First Kings. As at all times, not excepting the present day, there were then many men who claimed to knowledge and power which they did not have. False prophets, they were, like the swarm of charlatans who now prey upon the credulity of the public.

And even as at the present time, when one appeared who was truly a Master of his subject, the envy and malice of those who found an easy living in their pretensions, was directed against him, and against his teachings. So, therefore, did the four hundred and fifty spurious prophets array themselves against Elijah, and worked to turn the tide of public sentiment against his doctrines.

But Elijah called for a test of their teachings; he called upon them to make a sacrifice of their material wealth, to draw the fire from heaven and consume the Bull upon the altar of the common good. But although they shouted until hoarse, leaped upon the altar in dramatic gestures, and prophesied through all the day until evening, nothing of consequence happened.

Then Elijah built an altar of twelve stones, after the manner of the ancient cromlechs, one stone for each tribe and zodiacal sign. Round about it, as the magical decanate of Taurus is associated with planting in the ground, he made a trench as great as would contain two measures of seeds. Such seeds, even as material things germinate spiritual powers when used with intelligent compassion, require moisture if they are to grow: therefore, were twelve barrels of water, one for each type of crop to come, poured over the altar, filling the trench.

When all was in readiness he called down the celestial fire which consumed the sacrifice, the wood the stones, the dust, and even licked up the water in the trench, as emotional energy is always consumed in any physical demonstration of mental power. Thus did Elijah show his skill; but it was the final result that demonstrated him a Master. The drought was broken, and shortly there was the sound of abundant rain.

True Mastership is never shown merely through the exercise of ability, however unusual it may be. Auriga in the heavens holds the bridle reins in his strong right hand, to indicate ability to control and guide the forces of nature. But this alone does not constitute Mastership. With his other hand he holds and protects a mother goat and her young. He possesses ability to harness the fire divine, but he sacrifices this power by which selfish possessions might be gained, in aiding those in dire distress. Even thus did Elijah use his skill for the benefit of a stricken land.

Whenever, as frequently, is brought to my attention the marvelous feats which are reported from far-off places—the walking on red-hot coals, long interment beneath the ground, knives and nails piercing the flesh without the flow of blood, and other wondrous things galore—by way of contrast I always think of Elijah. Especially, as is usually the case, when excuses are made for these wonder-mongers in their customary failure to help the condition of the miserable population around them.

I often wonder what Elijah would have said had someone remonstrated with him over the self-perpetuating handful of meal and cruse of oil, telling him that thus to interfere with the karma of the widow was to commit a sin.

It was during the time of drought, and before the episode of the trial of strength with the charlatans, who after the manner of certain wonder-workers of the East today, cried loudly and cut themselves with knives to induce the emotional frenzy necessary to their work. Elijah gave assurance to the starving woman that she should not want for food until the drought was ended.

Had the wonder-workers of his time been told of this help to the widow, or the bringing back to life of her son, no doubt they would have said that such procedure was contrary to divine law. For ever thus do those whose claims to spiritual power are unjustified, make excuses for their lack of alleviating action. Yet the Key-phrase for the Capricorn sign is, I Use; for the goat there pictured, or on Auriga's arm, is noteworthy for utilizing everything at hand for food.

Unusual power is no token of spiritual attainment. Those who have such power and use it only for self-aggrandizement have failed to make the sacrifice demanded of the one who followed in the steps of the great prophet.

Elisha was ploughing with twelve yoke of oxen before him, he being with the twelfth, or Taurus, when Elijah cast him his mantle. Whereupon he slew the oxen, boiled their flesh, and gave unto the people, and they did eat. Also for their benefit he devoted his other possessions. Thus did he demonstrate, before he was permitted to minister unto his teacher, that he understood the necessity of using whatever powers he should acquire for the benefit of the needy.

Phaethon, in the story from the Greeks, failing to control the power he sought to master, was hurled stricken into the river. But Elijah, striking with his mantle, walked to the other side dry shod. And when Elijah went heavenward in a chariot of fire, the power he once had used went to his disciple, whose immediate healing of waters to help a city in distress indicated his worthiness to wear the mantle. Thus the text is apparent: *The Function of a Master is to Control the Forces of Nature and Use Them for the Protection of the Weak and the Benefit of All.*

Gemini   ♊   I Think

Ursa Minor   II-II   Intuition

Canis Major ♊–♎ Fidelity

Ursa Major　Ⅱ-〰〰　Reason

Chapter 4

Story of the Three Bears

DAMON and Pythias.
It was held in ancient times that the Twins were the builders of cities and the founders of empires. Picturing the section of the zodiac related in a natural birth-chart to brethren, thought and travel, and ruling the hands and arms of human anatomy, the stories about them show skill in the use of tools, dexterity in war, and often relate to travel.

In Peru they were believed to have built the first city, the symbol for them there being a pile of brick; and Rome is held to have been founded by Romulus, after his twin brother, Remus, had been slain in a quarrel over building a wall. They had reached the site of the future metropolis as infants, drifting down the river in a boat which there found lodgement in the marshes.

The Romans thus regarded the heavenly Twins as exerting a special power of protection over them. Because they relate to travel they were frequently pictured with steeds, and Grecian temples thus retain them, riding side by side, armed with spears, on snow-white horses. The Romans, adopting the idea, struck a coin in their honor. The pence of the Good Samaritan was such a silver piece, on which the two horsemen were shown.

This protecting power of thought and skill was honored so greatly in the time of Imperial Rome that it entered into the customary oath. On our witness stands the Bible, as the sacred word of God, is considered the emblem of that high power which none should dare defy; but in olden Rome the solemn token of the sacred power by which they swore was Gemini. Passing to a less reverential generation, By Gemini, which to us is, By Jiminy, became a by-word of the street.

Six hundred years after the devotion displayed to David by Jonathan, and three hundred years after the founding by one Twin of Rome, lived Dionysius, the tyrant of Syracuse. The Pythagorean sect then flourished, and to those who joined its ranks, revealed the teachings of the still more ancient Stellar Wisdom.

Damon and Pythias were such followers of the great Samoan sage, developing their spiritual powers and learning about numbers and the stars from the same ordained instructor. Thrown constantly together in the school, a strong attachment formed between them, and their friendship grew as the horizon of their knowledge widened. The bond of religious brotherhood was strengthened by personal admiration.

Then Pythias, through some political indiscretion, came under the disapproval of the monarch and was condemned to die. He was a man of varied interests, and financial matters, due to his absorption in his studies, were rather at loose ends. Thoughtful of others, who might be left destitute by his sudden passing, and of debts that rightfully should be paid, he begged the tyrant liberty long enough to set right these various affairs.

Quite naturally, the one who had condemned him to death wanted to know what assurance could be given, if he were allowed temporary freedom, that he would come back, and be present on the day of execution. Whereupon friend Damon stepped forward, pledging himself, standing ready to be slain if Pythias failed thus to return. In this manner, therefore, was the matter settled.

Damon was kept under closest guard, and as the day approached, speculation ran high whether Pythias should die or Damon. Some thought the teachings of the initiates in the school to which they both belonged had so imbued the friends with a sense of honor that, even though his life be forfeit, Pythias surely must return. Others, more numerous and more highly vocal, expressed their belief, and backed it with a wager, that he had made good his escape, having fled to some foreign land.

On the death-day excitement ran high and a huge crowd gathered. Damon seemed the least concerned of all. And sure enough, as the time for the fateful ceremony drew near, here came Pythias striding through the gathering, to take his place before the executioner, true to his word and true to his friend.

So impressed was Dionysius with this loyalty of friend to friend, and with teachings which gave so high a sense of honor, that not only did he free Pythias, and spare his life, but he also asked to be admitted as a member of the Pythagorean order.

No less dramatic, and also concerned with the absence of one, is the Greek story of Castor and Pollux, after whom the heavenly Twins are now named.

They fell in love with the daughters of Leucippus. But as these maidens already were betrothed to the sons of Aphareus, resentment was expressed by these earlier suitors toward the Twins. At last the rivalry ran so high that insult was passed, resulting in a challenge to battle. In the course of the ensuing fight Castor was slain.

So great was the attachment of Pollux for his brother that he walked up and down the earth, disconsolate and filled with sadness. Interest in life had departed, and he longed to die, but this he could not do, for unlike the absent brother, he was immortal.

Jove, from his Olympian heights, perceiving the vast distress in the heart of the surviving Twin, took pity and permitted Castor to share his brother's immortality. Yet in granting this favor he made the stipulation that but one of the two could be on earth at a time, the other remaining meanwhile confined in Pluto's dark realm.

The mind of man, after the manner thus described, is acknowledged to be two, the objective and the unconscious, linked inseparably so long as earthly life shall last. The objective mind being dependent upon the physical brain for expression, is, like Castor, subject to the forces of death. But the unconscious mind, persisting in the astral realms after the dissolution of the physical, like Pollux, is, in truth, immortal.

The conscious, or objective mind, embraces those states of consciousness, thought, feeling, and visual images, which, through the etheric energies that connect the four-dimensional and the three-dimensional form, impress themselves strongly on the physical brain. Castor is mortal, because when the physical brain ceases to function he exists no more.

Yet when Castor is on earth, when the objective mind is active as in the fully waking state, the unconscious mind, Pollux, is below the threshold of consciousness, unable to express except imperfectly on the physical plane. He is chained in the realm of invisible forces, in Pluto's dark domain.

But when Castor finishes his daily sojourn, and departs through the processes of sleep, himself to enter the realm of darkness, it is then that Pollux holds full sway. In dreams the unconscious mind finds experiences such as it desires, visits the halls of learning, and weaves a pattern of phantasy which, more frequently than not, is all the memory it brings back to relieve the monotony of the waking state.

Jonathan and David were like Castor and Pollux in the eternal bond of their affection. And just as David was wont to soothe the troubled spirit of King Saul by playing on a harp, so is that harp still pictured, as anciently, held by a heavenly Twin.

When Saul sought the life of David, it was Jonathan, who loved David as his own soul, who saw to it that he escaped. He made a point of reporting to him every whim and purpose of his father; and on one occasion when the peril was most high, he devised a means by arrows, that David should be enlightened that danger threatened.

A place was appointed where David should come in hiding to receive the signal agreed upon. A bow and arrow are still to be seen clasped in a Twin's hand, and the robe is there also which was given to David. Three arrows were to be shot, as if Jonathan were practicing at a mark. If he spoke to the boy with him saying, as he started to retrieve the shots, that the arrows were this side of him, David was to know that he was safe. But if he said, as he was compelled to do, that the arrows were farther on, it should be a signal for David to depart in haste.

On still another occasion it was his wife, Michal, who saved David from the wrath of her father. This was accomplished by using a pillow of goat hair, and covering it with cloth, as if it were David prostrated with a fatal illness. The bed was brought to Saul at his command, with expectation that he would hasten the demise, but the one he thus sought to destroy had meantime effected his escape.

Thus again was the goat employed, as so often is the case, to symbolize the power of use. David possessed ability, and after the manner of the adjoining decanate of Taurus, in which a goat and her kids are pictured in association with the Master, Elijah, it is made plain that his powers were not being employed for selfishness, but for the good of the nation.

So long as David worked constructively, so long as his thoughts were directed to the accomplishment of some good end, he was helped by those nearest to him. And to the extent that any other person is able to live a completely constructive life, will he also receive the maximum benefit from his environment.

Nor is the harp pictured with the heavenly Twins without great significance; for to the extent thoughts are joined harmoniously, as were joined Damon and Pythias, Castor and Pollux, David and Jonathan, do they enter into beneficial compounds. Thoughts that are born at the same time, that are presented to the consciousness in association, become linked together in such a manner that they present a united action. The thought-cell so formed works from the four-dimensional plane, with such energy as it possesses, to attract events relating to it into the life. To the extent there are discords present it attracts misfortune, but to the extent there is that harmony which the harp symbolizes, does it work to attract events which are fortunate into the life.

The Key-phrase for that section of the zodiac where the Sun is from May 21 to June 22 is, I Think. The text, therefore, is: *Thoughts Are Man's Most Potent Builders.*

The Wee Small Bear Whose Porridge Was Just Right

Way to the north, where they may be seen circling close to the celestial pole, is the constellation of the Big Bear and the constellation of the Little Bear. A Middle Sized Bear is not shown; for the middle decanate of Gemini, instead, is pictured far to the south as a good sized dog.

Not only are we led to expect, because Gemini is the natural ruler of thought, that the constellations picturing its decanates shall relate to mental processes, but the stories of David and Jonathan, Damon and Pythias, Castor and Pollux quite prepare us to recognize in the bears a further elaboration of teachings relating to the two types of consciousness.

Bears, in addition to unconquerable restlessness, and their habit, like mind, of devouring everything presented that has possibilities as food, have unusual feet. They are plantigrade, as is man, walking not upon their toes as most beasts do, but upon the soles of their feet. The feet of a bear are mentioned in Revelation; and in Second

Samuel, 17, it speaks of men that are chafed in their minds as a bear robbed of her whelps in the field; indicating recognition of this largeness of understanding and restlessness which associates the bear symbolically with types of mental activity.

Taking the two bears to signify objective thought, which in its latest development becomes reason, and unconscious thought, which in lower forms gives rise to instinct and in man to intuition, next must be decided which bear relates to the latest form of thinking. If we follow the simple system employed by the wise ones of old in their starry portrayals as similarly we followed it in learning the order of pictorial succession, we are led to conclude that the mental activity which first developed is that which also appears first in the constellated pictures.

The Little Bear, exemplifying that section of the Sun's warm path from May 21 to May 31, coming first, reveals something of import regarding the unconscious mind. Just what that something is, let us try to learn from legendary stories about the little bear.

Some American Indians recognize the constellation as a Dipper and some as a Bear. Because of its form, just as Whites do, they often refer to it as the Little Dipper. But in general throughout the world the Pole Star, at the tip of small bruin's tail, is given a place of special honor.

One legend of wide diffusion among the American tribes is that once a hunting party of Indians lost its way and its members were in grave doubt as to the direction to go to reach their home. It was such a serious matter that they very earnestly prayed the Great Spirit to give them proper guidance. No sooner had the prayer been finished than a little child appeared in their midst and proclaimed itself the spirit of the Pole Star.

Following it, as plainsmen and woodsmen commonly at night look to the Pole Star to give them direction, they were guided safely to their home; and ever since that time Indians have recognized the orb, whose spirit is like an innocent child, as the star which never moves. When they died the huntsmen who were thus guided were carried up to heaven where yet they may be seen as the stars of the Little Dipper constellation.

Now that which is ever the same, changing not, but immovable, and which like the Pole Star is the best of all guides, is Truth. It is the

Rock of Ages, upon which any lasting church must have foundation; the rock which the Psalms proclaim is higher than I. Thus to the Greeks was the Pole Star known as Mount Olympus, the abode of the gods; a mountain so high that birds could not fly to the top of it, nor clouds collect upon its summit. Truth is never cloudy, nor can the thoughts of men ever soar to its utmost height.

The Big Bear in the sky, by means of its pointers, indicates the way to Truth, but the tail of the Little Bear actually touches it. As the Pole Star is reached by the Little Bear's tail, so are there faculties of the Unconscious Mind by which Truth can directly be apprehended.

The Objective Mind, with its mature powers of Reason, is a long way removed from the infantile stage. Not only is it full grown, but also sophisticated and often ruthless. Suggestions offered it are met with skepticism. But the Unconscious Mind, as dream life reveals, is not so critical. That which Reason, when it is brought to bear, calls impossible, takes place in the phantasy of dreams. For that matter, it also takes place in the reality of the four dimensional realm, where the restrictions imposed by three-dimensions no longer hold.

This naivete with which the Unconscious Mind accepts conditions that the Conscious Mind rejects as illogical leads to associating it symbolically with a little bear or a little child. As the Indian legend indicates, so the Bible also asserts, that the kingdom of God must be received as a little child. There is a faculty of the unconscious mind which feels assured when things are right.

Thus did little Goldilocks, in the nursery tale told over much of the globe, always find the possessions of the Little Bear just to her liking. The Things which belonged to the Great Big Bear were too coarse and rough for her; and those of the Middle Sized Bear were also uncomfortable; but the Little Bear's were just right.

You doubtless remember Goldilocks, the little girl who lived near a forest covered mountain, like Mount Olympus, and often went for a walk in the woods.

One bright and sunny morning she had gone farther than usual, picking the pretty flowers, when she came to a house, and as the door was unlocked she entered; much as we enter the physical world. But this was the house of the three bears. We call them Reason, Impulse and Intuition.

The bears were out for a stroll in the woods, while the porridge which Mother Bear had made—and what a porridge Impulse often makes of life—had been left, already poured in bowls, on the table to cool. So as Goldilocks was hungry she sampled the food. The great huge bowl of porridge was too hot, the middle sized bowl of porridge was too cold, but when she tried the little wee bowl of porridge, it, like the Intuitional appraisal of life's experiences, was neither too hot nor too cold, but just right.

After eating her fill she tried the chairs. The great big chair was too high for her, and the middle sized chair was too low, but the little wee chair was neither too high nor too low, but just right. These were not immobile chairs. They were such as typify action; for Goldilocks rocked and rocked until the little chair broke all to pieces, as in the end man's body always does.

Then she went upstairs where there were beds; beds that symbolize rest to the body after the assimilation of grueling experience and the destruction of physical tissues through the monotonous rhythm of the daily toil. The great huge bed of Reason was too high for her; for the reasoning process is a foe to sleep. And the middle sized bed of Impulse was too hard; she would have tossed and turned if she had attempted to rest there. But the wee little bed was just right; for the Unconscious Mind has full charge in slumber and Intuition can then impress its guidance through the avenue of dreams.

Such impressions are more easily recognized in the moment of waking. Of course, Intuition often is active at the very moment some situation is presented, giving instant appraisal of its possibilities and its outcome. But more often than not the Great Huge Bear of Reason so intrudes its ungainly force that the wee small voice of Intuition can not then be heard. But if listened for, it can be heard readily in that transition state between sleep and waking.

When the three bears came home it was the Little Bear that discovered Goldilocks in his bed, and spoke in a wee small voice. Whereupon—just as Reason and Impulse rush in when one starts to awaken—the two larger bears rushed over to the bed, making so much noise that they frightened Goldilocks, and she jumped out the window and ran safely home, despite the Little Bear calling to her to come back and play with him.

No time is quite so easy, as a rule, to hear the voice of Intuition as in this transition from the sleeping to the waking state; but its promptings must be carefully listened for and noted before thoughts begin to clamor in the mind.

It is because Reason and Impulse so often intrude and create a clamor that the promptings of the unconscious mind should be subjected to whatever method may be available to check their accuracy. Like the Little Bear's tail, Intuition, which is the Key-word for the decanate this animal pictures, is in constant touch with the Pole Star, Truth. But its voice is easily deflected and is often misunderstood through the crowding influences of other forms of thought.

Not that the unconscious mind is able to apprehend all there is to know; but, because it draws information from the reports of both the physical senses and the four-dimensional senses, having access to both realms, its possibilities of acquiring information are vast. In the astral realm the process of tuning in on the knowledge desired makes the more laborious methods of earth quite unnecessary.

When the unconscious mind realizes what is expected of it, it will endeavor to meet the expectations, traveling in sleep, using the faculties of clairvoyance and clairaudience, and the tuning in process to acquire Information.

Yet after it has collected facts from both the outer and the inner plane, and from them has formed correct conclusions, there is still the more difficult problem of getting recognition from the objective consciousness. Only through training can its voice be heard. Yet the text is clear: *Only Through the Intuition Does Man Contact the Real Underlying Truth of Things.*

Why a Mad Dog Shuns the Water

The marriage-decanate of Gemini, so called because it has a sub-influence ruled by Libra, the marriage sign, is pictured by a dog. This dog is not fat and plump. Thought, to which the sign as a whole relates, is swift, therefore, this dog is long of leg and speedy, like a hound.

Character is the real man, the whole man, and represents a fusion, or marriage, between the unconscious mind and the objective mind, whose powerful activities are portrayed by the bears. And because character is the truly important thing, in placing its pictographic symbol in the sky it might be expected that the ancients would use in its portrayal the most conspicuous of all the stars. Sirius, the star in the mouth of the greater dog, is the most brilliant star in the whole expanse of sky.

Joining, as it does, the Reason section of the zodiac with that section relating to Intuition, one can not help but wonder how much the ancients knew regarding it, how much was coincidence, and how much was an intuitive recognition of the real nature of the Dog Star, Sirius.

The star, like thought and like the hound, has a rapid proper motion. That is, relative to other stars it is moving at tremendous speed. And it is not one star, as to the naked eye it appears, but Twin stars, united, or married, by the mutual pull of gravity, and thus revolving around a common center; bound together by a tie as inseparable as that which held Castor and Pollux.

But more amazing still, the companion star, the smaller of the two, has a density incomparable to anything known on earth. Forty thousand times as dense as water, more than a thousand times as heavy as platinum, an amount of it such as might be placed in the pocket of a boy weighs not less than a ton.

Like planets revolving around the Sun, and with space between as large in proportion, the electrons of all atoms of matter revolve around the nucleus at the atom's center. And it is supposed that the pull of the nucleus at the center of the atoms on the companion star of Sirius, under conditions which are not understood, became so great that the atoms collapsed. The positive and negative charges entered into a still closer embrace to form a type of substance that no longer can be considered atomic; a substance having a distinctly different character to anything existing on the earth.

Very much as electrons and protons, united in a miniature solar system, are part and parcel of every atom of matter, so while man functions through a physical body the conscious and unconscious minds unite to contribute to his character.

As the dog is an animal which frequently gives warning of danger, like the voice of conscience protesting against the trespass of wicked deeds, and as both reason and intuition unite to apprise of other peril, so the Dog Star in ancient Egypt gave warning of the flooding of the Nile.

In the spring of the year this brightest of stars is visible just after sunset. But each evening it sets about four minutes earlier, so that as the season advances it is closer and closer to the Sun, until there comes a time when it is so close to the orb of day that it can no longer be seen. Then some fine morning, to anyone ambitious enough to be up, it may be seen as a morning star, heralding the approach of the rising Sun.

This first visible appearance of Sirius before the Sun was of great importance to the Egyptians because it timed the yearly approach of an event which to them meant life or death. They were an agricultural race, dependent upon the harvest for sustenance. That harvest, in turn, depended upon the flooding of the Nile.

The raising of crops, year after year, on the same piece of soil is made possible only when the elements removed are in some manner replaced. It is customary for men to spend time and money thus to prevent the wearing out of their ground. But in Egypt, each year, the Nile did this for them, overflowing its banks, depositing a thin layer of rich new silt, and in addition giving the farms a very necessary soaking.

Egypt was dependent for her life upon this flooding of the Nile. The civilization which persisted for thousands of years was made possible by it. Is it any wonder then, that the brilliant star which heralded this event should have received unusual homage!

Its first visible appearance before the Sun marked the commencement of their year. It was the first of the month of Thoth (Mercury). Were this not known historians would have a sorry time with ancient chronology. It serves them as the reference point from which to calculate the past.

There was a vague year of 365 days and a Sothic year of 365¼ days. The coincidence of the two calendars after 1461 vague years or 1460 sothic years gave them a Sothic period. And it is on record, fortunately, that one such Sothic period commenced on the first day of Thoth, in A.D. 139.

Each year it was the custom, on this first day of the month of Thoth, for the Pharaoh or one of his sons to go early to the temple. Then, just as Sirius came into view, and its rays shone through the temple and fell directly upon the shrine, to make an offering of papyrus and of lotus flowers. This officially commenced a festival which the populace celebrated with fervor and pageants of splendor.

When Sirius thus rose ahead of the Sun, Etesian winds were

piling moisture from the Mediterranean against the interior mountains, and soon the resulting rains would bring inundation. It was time, so the dog in the sky warned them, for farmers to move their household goods to higher ground until the flood had passed and it was safe for them again.

Thus the constellated dog may be seen keeping a watchful eye on the rising river. And although, due to the precession of the equinoxes, the time of this event is now earlier in the year, when the Greeks and Romans first contacted the Egyptians, the first visible rising of Sirius before the Sun commenced the close sultry days of summer, which because of this were called dog days, and are still so termed in many parts of the world.

Canis Major is a friendly dog with his master's welfare dominant in his heart. Ever faithful to the trust imposed in him he willingly risks his life in the protection of his human friends. The Sun is in the Fidelity decanate he pictures from June 1 to June 12.

As man looks up to God in service and devotion so does the faithful dog look up to man. No other animal habitually displays these qualities which in their fuller bloom become the flowers of religion and altruistic action.

As pictured in the sky he is not fleeing in terror from the rising water. He is merely warning that temporarily it is better to repair to higher ground. The soil can bring forth its fruit only when it thus has been moistened; and the earthly life of man acquires a healthy harvest only when the finer, kinder qualities of affection have softened its hard, dry selfishness.

The great dog in the sky portrays the character of man, which warns him when the emotional tide runs high enough to bring him peril; and leads him back again to moist and fertile ground when there is safety.

But when he develops fear of water, when the character no longer is swayed by the softer, kinder sentiments, he, himself, becomes a greater peril. To turn loose the dogs of war, was a customary expression in the days of ancient Rome. And when the character of a people develop madness, as a dog develops rabies, it seeks to find expression in acts of military aggression.

Hydrophobia means to have a fear of water, and those engaged in war must of necessity shun contact with those finer, kinder emotions which give quality to the soul and build for it an enduring spiritual body, such as symbolized by the stellar river. Instead there is the cruelty and wanton destruction so well expressed by the mad dog which tradition says thus shuns the water.

This is the worst of the whole affair, that one nation in the world affected with this military madness endangers every other nation. As a dog with the rabies bites right and left with no discrimination, so one jingo nation infects the others. None can disregard the threat of its armament. And each thus infected country, strengthening its powers of destruction, becomes a source from which the malady spreads to others who are fearful of its possible aggression.

And so, from one country to another, does the disease move forward. Nor apparently is there any prevention of the spread of this dread madness except through the restraint of the nation where it develops, suppressing it at its source.

Still another form occurs within a nation. Reasonable hours of labor, reasonable wages, and kindly working conditions for those employed are the dictates of proper character and in the interest of the universal good. But one firm developing the cruel traits of competitive madness, lowering wages, lengthening hours, making living conditions impossible as one nation infects another with vast expenditure for armament—compels other firms in the same business to develop like methods to prevent being bankrupt.

Mad dogs of industry and mad dogs of military aggression must be restrained for the protection of all, themselves included. But such madness primarily is that of character. There is no real benefit to the individual that can be purchased at the expense of the universal good. It is a sign of hydrophobia when, within the law or without it, the attempt is made to racketeer.

The good of any man resides in his character, and his character is sound only so long as it has due regard and sympathy for the interests of others. The text therefore may be expressed in the words of the bard of Avon: *"This Above All; To Thine Own Self Be True; And It Must Follow As the Night the Day, Thou Canst Not Then Be False to Any Man."*

When the Giants Made an Assault on Heaven

In the long ago there was a race of giants whom the Greeks called Titans. They were very powerful and became arrogant with the knowledge of their strength. In this they were not unlike some scientists of the present day, who triumphant in their conquest of certain laws of matter, believe no information of importance, of a different nature, can lie beyond their ken.

So certain of themselves did these giants become that they decided to storm the gates of heaven and dethrone the gods who resided there. That is, like Soviet Russia at the present time, they deemed there was no power superior to the physical. Brute force and intellect seemed to them supreme, and in their atheism they sought to overthrow the very judgment seat of God.

Still further back in Bible times another race of men had kindred thoughts. The sign Gemini, the third decanate of which is pictured by a Giant Bear, relates to building, the Peruvian symbol for it being a pile of bricks. Such bricks were used, as described in Genesis 11, on Shinar's plain to construct a city and a tower, whose top should reach to heaven.

The Sun while in this decanate of Reason, from June 12 to June 22, like the laid brick tower of Genesis, the barrows and pyramids of various lands, and the mountains which the Titans piled up in their invasion of the dwelling place of God, mounts higher and higher in the sky. Only at mid-day on the 22nd of June does it reach its highest, most northern, declination. This is the longest day of the year, the nearest approach of the earth to gaining perpetual light.

But the Sun, at the end of this giant decanate, ascends no higher. The Titans are defeated by the power of Jove, whose Sagittarian sign across the zodiac opposes to Intellect and Reason the mandates of true religion.

Gemini relates to thinking, but no less also to the expression of thought in speech. On Shinar's plain, therefore, the defeat of those who assaulted heaven with Babel's tower was accompanied by a confusion of tongues, and a scattering of forces, such as those born in this sign find often to defeat their ends. And the Titans, like scientists who pile up facts to refute the possibilities of an after life, to have other greater groups of facts piled over them, were buried under the very mountains they had erected; and their blood, as the essence of atheism always does, gave rise to a race of ruthless men.

It is not to be inferred from this defeat that Reason is without its proper use, or that the Titans had not a proper function. Reason should be used wherever possible to check the reports of the psychic senses and intuition. The two stars in the outer bowl of the dipper which mark the shoulder of the Giant Bear point directly to the pole star, Truth. Mariners and plainsmen and those who must find their way through the forest at night constantly use them to indicate the North Star which gives them true direction.

It was the assumption that objective consciousness and the reports of the physical senses which Reason commonly employs, were sufficient in themselves to acquire the whole of Truth that led the Titans to disaster. Reason, like the Pointers, only indicates the direction of Truth, which is really touched by the unconscious mind and the Intuition as symbolized in the Little Bear. Yet as affording a necessary means by which the accuracy of the findings of the other faculties regarding the inner world are tested, and when true their doctrines may be upheld, Reason has a fundamental work to do; for Atlas, one of the defeated Titans, henceforth was compelled to support the heavens on his head and hands.

This Atlas, one of the fabled giants associated with the larger bear, was the father of the Seven Sisters now translated to the Pleiades. Six of these well-known stars are plainly visible in the shoulder of the Bull; and keen eyes can see the seventh, and perhaps the eighth and ninth, Atlas and Pleione, father and mother of the famous girls.

Alcyone, Maia, Merope, Taygeta, Asterope and Cleaeno were quite proper in their conduct, and in due course of time, according to the conventional standards of their kind, were married to immortal gods and lived in respectability. But the seventh sister, Electra, was of a different turn, and had a disgraceful affair with a mortal lover. So great was the shame her sisters felt for her that her light died out, leaving but six stars to be seen by common eyes.

Suffering from the disdain of these sisters, and still disconsolate over her lover who, being mortal, had died, she wandered far away and became lost in the cold region of the north. Thus did the Greeks identify the naked eye star, Alcor, in the constellated Great Bear as the Lost Pleiad, who previously had been Electra, and in addition to marrying a mere mortal had veiled her face at the burning of Troy which had been founded by her son.

The Seven Sisters, through their residence in the Bull of material possessions, indicate their attachment to physical things. But Electra went beyond mere desire for the tangible things of life and formed so intimate and persistent a longing for such things that it veiled the light of their transitory nature from her inner sight.

Like many another who has formed too strong a love for that which is mortal, she wandered in the region of cold intellect, and found her final abode in the lair of the icy giant, Reason.

She was like the soul who can not turn from the thoughts of earth to higher things, even at the time of mortal passing, and thus remains earthbound for a period after death.

It was at the period of the summer solstice, when the Sun has reached the end of the decanate pictured by the Giant Bear, that the Maya and the Aztecs built special fires atop their numerous pyramids. Symbolically, because the Sun was then nearer to them by declination, this represented the closest approach of the deific spirit to the earth. The day was easily ascertained; for it was the time when at noon a stake cast its shortest shadow.

This northmost position of the Sun on earth, because thus so simply found by watching a shadow, was the index more commonly employed to mark the precession of the equinoxes, and thus to indicate the time of vast changes on the earth, including cataclysm. That is, when the decanate pictured by the Great Bear, representing the Tower of Babel, moves to a point in opposition to the Pleiades, associated with the decanate pictured more completely by the frightened Hare, such changes are at hand.

At Uxmal, in Mexico, to indicate this relation between the solstice Sun and the northern constellation, seven pyramids were so arranged as to represent the seven bright stars of the Great Bear. The Mound Builders also had altar fires atop their piles of earth; and those who make a study of the origin of words report that such mounds in the British Isles, through "berw," the ancient name of bear, have now come to be known as barrows, after that animal, and that the Welsh name for hill, "bryn," is the original of the popular name, "bruin."

At least, when Ireland was converted to Christianity one of the most difficult tasks of the good Fathers was to abolish the ancient custom of lighting fires on the tops of towers, pinnacles and conical hills in honor of the Sun. The pyramidal temples of Bel (the Sun) scattered throughout the world relate to its solstitial position. A belfry is now a cupola in which a bell is suspended, was once a tower of refuge, and at an earlier date was derived from words having to do with Bel-fires, that is, places where fires were kindled in honor of the Sun.

A pyramid of soil or stone is a high point on the earth; and some of them, those more carefully constructed, were so built that the inclination of the northern side was in line with the solstice Sun, so that on the longest day at noon no shadow would be cast, but the Sun apparently would perch like a ball of fire on the summit, when viewed by those at the northern base. Thus on this day was spirit symbolically joined to matter.

The pyramid or tower, as the highest edifice of man's construction, well represented the apex of his physical attainment, the highest point reached by the objective mind. But such a physical structure in itself was limited in its function. It was like the legendary Atlas who failed in his attempt to storm the gates of heaven; but was given useful employment holding this celestial region on his head and hands.

This, I believe, quite accurately describes the function of physical life, the hardships of which compel the development of the power of Reason as an effective means of escaping painful penalties.

Pain is the warning that the organism is not fully successful in adapting itself to its surroundings. And to escape the pain, the organism struggles. When it is successful in making the proper adaptation, the pain ceases and pleasure is felt instead. Pleasure is the signal to an organism that difficulties have been overcome and that all is well.

Ants and bees readily sacrifice their lives for the good of their fellows, a dog will die for his master, and many mother animals will defend their young to the death. We can not, therefore, place man on a pinnacle due to his altruism. But in the exercise of intelligence, especially Reason, he is as high above other creatures of the earth as a pyramid or tower is above its surroundings.

Yet Reason does not perceive all. When we approach an object from one side we may see all that can be seen from that direction, but not all that may be seen from the other side. Reason and Intuition thus approach knowledge from different directions. While Intuition touches Truth, it does not get the view that Reason does, even though Reason only points in its direction.

Both the inside and the outside of things need to be known to possess complete knowledge. As for the Great Bear it indicates the text: *Reason Points the Way to Truth, and Offers a Valuable Means by Which the Accuracy of the Reports of the Psychic Senses Can be Tested.*

Cancer I Feel

Hydra ♋−♏ Revelation

Argo ♋︎♓︎ Research

Chapter 5 _____

The Ladder to Heaven

_____

ANGELS **That Go Up and Down.**
Even at the present day, when arbitrary forms of speech long since have displaced the more primitive use of universal symbols, it is not uncommon to refer to the highest point as nearest heaven. The highest point in the zodiac, the place for which pyramids and mounds were erected, is the dividing line between Gemini and Cancer. Fires were lighted on these eminences to signify the Sun had reached its greatest elevation; that is, had reached the very gate of heaven.

If there is a special gate to heaven, to which in ancient times great homage was paid, we moderns should not be ignorant of its nature. Peter, who is pictured in the sky as Cepheus with his foot upon the rock of Truth, the Pole Star, against which the gates of hell, at the opposite side of the zodiac, shall not prevail, is reputed to hold the keys to the kingdom of heaven, as related in Matthew, 16. But it were better for our purpose to go much further back; back to the dream of Jacob as described in the twenty-eighth chapter of Genesis.

The degrees of the zodiac are not unlike the rungs of a ladder which arches the sky, extending from earth to heaven. Jacob dreamed of such a ladder set up on the earth, and the top of it reached to heaven; and angels of God were ascending and descending on it. Thus do the Sun and the various planets move higher and higher in the sky until they reach the first of the sign Cancer and then start their descent to lower declination.

This sign Cancer, where the Sun may be found from June 22 to July 23, is the natural ruler of the home and family. Therefore, next in his dream he is told that his children will be many and that in them all the families of the earth will be blessed. But when he awoke he was frightened, saying, "this is none other but the house of God, and this is the gate of heaven."

As angels more commonly are considered, instead of their going up to heaven from the earth, and the returning from that superior region, we should expect them to come down from heaven and after their visit on earth to return again to that higher plane. But in Jacob's dream they were going up, as the Sun ascends to reach the sign Cancer, and then coming back to earth, as the Sun again descends after it reaches that family sign.

This going up and coming down, which the Sun is observed to do each summer, evidently signified to those who traced the starry pictures in the sky and gave to each a story, a going up and coming down which was suggestive of the movement of those intelligences which have no physical form, and which, for want of a better term, may be called angels.

Although the place where a person commonly sleeps may be regarded as his home, the action of Jacob after awakening, of setting up a stone to be the house of God would be difficult to understand were it not that other contemporaneous peoples, in various parts of the world, were also accustomed to set up pillars, pyramids and towers to commemorate this nearest approach of the spiritual symbol, the Sun; which, in this position, marks the commencement of the home sign, Cancer.

It was the belief of the better informed of these people that the soul made progress by gaining experiences in one physical form; passing at its dissolution into the astral world, as Jacob saw the non-material beings do in his dream, and after a period of experience and assimilation in the astral world, descending, as Jacob saw them do, to occupy another, but more complex, physical body on the earth.

Every such form occupied constituted one rung in the soul's evolutionary ladder. It could be gained only through the offices of parents who provided it opportunity to have a new physical body.

Every physical cell, every germ or shoot which develops into bacterium, plant or animal is dependent upon parenthood for its existence. Without parenthood there could be no opportunity for evolutionary progress, no successive rungs which more complex life-forms provide, no avenue to reach the spiritual development which opens wide the Elysian gates. As the commencement of Cancer marks the highest declination of the Sun and the boundary of the place of home, so also, as signifying parenthood, it is in truth the very gate of heaven.

This coming back to earth, and the coming back of the Sun toward the earth in declination, needed some object to represent them in the sky. The Crab does not move directly forward, as other creatures are wont to do, but has a backward, sidewise gait. Its motion thus most fittingly represents the backward motion of the Sun.

Nor is it without significance that the preceding compartment in the zodiacal circle, which is touched by this gate of the above, is Gemini, the section ruling thought. As the Key-phrase to Cancer is, I Feel, we have quite appropriately, Thinking and Feeling in immediate contact with the highest point of the celestial circle, and thus leading to the heavenly gate.

Thoughts enter into compounds which are harmonious or discordant according to the Feeling at the time they were brought together. If the feeling was that of discord, the thoughts so united tend to attract into the life the very opposite of heaven; they attract misfortune and distress. But if the feeling which accompanied their union was of a pleasant turn, to the extent such harmony was present do the thought-cells then composed, work to attract fortune and happiness into the life.

A similar process is at work with lower forms, in fact, wherever life exists such processes are at work; although the states of consciousness experienced can hardly be dignified by the name of thought. Yet lifeforms on every plane, and in every stage of progress, have experiences which are registered in their finer forms as states of consciousness.

These states of consciousness, however lowly and simple they may be, constitute the experiences of that form. They are registered in the astral counterpart, and combine to form the psychoplasmic cells of that finer body; and these, in turn, determine the experiences which will be attracted to it.

Whether lowly or highly evolved, whether to a single cell of protoplasm or to an educated man, every experience that comes to a life-form adds just that much energy to its finer body. As a man, when hypnotized, or under psychoanalysis, can recall any experience or thought of his past, so the four-dimensional body of every organism is a complete record of all that has happened to it, and its mental and emotional reactions to these occurrences.

Thus it is that every form of life is moving forward toward the acquisition of such abilities as will fit it to perform the particular function in the cosmic scheme of affairs, that it has been called into differentiated existence to fulfill. It attracts to it, by virtue of its original polarity, the type of experiences that afford it the proper trend in education. It does not have just the same experiences that some other does; because it is not being educated to fill the same cosmic position.

Its experiences in one form of life, however, give its thought-cells, or unconscious mind, ability to handle certain situations. It learns how to gather together the material elements and build a certain kind of physical body. And then, when the body dies, as seen in Jacob's dream, it ascends to heaven; that is, passes to the astral spheres.

In this astral realm there are other opportunities for experience and progress. Life is never stationary; it is ever moving, always gaining new experiences, whatever may be the plane. These experiences however, are of a different sort. They are four-dimensional experiences; experiences also of reorganizing what has been gained in the preceding physical body.

Then, when the vibratory conditions are right, the life-form which has continued its progress on the astral plane, is attracted again to earth, descends the ladder as in Jacob's dream, to enter another physical form; a physical form which is a step in advance, perhaps a long step in advance; due to its assimilation of previous experiences.

Successively, it ascends to the astral plane and then returns to earth, as the angels moved up and down; but each physical form, due to its acquired experiences, is a step in advance, and each ascent to the astral is a more conscious existence. Birth and death and birth again are the rungs of the ladder which lead man to his spiritual estate; and the gate through which he must pass to enter that estate is the gate of parenthood.

The benefits of parenthood, if its offices are well performed, are not confined to those conferred upon the offspring. Like most of the better things of life when given, the giver receives an equal advantage. As iron when cold gives forth no glow, yet becomes luminous with light when sufficiently heated, and thus imparts a motion to a substance finer than the physical, that is, to ether; so the warm sympathies of parenthood transmit their energies to substance still finer than the astral and tend to the construction of a truly spiritual form.

To the extent feelings and emotions are present which have for their chief concern the welfare of others, do they displace thoughts and emotions which revolve around the self, such as are represented by the Giant Bear; and to the extent the tender emotions of the family ties find expression do they displace the domestic discord of the Giant Crab.

Greek legend says that while Hercules was performing one of his great labors, battling with Hydra in the Lernean marshes, a huge Crab attempted to drag him down through seizing him by the foot.

Many another worker has similarly been hampered in life's struggle through domestic misunderstanding. Strife and discord in the home have a peculiarly effective way of confusing the mind and retarding effort. They are powerful to pull the individual down. But domestic harmony is equally as effective to raise him up. The text, therefore, becomes: *Parenthood Tends to Displace Selfishness With those Tender Affections that Most Quickly Strengthen the Soul and Build the Spiritual Body.*

The Misfortune of Old Dog Tray

Long have the bards sung of the Inconstant Moon, whose face each night is different from the last; who rules the ever-changing ocean tides, and in the birth-chart of man is found in that department of his life most given to ebb and flood. Might we not expected, then, that the Moon's own decanate of the Moon's own sign, Cancer, should picture in constellation and in story, some spiritual doctrine relating to family life, which the sign as a whole governs, as influenced by unjustified change?

And we should have a right to expect, I believe, that the teaching should chiefly revolve around a danger to be avoided, rather than an advantage to be won; because when the Sun enters this particular decanate, or 10 degree section of its path, it undergoes its greatest derogatory change. Until it reaches the point pictured among the constellations by Canis Minor it increases in power, the days get longer and longer; but the moment it touches the Little Dog decanate it begins to fail; its power diminishes, and the days become shorter and shorter. Its life is no longer what it used to be.

It should not be inferred from this, however, that people born from June 22 to July 2, are less faithful in their family vows than others. Their love of home and their devotion to it is even remarkable. The changeableness to which they are subject relates to their feelings. Their emotions are like the tides of the sea, flowing in during one period, shortly to turn and flow out during the next. Although the message the constellation conveys points to the dangers of moral laxity, the trait which most clearly distinguishes those born when the Sun is here is stated by the Key-word, which is Moods.

Cancer is the first of the watery signs, and thus relates to baptism. That is, the Sun, as symbol of deific power, as it makes its annual pilgrimage, must go into, and come out of, the water sign Cancer before it can return to its own home in the next sign, Leo. It is not the sign of death, but in a natural birth-chart rules the conditions at the end of life; and thus signifies, as baptism does, a readiness and willingness to enter upon a new and higher form of life, a willingness to enter the Father's fold.

When the ancients sought to find an emblem of the Savior in the sky, most naturally they selected the brightest of all the stars, the great star Sirius, which was venerated especially in Egypt because it gave warning of the flooding of the Nile, which in turn made possible the raising of crops, and thus gave new life to the people.

This star, in turn, had its own announcer. Sirius comes first in zodiacal longitude, which determines the order of its pictorial succession; but due to having a northern rather than a southern declination, Procyon, the Little Dog Star, to people of the northern hemisphere, always puts in an appearance above the horizon first. When the Little Dog Star appears it is known that the Great Dog Star shortly will follow. The baptizing star, chief luminary to picture the water-decanate of the most watery sign of all the zodiac, thus announces one still greater who is to come.

The great baptizer of Bible times, John preached incessantly against moral transgression, saying, "And now also the axe is laid unto the root of the trees; every tree therefore which bringeth not forth good fruit is hewn down, and cast into the fire." In fact, he lost his life through pointing out to Herod the evil which would follow his domestic sins.

Herod's brother Philip had a wife. But instead of treating her as a sister, Herod violated the sanctity of his brother's home by taking this woman and marrying her himself. The wife he thus obtained by breaking up his brother's home was called Herodias; and by her subsequent conduct we may be sure that she not merely sanctioned this proceeding, but also chiefly engineered it.

She was that type of woman who obtains her ends through craft and subtlety, to whom loyalty is unknown, and stops at no sin nor violence to prevent her ambitions being thwarted.

Therefore, when John remonstrated with Herod on the evil thing he had done, and placed the proper measure of blame on Herodias, she schemed and plotted to take his life. And it is not amazing, as the power of the Sun is cut off as soon as it reaches the family decanate of the family sign, that John lost his head through a plot involving the whole domestic group.

Herod, mindful of the wishes of the people, who rightfully regarded John as a very holy man, had no intention of killing him. But Herodias had a daughter who danced very well, and she conceived the idea of using this daughter to have John destroyed.

When Herod's birthday rolled around, therefore, and he had invited high captains and other notables of his realm to be present at his home, he was desirous of impressing them through affording excellent entertainment. He was more than pleased, consequently, as things began to get a bit dull, when just at the right moment, the daughter of Herodias put in an appearance and danced so engagingly that all were loud in their praise.

As pride welled up within him, and rather off his guard with the excitement of the celebration, he swore an oath that he would give the girl anything she asked, even to half his kingdom. It had not occurred to him that she would make some unreasonable demand. But when, instigated by her mother, she did betray his spirit of generosity, to have failed to keep his oath would have lost him the esteem of all those present.

Therefore, when the girl asked for the head of John, to save his own face, he ordered it brought to her, that she might carry it to her wicked, plotting mother on a platter.

Herod may not have been a model man, but like Old Dog Tray, he had to take the blame also for the transgressions of his close companions.

The Old Dog Tray story is told in many lands. He was not at heart wicked, just a dog with certain weaknesses of character, too easily influenced by his associates. He had never killed a sheep in his life, and had no intention of thus betraying the trust placed in him by his master.

But there were other dogs that had no such scruples. They lay about all day, taking it easy and warming themselves while they dozed in the sun. But when darkness fell they gathered into a roving marauding band, scouring the countryside in search of sheep to kill, on which they feasted, returning to their homes before the break of day.

Tray was not a murderer of sheep, but he loved company, and on a particular night when many sheep were killed had gone along, more for the sake of companionship than with any thought of adventure. By this time the owners of the sheep had become so thoroughly aroused that they had placed a watchman to observe which dogs left their homes at night to join the outlaw pack. Tray was absent from home, and was seen to join the others before the crime took place. He, therefore, was rounded up and paid the penalty of death, along with the guilty rest.

Long before the time of Herod another Hebrew king, Ahab, had a wife whose name has come to be used as a synonym for infidelity and wickedness. Jezebel influenced Ahab to commit all manner of evil, and it was prophesied, therefore, that she should die and that the dogs should eat her flesh; a prophecy that in due time was fulfilled, as related most dramatically in Second Kings.

The dogs that thus devour are the emotions which ever accompany wickedness. The feelings which are present as the companions of thought determine the type of compound which is formed in the thought-cells of the structure of the finer body. Treachery, sooner or later, brings a reward of sorrow through the events attracted by the thought-cells thus formed. Hate gnaws at the very bones of the hater, attracting malice from others, and through its action on the ductless glands, destroying the mineral balance of the body.

Ever-changing moods and fretful inconstancy within the domestic circle attract a train of woes that consumes the energies and leads eventually to some disaster.

The Greeks portrayed the devouring effects of unhallowed emotions quite clearly in their story of Actaeon. This legendary person had fifty dogs with which he hunted in his leisure time. One day, as with his dogs he came out of the forest into the vale of Gargaphia, quite by accident he discovered Diana, the Moon, bathing there with her nymphs.

Instead of beating an immediate retreat, as modesty dictated he should, his emotions overcame his finer nature. But Diana perceiving his approach, thereupon transformed him into a stag. In this stag the dogs could not recognize their master, but considering it their natural prey, they tore him quite asunder.

The Law of Affinity is inexorable. That which we have within ourselves, and that only, do we attract from our environment. The discord may be due to weakness, as it is represented in the story of Actaeon, rather than to malice; yet whatever its cause, if it is a portion of the character, built into the finer body through emotional associations, it will attract a similar discord from without.

We can not do injustice to another, or like Herodias, harbor thoughts of revenge, without building into ourselves the nucleus of the very condition thought about. The plot, the very wish that injury may befall someone, builds cells of a similar quality within ourselves, which, because of their discordant composition, because given a feeling of malice, not only work from the four-dimensional plane to bring about the injury contemplated, but due to their essential vicious nature, also work to attract misfortune to ourselves.

Both the ductless glands of the physical body and the thought-cells of the four-dimensional body, take their orders as they come. It is not within their ability to reason and make decisions; only to obey. If, therefore, the thoughts are evil, or the emotions run wild, they act as thus directed, unaware that destruction follows to their master. The text which the decanate thus suggests is: *The Wages of Sin Is Death.*

The Snake Which Had Too Many Heads.

The people whom we meet from day to day, not less than those with whom we make a casual acquaintance, leave us with a distinct impression of their characters. Certain points of strength stand out, and certain points of weakness. Even those we most admire not infrequently have special traits that lessen their personal attractiveness.

We have all met the perennially apologetic individual, I am sure. The one who has ability sufficient for accomplishment, but who is fearful to make the attempt. When called upon to take some small responsibility he shrinks from it, asks that someone better qualified should do the work, or if he accepts it, makes it plain that, although he will do his best, he feels himself unqualified. Our psychologists have a label for this complaint. They call it an inferiority complex.

Closely akin to him, although quite the opposite in his expression, is the braggart. His pleasantest pastime consists in telling people how great he is, what wonders he can do. He is always the hero of his own stories. Whatever he does, be it really great or small, the part he has had to play is given undue prominence in the telling. Because inside himself he feels inadequate he ever thus presents to others a false front, in the effort to impress them with his own superiority. But psychologists say this attitude also is in reality the expression of an inferiority complex.

A third type of person we all know—in fact, we can not completely avoid him—actually believes himself of quite superior stuff to other individuals. He is ever eager to appear before the public, but when he does, as the current sporting expression goes, he always plays to the grandstand rather than offer support to his associates in their team work. He strives for the plaudits of the multitude rather than seeking satisfaction in more obscure but worthy service. The psychologists say such an individual is afflicted with a superiority complex.

Other traits of character there are also, perhaps a hundred of them, that derive from these main stems; branching out as ugly heads to mar the symmetry of action. Yet it were an unprofitable thing to draw attention to these defects, which in greater or less degree we find so common, were it not that in olden times they apparently were so well understood, and that the only remedy so far discovered is set forth most clearly in the story of the constellated Hydra.

Although, according to the mythology of the Greeks, Hydra originally had a hundred heads, only one of them was immortal. It may be assumed, therefore, that the head yet to be seen on the constellated figure is this deathless one.

Likewise, it has been found by modern psychologists, through wide experience with hypnosis, psychoanalysis and innumerable specially devised tests, that there is one head, or governing attribute within the unconscious mind of man which ever dominates the soul; which never is relinquished, and which never takes a second place so long as life shall last. More commonly it is referred to as the desire for significance. It is the inner urge to be and to accomplish.

Within each form of life there is a vital urge, an impulse that causes it to cling to life, to struggle onward, to climb upward, to express itself and to maintain its own identity at whatever may be the cost. In human terms we speak of the group of thoughts thus expressing as the Power Urges. They are mapped by the Sun in a chart of birth.

Because this urge for significance is chiefly that which impels the individual to struggle to survive, and without which he relinquishes his hold on life, it is that factor within the human mind which resists most strongly the effort to remove it, or to cause it to take a subordinate place. When it is quoted that self preservation is nature's first law, it is implied, as psychologists have found to be the case, that the individual holds most tenaciously to the importance of himself.

In his contact with the outside world, however, this sense of his own power and importance often suffers considerable shock. Especially in the childhood home is he surrounded by those whose abilities are greater. These through their attitude may cause the child to feel quite inadequate to meet that which is expected of it. Regardless of its abilities, for the child's experiences are not wide enough to afford a basis of sound comparison, its repeated failure to live up to its own expectations, which are those implied by the attitude of others, may give rise to a chronic feeling of inferiority.

On the other hand, the child who is constantly told how bright he is, whose parents place him in the limelight on every possible occasion, and in spite of mediocre performance give him unstinted praise, develops an undue feeling of his own importance. Too limited in experience to judge by outside standards, as his home and parents constantly offer the suggestion that he is made of better stuff, he accepts their statement as the truth and nourishes a chronic feeling of superiority.

Because in childhood the mind is more plastic and impressionable than at any later date, the suggestions offered by parents and others in the home are of far more importance, as a rule, in the development of chronic states of feeling as regards its own significance, than the experiences of a later date.

Yet whether the objective mind and certain thought-cells of the unconscious mind accept the suggestion of superiority or that of inferiority, there is always a central nucleus of the unconscious mind—those thought-cells most closely allied to the individuality—that never do accept the suggestion of their own inferiority.

In spite of any evidence to the contrary they hold tenaciously to the attitude that the individual is significant in the scheme of things, that he possesses qualities of value, that in reality he is not an inferior being. They hold to this tenaciously, because when this inner attitude is displaced, when this Power Urge nucleus of the individuality accepts defeat, when the soul itself admits its lack of worth, no longer is there any hold on life, nothing left which makes an effort to survive.

When, therefore, there has been developed through any experiences, of which the usual source is the home, a chronic feeling of inferiority, the individuality thought-cells of the unconscious mind refuse to accept this and devise various subtle ways by which to save their face.

The apologetic person, in the Power-Urge section of himself, expects greater things of himself than of others. He feels that he should be more perfect than the common run of mankind; hence he apologizes because of his performance, though quite as good, or better than the performance of others. He shrinks in fear from responsibility because if he did not make a great success of it, this would be a shock to his interior sense of superiority.

The boastful individual, because of his desire for significance, which in actual life he fails to attain, compensates by trying to impress others with his superiority. He presents himself as he would like to be. But while this may fool the central cells of his unconscious mind, it seldom fools the public.

The person with a superiority complex, after he leaves the parental roof and faces the world, still feels superior; but, because he fails to mold circumstances as he believes he should, his unconscious mind must ever find new alibis, for this lack of success. His failure to accomplish more than others, to save the face of his central unconscious mind, is ever laid to hard luck. He never gets an even break with others. He thinks himself imposed upon, and that his merits are never properly rewarded.

These types are only three of the more easily recognized misadjustments, of the hundred that might be mentioned by which the unconscious mind compensates by subterfuge for failure to make a correct appraisal of its own relation to life.

To readjust these mental factors was one of the twelve great labors of Hercules. The huge sea serpent, Hydra, pictures the Revelation-decanate of Cancer, where the Sun is located from July 2 to July 12. This creature of the middle-decanate of the home-sign, according to Greek legend, not only had a hundred heads, but even as when a complex or a repression of the human mind is violently slain it crops out in other types of expression, when one of the sea serpent's heads was cut off, two other heads immediately grew to take its place.

Hercules solved the problem of these abnormal growths by securing the aid of a companion, such a companion as befits a home. When he clubbed off one of the unseemly heads, Iolaus seared it over with a hot iron to prevent another from growing.

The final head, however, was immortal, as is the desire for individual survival and significance. Wisely, therefore, instead of attempting its annihilation, Hercules buried it under a rock, symbolic of the "rock of ages," the Pole Star, Truth.

Whatever may be the unseemly desires within the unconscious mind, they can not successfully be repressed. Merely to deny them expression is to have them show two different heads where there was one before. But their energy can be utilized, and made to perform constructive work by applying the hot iron of discrimination, sublimating it through wise appraisal which directs it to find full expression in more highly acceptable ways.

Quite correctly the Individuality of man refuses to consider itself inadequate, inferior and of no consequence. The soul of each was brought into existence with a definite and essential work to do. Quite correctly also desires for expression refuse to subside. Whatever their nature they represent energies which diverted can be turned to constructive use.

Any attempt to annihilate a desire, to merely ignore it, or to suppress it, fails, because the energy is still within the finer body and must express either in acceptable or unacceptable ways. The text therefore is: *Not Through Slaying Desire, but Through Sublimating It to a Higher Plane of Manifestation, Does Man Make Soul Progress.*

The Ship Which Brought Them Safely Home.

If we turn back the leaves in the book of earth's past, before long we reach pages in which fact and tradition are so inseparably blended that one can not be discerned apart from the other. To perceive where one ends and the other begins thus often becomes a hopeless task. This seems particularly true in reference to the various accounts of the flood.

One who has stood on high mountains in various regions of the land and observed close to their summits—or further down where erosion has failed to remove them as it has on top, scouring them off down to the granite core various rocks of sedimentary origin, realizes that there is some foundation for the story of the great inundation. There are but a few choice spots in all the world that show no evidence of having been at some time in the past at the bottom of sea or lake or ocean. Sandstone, limestone, shale, and all their innumerable derivatives, are formed only in the presence of water.

Gradual subsidence of certain areas accompanied by gradual elevation of others may account for much of this; but there is evidence also of occasional cataclysmic change. Yet when we contemplate these, especially of modern geologic time, the accurate history of the rocks grows dim and human tradition emerges as of more significance.

Traditions of a widespread flood are almost universal. Linked with the story of creation as written on the oldest cuneiform tablets known is an account of it. American Indians have their version of the story; and the Tro-Cortesianus, one of the three Maya books which alone escaped Spanish vandalism, being smuggled into Europe, links it with the sinking of an ancient land from which we inherit stellar wisdom. A translation of this Maya document reads:

> In the year 6 Kan, on the 11 Muluc, in the month of Zac, there occurred terrific earthquakes which continued until the 13 Chuen

without interruption. The country of the hills of earth—the land of Mu (some translate this Atlantis)—was sacrificed. Twice upheaved, it disappeared during the night, having constantly been shaken by the fires of the underneath. Being confined, these caused the land to rise and sink several times in various places. At last the surface of the earth gave way and the ten countries were torn asunder and scattered. They sank with their 64,000,000 inhabitants 8,060 years before the writing of this book.

Quite similar in their purport are the accounts contained in the Timaeus and Critas of Plato, where the civilization of Atlantis is mentioned and the story is told of its sinking, as related to the Greek law giver, Solon, by an Egyptian priest. After describing it in much detail, and asserting that the world had been many times scourged both by fire and by water, the priest told Solon of the sinking of the western land in a single night some 9,000 years before.

These times of greatest cataclysm, according to the stellar traditions of the past, take place when the equinoctial pointer, which is the index to evolutionary progress, reaches the stations of most critical change in its backward circle of the stars. These points are the dividing line between the fixed fire of Leo and the movable water of Cancer, and the opposite position of the zodiac where the fixed air of Aquarius joins the movable earth of Capricorn.

These two points reached annually in the journey of the Sun mark the extremes of temperature. The hottest weather of the year commonly occurs about July 23, when the Sun moves from Cancer into Leo; and the coldest weather of the year usually may be expected about January 20, when the orb of day leaves Capricorn to enter the sign of the Man.

The Vernal Equinox in its movement through the signs, however, goes in the reverse direction, so that it moves from Leo into Cancer, from fire into water, from the decanate of the red-hot crater into the decanate pictured by a ship.

When the Equinox thus crosses from fixed fire into movable water, and the Sun at the time of the Vernal Equinox goes down in the west as if submerged, the Waterman rises in the east, triumphant, and starts pouring water from his urn down upon the earth in torrential floods. And as timing this event, the Pleiades, which are often called the doves, are then directly overhead.

According to the latest and most refined astronomical calculations, the complete precessional cycle requires 25,868 years, instead of the round number, 25,920 years, which the ancients more commonly employed. If, therefore, as both tradition and the pictures in the stars hold forth, the period when stresses and strains are such as to make watery cataclysms probable relates to the passing of the Vernal Equinox from the decanate of Crater in Leo into the decanate of the Ship in Cancer, the dates are not difficult to ascertain.

Taking 1881 as the date of the Equinox passing from Pisces back into Aquarius—that is, 30 degrees back from the place where in ancient times it had been ascertained that the commencement of the circle of stars coincided with the commencement of the circle of signs—it must have passed back into Cancer from Leo just five signs earlier, and will again reach such a point seven signs later.

Five-twelfths of 25,868 gives 10,778 years before 1881, or 8,897 B. C. as the date of the last such period of watery cataclysms. And seven-twelfths of 25,868 gives 15,085 years after 1881, or 16,971 A. D. as the next such period. On these dates, at least, at the commencement of the astronomical year, as Crater goes down in the ocean and the Pleiades are overhead, the Waterman comes up with his urn as if to pour torrents down upon the earth.

The traditions and stories of this olden flood, wherever they are found, are linked with the wickedness of men. This wickedness is not of the usual kind, but always has to do with strange and abnormal psychic phenomena. Atlantis sunk, so the tradition goes, because of its devotion to magic of the blackest sort. Those who had gained the ability to use occult forces no longer used them for the welfare of the people, but chiefly to gain in power for themselves. The populace was enslaved by unseen forces.

In the time of Noah also, a similar condition obtained. The sixth chapter of Genesis relates incredible things about the diabolical influence upon the lives of the people of beings that rightfully belonged to a different plane.

Those who go to the seance room expecting to surrender control of themselves to entities about which they have no knowledge should again read this ancient story. The ship, or ark, picturing the Research decanate of Cancer, where the Sun may be found from July 13 to July 23, indicates that the etheric sea of such a situation favors the production of strange creations; but it also indicates that it is safer not to become immersed in this Psychic Research sea.

Warned by their knowledge of the stars, the wiser ones of Atlantis are said to have departed to foreign shores. Likewise warned was Noah, and as the account makes clear, neither he nor his family took part in the current psychic abominations.

Instead, they ever kept alert, always avoided those who followed practices that included loss of self control. Their souls were stable and sound, like the Grecian ship which carried Jason and his companions on the famed Argonautic Expedition for the recovery of the Golden Fleece.

This Golden Fleece of eternal life, symbolized by the ruler of gold, the Sun, in its exaltation, the sign of the Ram, is well worth sailing for, well worth all the Research that may be devoted to learning how it may be secured. But it is not to be obtained by loss of self-control, and not by a complete discard of caution.

There is a right way to investigate the conditions and possibilities of the unseen realms, those regions where man must make his future home. But when the ark first touched the land Noah did not throw caution to the wind and rush forth. First a raven and then a dove were sent out that the conditions which there prevailed might be learned without danger. Nor did Noah remove the cover of the ark until, without chance of being drowned, he had ascertained that the earth was dry

Not birds, but radio waves, are now used as messengers. The nervous system of man is an organic receiving set, over which he can receive communications from other planes. With properly developed poise he can tune in and out much as he desires, and without the danger of some other entity in control.

If, as when the raven was sent from the ark, no message is received, or if it be inimical, if he retains poise he can tune off the station. But if, instead, he steps from his steady bark and permits dark waves of unknown origin to sweep him off his feet, so that, no longer is he able to determine what he can do, he has relinquished his ship of safety.

The right and the wrong way to accomplish a given thing may seem closely allied. Particularly may this seem true in the field of Research so long as that which is desired seems identical. Yet the result to the individual of using the correct method of approach is the difference experienced by those who entered the ark, or departed on board ship from the land of Atlantis, and those who felt the full force of the deluge.

Argo encourages rather than disparages the effort at research into the forces and regarding the entities of the invisible plane; a tendency outstanding among those born while the Sun is in the section of its annual cycle thus pictured. But it also offers wise council as to the method by which such voyages can be attempted in safety. Each mariner should keep his hand firmly on the helm. The text, consequently, is: *Poise is the One Safe Haven of the Soul, therefore,* "Under All Circumstances Keep An Even Mind."

CRATER   ♌-♌   Rulership

CENTAURUS ♌-♐ Reformation

CORVUS ♌-♈ Ambition

Chapter 6

Is There A Santa Claus

WHEN Samson Lost His Strength. Daniel had quite an adventure in a den of Lions and the Greek Hercules was compelled to strangle such a beast, but at a still more ancient date heroic Samson tore one quite in two, at the time when love first came into his life.

To picture that section of the sky where the Sun holds forth in all his courage and all his strength from July 23 to August 23 each year, the section which in the natural chart of man relates to offspring, to pleasures, to gambling, and to affairs of the heart, the ancients chose the king of beasts, the dauntless lion.

Samson was one of those unfortunates to whom our sympathies go out, present in every community and in every period of the world, who loved not wisely but too well. He was a good chap, but always unfortunate in his love affairs.

His intentions, as a youth, were honorable and just. He met a young woman who found favor in his sight, and being in love with her, sought in honor to make her his wife. But his parents were opposed to such a match. This woman was of a different faith, they wanted nothing to do with her, and so Samson's troubles began.

A Lion, related astrologically to the house of pleasure, is a universal symbol of desire. If the desire be spiritual the creature is represented in its beneficial sense, as when Christ is termed a Lion of the tribe of Juda; but if the desire be gross, such as leads to destruction, the beast is shown antagonistic, as when the devil is mentioned in the Bible as a roaring Lion.

Thus when Samson, in love with the girl, was met by a young

lion which roared against him, it is to be inferred, especially as his parents disapproved, that he was beset by passions which raged within. But, as is set forth at considerable pains, his life up to this time had been without blemish in thought or action, his mother being carefully instructed even before his birth.

The young Lion thus was easily conquered, and whatever his thoughts for the moment may have been, they were quickly vanquished by those of a highly spiritual kind. No type of nourishment is quite so high in its symbolical significance as honey, ruled by Venus, and made from the nectar of flowers. It thus represents a spiritual food.

Genius in every age and clime has been inspired by love. As the love is exalted so does genius soar to higher levels of expression. Love has creative power, therefore Samson, having again talked with the girl of his choice and exalted by his adoration, partook of spiritual nutriment, tuned in on energies which brought him spiritual strength, as symbolized by the honey he found and ate, which the bees had made in the carcass of the roaring lion he had slain.

The conversion of the roaring lion into honey with which he fed his soul, and which also proved acceptable to his parents, is expressed by psychologists of the present day as the sublimation of desire.

As already pointed out, in practical astrology the sign Leo is related alike to love affairs, to gambling and to entertainment. Therefore it was quite in order, from a symbolic point of view, that the culmination of Samson's first love affair in marriage should be celebrated with a feast to which other young men were invited, and that this, in turn, should lead to gambling.

The riddle proposed by Samson, on which the wager was laid as to its correct solution, is the riddle with which every person is confronted, and on the solution of which depends his life's reward. Samson knew the solution of the riddle; but as events later transpired they show, like many another, that he did not always practice what he knew.

With the thought in his mind of the lion he had slain, out of which he had obtained honey, he said to those who came to his entertainment, "Out of the eater came forth meat, and out of the strong came forth sweetness."

In the sense of Samson's riddle only those who have can give to others; and those who have the energy to benefit their associates must acquire it from some already existing source. Even the vegetables from the garden are eaters; for they consume water and minerals from the soil and carbon from the air.

This is generally recognized; but in the second part of his riddle Samson went beyond the commonplace. Not the observation that only those of outstanding abilities are able to be of much help in the progress of the world as such. But when he implied that spirituality, as symbolized by the honey, depends upon strength, he sets forth a great truth.

Moses made use of material wealth for spiritual purposes. But here is a teaching that desires, even the roaring desires which Samson met on his visit to the Philistine woman, can so be used. In fact, the implication is that desires such as are symbolized by the lion are the source from which spiritual powers most readily can be derived.

The Key-phrase of Leo is, I Will, and people born when the Sun is in this sign commonly exhibit more than the average amount of that fixity of purpose which goes by the name of will power. Yet power of will itself is dependent upon ability to keep the desires focused on the objective to which once they were so strongly attracted that a decision to follow some line of conduct toward their realization was made. Therefore, the stronger the desires are which an individual has, the greater will be his will power if he can keep them, instead of running wild, turned into some particular channel of his choosing.

In order to accomplish this there must be the willingness, when occasion requires, to face disagreeable situations. Such willingness is called courage. Courage is of different kinds. Samson had the courage to meet physical peril of the most dangerous sort; but not the courage to resist the pleading of a woman, even though it meant his certain ruin.

For that sweetness which comes from the strong, which is the manifestation of spiritual growth, the desires must not be diverted from their lofty aim through wavering in the face of obstacles. To desist, to give in to another knowing such yielding to be wrong, is moral cowardice. In spite of Samson's physical courage he was a moral weakling; for when his newly acquired wife tormented him to tell her the secret of his riddle, after a time he grew so weary of her complaining that he took the line of least resistance and told her all.

She, telling those who sought to solve the riddle, caused him to lose his wager. And although at some later date, linking the common rulership of love affairs and gambling, some one coined an ameliorating phrase that to be unlucky at cards is to be lucky in love, Samson's experience, like common observation, brings its complete refutation. He lost not merely the gambling stake, but his wife as well.

One might think that one experience of this kind would have been enough for Samson. Yet in our daily contacts of life such failure to profit by experience is a matter of common observation. A certain weakness is so strong, as the birth-chart reveals, that the individual makes the same blunder over and over again. It is one of the functions of astrology to indicate how this can be avoided.

In Samson's later, and even more disastrous love affair, the source of his strength, the cause of its loss, and how at last it was regained are set forth still more clearly. But this clarity is present only when hair, which like honey is ruled by Venus, the planet of love, is recognized as a common object used in universal symbolism.

When Delilah implored Samson to tell her the secret of his strength he tried by means of subterfuge to throw her off the track. He told her that if he were bound with seven green switches he would be unable to break them. So she bound him thus, and called as if shouting to his enemies; but he broke the switches with the greatest ease.

As she continued to nag him for his want of trust in her, later he said that if he were to be bound with new ropes he would be unable to free himself. But when she trussed him up with such strands, and called to his enemies who lay in readiness to capture him, these also he broke like threads.

Then he told her that if she were to weave the seven locks on his head it would render him helpless. Yet when she had done this, and fastened him by the hair to the loom, and he awoke, he went away, carrying the pin of the weaving beam, with no more difficulty than he had before.

Finally, however, the moral cowardice of the man caused him to yield to her entreaties, and he told her all he knew; that his strength was in his hair. So she shaved his head and his strength departed from him. She called his enemies. They put out his eyes, placed him in fetters, and made him do the grinding n the prison house.

The seven locks of hair which she shaved from his head are of the same symbolic significance as the honey taken from the lion's carcass; for both hair and honey are ruled by the planet of love. But here, instead of acquiring spiritual energy through the sublimation of his desires, he is represented as having lost the energies he already possessed through moral cowardice.

The seven locks which were shaved from his head were symbols of great desires, which, so long as present furnished the energy for tremendous undertakings. But when, through lack of courage to resist that which deflected him from his purposeful course of life, he permitted himself to be shorn of desire, in other words, when he gave up to the importunities of life, his strength went from him.

Yet later, when his hair grew long again, symbolizing desires that could be converted into will, and they had taken him into a house where his enemies were collected that they might have fun with him, he pushed down the pillars, bringing their destruction along with his own demise. The text thus follows: *Any Accomplishment Truly Worth While Requires the Exercise of Courage.*

Fire and Brimstone Which Came Out of the Sky

In form, the cup placed in the sky is similar to those vessels used in ancient times, and in many regions of the earth today, for holding burning coals. This heat producing quality is quite understandable in light of the constellation's use to picture the fiery decanate of the fixed fire sign, the 10 degrees through which the Sun must pass from July 23 to August 3, when commonly the days are hottest.

Therefore it represents the fiery furnace into which, as related in Daniel 3, Shadrach, Mesach and Abednego were cast; the furnace which, for their special destruction, had been heated seven times hotter than was the ordinary custom.

So hot was it, and so great was the haste of Nebuchadnezzar to have these men—who fell not down in worship when all the people heard the sound of cornet, flute, sackbut, psaltry, and all the other kinds of music which Leo rules—consumed in flames, that those who threw them in perished of its heat. As the desires which Leo rules, when their associates are bad, burn the flesh and sear the soul, so did the unregenerate worshipers of lust perish by the fiery furnace.

But the three companions who refused to bow the knee to sensual pleasures, who still earlier with Daniel had refused defiling food, had formed spiritual associations for their desires. Thus when Nebuchadnezzar looked into the furnace where they had been cast, instead of men who had been bound and thrown into the flames, as desire is wont to bind and burn its own, he saw the three walking about unhurt, and with them was a fourth, who appeared like the Son of God.

In very truth, it is that with which desire associates that determines its power to injure or protect. If its associations are spiritual, as those of the three companions are revealed to have been, it consumes and destroys as related in this story from the Bible.

Still further back in Bible times, but not back so far as Noah, the cities of Sodom and Gomorrah perished because of licentiousness. They were wiped out not by flood, but by fire and brimstone from heaven. Yet even as Shadrach and his companions escaped unharmed, so did Lot and his two daughters escape the holocaust of that time.

This again recalls the universal tradition that the world at times is swept by floods and at other times by fire. The period of such cataclysms, according to the stellar doctrine of the past, is when the Vernal Equinox moves backward from the fixed fire of Leo into the movable water of Cancer; or when it passes back from the fixed air of Aquarius into the movable earth of Capricorn.

Either as to the time or the particulars of the two types of cataclysms we have nothing more definite than tradition. But that some such cataclysms really did occur, wiping out early civilizations, there is increasing and positive evidence to show.

At the time this is being written (1935) the latest such conclusive evidence is that furnished by the explorations of F. A. Mitchell-Hedges in Central America. There he has found thousands of relics—which have been presented to the Museum of the American Indian, New York, and to the British Museum, London—of a civilization infinitely older than that of the Maya or of the Inca.

While a different culture from that of the Maya or the Inca, the similarities caused the British Museum in an official statement to express the opinion that it is an ancient culture from which the ancient forms of culture were differentiated over Central America.

The director of the Museum of the American Indian, Heye Foundation, New York, wrote Mr. Mitchell-Hedges in part:

> Your own observations, and the United States Government surveys in Nicaragua, prove conclusively that at some remote period a tremendous earth movement of cataclysmic force must have taken place in that part of the world ... and your excavations have actually unearthed the cultural artifices of a prehistoric people that existed prior to the great earth movement ... and your discoveries open up an entirely new vista in regard to the ancient civilization of the American continent.

Mr. Mitchell-Hedges says his research has revealed that at some remote time a great land area stretching eastward from Central America sank and was engulfed by the sea, and that during this gigantic geological readjustment a portion of what had been sea-bed was heaved upward to become land of considerable height within the area now known as Central America.

Volcanic action of magnitude must have accompanied this cataclysmic change, during which his evidence goes to show, a great and cultured race of men were destroyed. A few, fleeing to the tops of mountains and upland, were able to survive for a time on the newly made islands, where they left behind the imperishable objects of their own handicraft, from which Mr. Mitchell-Hedges, with the support of the two great museums mentioned, is endeavoring to reconstruct their life story.

As to the date at which this pre-Mayan civilization existed, he believes it flourished not later than 15,000 B. C., and possibly that it dates back of 25,000 B. C.

It is not a legitimate function of tradition, even of stellar tradition, to set dates of events in the past that should be left to the painstaking research of archaeologists. Yet it may not be amiss to determine the date when, according to stellar tradition and the pictured constellations, the last period of great cataclysms by fire took place. If Mr. Mitchell-Hedges is correct in his opinion that the cataclysm of which he finds the remains happened over 15,000 years ago, this would take it back of the time of the period of floods, back of the time when the

Equinox passed from Leo into Cancer. Therefore, we should look to the opposite point; to the time when the Vernal Equinox passed from the fixed air of Aquarius into the movable earth of Capricorn.

Such a position not only indicates that whatever happens to the water it is the land which moves first but that when the Equinox thus crosses from fixed air into movable earth, and the Sun at the time of this Vernal Equinox goes down in the west as if submerged, the Fiery Furnace, Crater, rises in the east, triumphant, and starts pouring fire down upon the earth. And as timing this event, the Pleiades, which are often called the doves, are then directly on the midheaven not at sunset, but at the rising of the Sun.

According to the latest and most refined astronomical calculations, the complete precessional cycle requires 25,868 years, instead of the round number, 25,920 years, which the ancients more commonly employed. If, therefore, as both tradition and the pictures in the stars hold forth, the period when stresses and strains are such all to make fiery cataclysms probable relates to the passing of the Vernal Equinox from Aquarius back into Capricorn, the dates are difficult to ascertain.

Taking 1881 as the date of the Equinox passing from Pisces back into Aquarius that is, 30 degrees back from the place where in ancient times it had been ascertained that the commencement of the circle of stars coincided with the commencement of the circle of signs—it must have passed into Capricorn just eleven signs earlier, and will again reach such a point one sign later.

Eleven-twelfths of 25,868 gives 23,712 years before 1881, or 21,831 B. C. as the date of the last such period of fiery cataclysms. And one-twelfth of 25,868 gives 2,156 years after 1881, or 4,037 A.D. as the next such period. On these dates, at least, at the commencement of the astronomical year, as the Man goes down in the ocean Crater comes up and so turns as if it were pouring fire and brimstone down upon the earth.

In the various stories from out of the past in which this fiery furnace figures many who are subject to licentiousness perish, but others more pure in heart are saved. It is not the zeal with which they live that causes the destruction of some; for neither Lot nor Shadrach and his companions, were negative people; but their zeal was directed constructively. It is not the finding of pleasure, but the seeking for pleasure in the wrong things, that leads to dissolution.

Because action flows so spontaneously and without friction toward those things in which pleasure is found the most successful way of defeating the pull of forbidden desire is to cultivate a still keener pleasure in more beneficial things. When the pleasure to be found in these is greater, the thoughts will turn in this direction, and the forbidden impulses will die for want of nourishment.

The attitude toward nearly everything in life has been conditioned through the experiences associated with it. To the extent the experiences with a certain type of activity have been painful does thought of it bring distaste to the mind. To the extent its associations have been pleasurable, do these become linked to it in the mind as an inseparable part of it, exerting a distinct attraction.

Through following the methods indicated by an understanding of this principle it is possible to cultivate a distinct liking for almost anything. There are always many phases of a thing, which if sought for, can make it appear in a pleasurable light. Even the thought of the advantage of having a will power strong enough to continue what otherwise is a distinctly unpleasant activity, may, and often does, so strongly associate the activity with thoughts of satisfaction that the activity in time becomes a pleasure. In fact, it is only through the advantages that are associated with it that people commonly learn to take pleasure in hard work.

People born while the Sun is in this first decanate of Leo commonly have a desire for, and some ability in Rulership. The text derived from Crater is: *To Learn to Like Anything, Associate With It as Many Pleasurable Thoughts and Sensations As Possible.*

Why Santa Claus Comes Down the Chimney

The very first glance at a chart picturing all 48 of the ancient constellations, such as that illustrating chapter 1, brings to the attention that two of the constellations, quite far apart in the sky, portray the same mythological creatures. Part horse and part man, the only difference between Centaurus, which pictures the Sagittarius-decanate of Leo, where the Sun may be found from August 3 to August 13, and Sagittarius, which pictures the sign where the Sun may be found from November 22 to December 22, is that Centaurus is armed with a shield and spear, while Sagittarius has a cloak and uses bow and arrow.

This identity of the pictured forms at once suggests that the ancients who placed these pictures in the sky to convey information in terms of universal symbolism, desired that these two sections of the heavens be closely linked in the teaching they wished to give. It certainly is not coincidence that one larger and one smaller section of the zodiac should be represented by similar creatures; or that those chosen should indicate the human qualities carried by a horse. Rather, especially as the huntsman and the spearman face as if each were traveling toward the place of the other, it signifies that there is a movement of the same type of influence from one station in the zodiac to the other.

We are bound to infer, therefore, that the teaching signified, and the traditional story left to give more detail, includes a movement, a carrying from one place to another—else why the horses' legs?—and that its comprehension requires several stations in the zodiac, the two most important being those pictured by the roving horsemen.

If we follow the simplest and most obvious method, which is that always employed by those who traced these doctrines in the sky, it will lead us to commence with Sagittarius because it pictures 30 degrees, and is therefore more important than Centaurus which pictures only 10 degrees of space. We may be sure, however, that a child or children will play a part in the story, because the smaller influence relates to the middle-decanate of Leo, which has natural rule of children.

Sagittarius, ruled by Jupiter, and the Sagittarius decanate of Leo, also having Jupiterian rule, are known to relate to gifts. Astrologers say that what Jupiter brings comes freely as the result of goodwill rather than through work as is the case with Saturn.

Hence it is that immediately after the Sun leaves the Sagittarius sign in winter is the time when gifts are made. Christmas is not on the day when the Sun reaches its farthest declination south, which is the day when it crosses from the manger of the horse to the manger of the goat, because for three days it remains at this lowest, most southern, point before starting back to bring new life and light into the world.

Giving it three days grace after December 22 insures that on Christmas day the Sun will be moving northward in declination and that the days will have started to get longer. They will thus continue to lengthen until June 22, when the Sun reaches the topmost point of the home sign, Cancer.

The topmost part of a home is commonly the chimney. Therefore the Sun, in coming to the home from the place where Jupiter brings his gifts on the line dividing Sagittarius and Capricorn in winter, must touch it first at the highest spot, the chimney. And to reach it, he of course comes through the air.

In vain you will search the Bible for mention of Christmas tree or Santa Claus; yet that they are linked traditionally with the Centaur picturing the middle-decanate of the section of the heavens relating to children seems certain; for on that day when they are prominent it is said a child was born. Born in a stable underground as the Sun yet represents; for it has reached its lowest point when between the horse and goat, from which time it starts to gain new strength.

Santa Claus, like the horsemen in the sky, one of which relates to the time of winter's cold and the other to the heat of summer, portrays two seasons of the year. His garb is chiefly red; for as representing the constellated Centaur is he not next the fiery furnace, Crater, where the heat glows fiercest? Yet also, to denote the snow of winter, the trimming of the garb is spotless white.

The gifts he brings at Christmas time are tokens of still greater gifts to come, they are the promise that abundance will follow after the time of winter dearth when the heat from the Sun will have had time to ripen crops again. Still ahead, even though the days have started in their lengthening, is a period of privation and cold. Stored supplies may become exhausted, giving rise to dark despair; yet even at the entrance of this period does he give promise of better days to come.

In his jovial manner and rotund figure he expresses the Jupiterian quality of Sagittarius, from which the Sun has just moved at Christmas. This is the sign of religion. And even as Santa Claus brings promise of material gifts; so religion brings an equal cheer and promise of spiritual blessings after the hard dark days of earth are done. Yes, the days are darkest about Christmas time. They are like those other days when hope so fades that nothing seems worth while. Therefore is it fitting that there should be joyous news of a happy future life.

Santa, however, not merely represents Jupiter's winter sign, but also a decanate of Leo, sign ruled by the Sun. And anyone who has viewed the radiant rising Sun on a cold and frosty morning will remember the resemblance to Santa's red circle of a face.

Yet the youngsters of the land, whose special joy he is, would not recognize the rotund fellow if divested of his whiskers. They are an essential part of his makeup because at Christmas time the Sun has just moved into Capricorn, and chin whiskers are the especial adornment of a goat.

Horses customarily draw sleighs, therefore Sagittarius and Centaurus well could qualify; but as still more significant of the cold bleak winter days, reindeer are now used to take their place. They are more accustomed to ice and snow.

Before this sleigh—which coming from Sagittarius, the Jupiterian sign of abundance, is filled with good things to overflowing—can get to the fireplace, Crater, it must land on top the house at Cancer. And thus really does the Sun. For after touching the highest point it reaches, which is where it enters the home-sign Cancer, it immediately starts descending, as if going down the chimney, until it passes into the decanate pictured by Crater.

It does not tarry in this fireplace, or hottest decanate of the zodiac, however, but at once moves into the decanate pictured by Centaurus, the other horseman of the sky. The feet, it is true, are ruled by Pisces. But ask any small boy or girl—such as is ruled by the Leo section of the sky—if it is enough to hang up the mere feet of stockings on Christmas evening. If I remember rightly, there is usually a hunt for stockings that are long and ample, such as come well up on to the thighs. And it is the legs thus covered by the longer hosiery that Sagittarius rules, and of which its decanate in Leo also must partake.

The horseman of Leo is not the gift, but the one who brings it; for it is the Sun at this time of year that ripens the grain in the field and the fruit on the trees. The gifts which the traveler from the north thus brings, while related to the children of Leo, are pictured in the next sign to it, in the harvest sign, Virgo. It is really the Virgin Mother, not Santa Claus, from whom the gifts more directly come.

The lady of the sky holds a palm frond in one hand and heads of wheat in the other; while Hercules, who pictures the middle decanate of the Virgo sign, holds in his hand the branch of a tree adorned with fruit.

The fruit thus shown is the fulfillment of the promise made at the time when the nights were longest, just as the Sun turned back from its farthest distance away. This promise was not made by using a tree when it was filled with fruit; because such are hard to find at Christmas time. It was made by using a tree symbolic of perpetual life, by using an evergreen tree. The fruit to come, when ripened through the heat of the Sun in Leo, was represented by presents on that tree. And it was spangled with stars and bedecked with lights as a token that the Sun, thus moving through the firmament, was on the way to dissipate the winter's darkness.

At this yuletide time of year, still further to connect the passing of the Sun from Sagittarius to the Centaurus decanate of Leo, the sign of love affairs and pleasure, it is the custom to hang mistletoe with the privilege of kissing whomsoever passes under it.

The mistletoe, like the Christmas tree, is of evergreen foliage, and thus symbolically promises everlasting life. But because it grows above the earth, apparently too pure and holy to touch the physical soil, it came to have a special spiritual significance. Its berry fruit, formed without polluting contact with the loam of earth, came to be looked upon as derived from an immaculate conception.

Kissing under the mistletoe even in times not remote was a solemn and binding ceremony. It was the token of a chaste affection and the promise of marriage. More than that, it was the promise that out of the love then expressed should develop a new and more spiritual type of life.

Such a life of spiritual endeavor, as Santa Claus and Centaurus clearly teach, is dependent upon what is done for others. It is the effort to give, rather than the effort to take, which promises a spiritual harvest.

After all, in the realms of the future, after we shall have passed from this mundane sphere, the physical objects men set their hearts upon will have less value than the tinsel and gilded baubles with which they decorate the Christmas tree.

Those born while the Sun is in the Reformation-decanate of Leo are often more energetic to bring beneficial changes. The text is: *It Is More Blessed To Give Than to Receive, and to Receive In Full Measure We Must First Give of That Which We Already Have.*

Why the Crow Turned Black.

One needs to know something of the habits and characters of crows and ravens to discern what the ancients must have had in mind when they placed one of these noisy, thieving, carrion-eating birds in the sky. Corvus is the name yet employed by naturalists to distinguish the genus embracing both birds, which are so closely allied that they are distinguished in the field chiefly through the noise they make. A raven has a coarse and croaking voice, while a crow vocalizes in a loud and raucous caw.

One who is familiar with the ways of crows and ravens could be sure that they would never be used as universal symbols of any commendable trait or habit. Their one claim to admiration is their unparalleled ability to look out for themselves.

Because they are destructive to crops, pulling the new sprouts of grain from the ground, and because in the cattle country of the West they do not wait for a crippled creature to die, but pick out its eyes and help themselves to its flesh as soon as they find it defenseless, relentless war has been waged against them by man. Yet so cunning are they that, with every hand raised against them, they are now more numerous than ever.

Before going further into the habits of crows, it should be explained that people born while the Sun is in the Corvus decanate of Leo, from August 13 to August 23, are no more apt than other people to partake of the undesirable crow-like qualities. It is true that they have great Ambition, and as a rule are exceptionally able to take care of themselves. But it is only the occasional individual who permits this Ambition so to dominate him that he comes to have no regard for the feelings and rights of others, and uses them unscrupulously to realize his aims.

Yet it was the function of the constellated pictures not merely to reveal those things which should be done, if one were to live the most satisfactory type of life, but also to point out the dangers along the way. And one of these dangers, to which many people are subject, and to which those born while the Sun is in the last decanate of Leo are particularly exposed, is portrayed by the character of the raven or crow.

When Noah, in the ark, badly wanted information, because the raven is so keen an observer he sent one forth to get it. It saw the condition, but instead of reporting back to Noah it flew to and fro. It took good care not to perish, but neither did it return to the ark, and to find out what he wanted to know, Noah had to send out a dove.

Spiritual Astrology

Even the feeding of Elijah was characteristic of the propensities of the bird. As related in First Kings, 17, there was great drought in the land, so that everyone was hard pressed both for food and water. Elijah had established a hiding place from his enemies by the brook Cherith; "And the ravens brought him bread and flesh in the morning, and bread and flesh in the evening; and he drank of the brook."

Where the ravens found the flesh is open to discussion; but bread already baked does not grow on bushes, even in the promised land. The only way they could have obtained the bread was to steal it. And as they are noted for such pilfering the inference is that they grabbed it when its owner was not watching, or at least without the owner's consent. Thus while Elijah benefited, someone else in this land of food shortage was deprived. Yet no blame can be attached to Elijah; for there was nothing to indicate he knew to whom the food rightfully belonged, or where to return it.

As the constellation shows this racketeering bird, he has alighted on the back of the water serpent, Hydra, and is in the act of tearing a piece of the living flesh from it, as in the cattle country of the West he works on stricken sheep.

Hydra is the longest of the constellations. It pictures the middle decanate of the sign of the home, Cancer; but also embraces in its length all four of the constellations relating to the different kinds of companionship; that is, companionship in the home, companionship in love affairs, companionship with employees, and companionship in partnership and marriage. We may be sure, therefore, that the characteristic which the ancients sought to portray by Corvus is one which quite commonly and quite painfully attacks and destroys these human associations.

Perhaps to get a clearer insight of this matter it will be well to turn to the Greeks. According to their account, Apollo, the Sun, was deeply in love with Coronis and was jealous of her conduct. This jealousy developed into a desire to spy upon her; and as most fitted to do such unethical gum shoe work, especially where love affairs are concerned, he selected a raven, which in that day was still of purest white.

Those who surreptitiously pry into the conduct of their associates seldom learn anything complimentary to themselves. It was almost a foregone conclusion, therefore, that the scandal monging raven would find something unsavory to tell. Although he partakes of other and forbidden food, chiefly he is a carrion eater. The more rotten the repast the better he likes it. So, true to his nature he came back to Apollo with gossip aplenty. His loudly wagging tongue took gross delight in relating, with spicy embellishments, all the details of a love affair between Corona and Ischys the Thessalian.

It might have happened today, with all their pictures in the tabloids, so true to common observation was the outcome. The malicious carrying of tales, the prying of inquisitive noses into what are no concern of theirs, all too often wrecks the budding of some fine affection; or, as in this case, brings grief and tragedy where peace and happiness should have laid their heads. Apollo, enraged at the reports of his sweetheart's infidelity, shot her through the heart.

The crow, of course, had nothing to gain but his own malicious satisfaction. Nor commonly is there any benefit to those who exaggerate the misconduct of others. It is a pity, therefore, that as the poet has suggested, the whole scandalmonger crew can not be painted red or blue, that all might know them; for something similar happened to the crow, and ever since that day he has been compelled to wear a cloak of black.

Because gossip which relates the amatory experiences of others is so common, as witnessed by the yellow news sheets, as well as by neighborhood propensities, more people should be informed as to its origin. Freudian literature makes it plain that those who find a suitable outlet for their own creative energies are never given to such gossip. They are very little interested in the love escapades of others because their own love natures have been completely satisfied.

In thinking about any experience there is a certain thought participation in it. In telling about the conduct of another, whether that conduct be commendable or the reverse, not only the one who does the telling, but also the one who listens, vicariously takes some part in the experience. Were this not true the movies would languish for want of patronage.

People go to the movies, and read fiction, chiefly to gain experiences vicariously for which they inwardly yearn, but which their lives are too narrow to permit. That which constitutes the strongest longing in their unconscious minds, is that which they enjoy most on the screen.

The office clerk whose most gallant act during working hours is to make entries in a book, inwardly longs for adventure. He is denied action and excitement in his life, and he goes to the movies to get them. He identifies himself with the dashing hero, delights in his valorous exploits, takes part in the downfall of the villain, and glories in the justification of those misunderstood. He goes home with a certain sense of satisfaction because a repression has been released.

The shopgirl whose life is devoted to pleasing customers over the counter, and who inwardly longs for romance, thrills with vicarious joy when the handsome hero on the screen, after surmounting terrific obstacles and facing dangerous hazards, at length triumphant, clasps the fair heroine to his manly breast. Nor should she be censured. To love and be loved is an imperative command of nature. Nothing is finer than honest love. And the shopgirl, identifying herself with the heroine, is able thus to realize in some measure a longing which is both beautiful and natural.

But the scandalmonger deals not with honest affection and in heroic and commendable actions. His tales are about illicit love. In telling and in hearing about, the morbid affairs of others, he takes part in them vicariously. Although he does not recognize this, and is the first to deny it, his unconscious mind identifies himself with the transgressor. Just as the office clerk finds some relief for his honest desire for adventure; just as the shopgirl is able somewhat to satisfy her honest desire for romance and glamour; so the gossip, through tale bearing and tale listening, is able to satisfy his desire for illicit, licentious, and ignoble conduct.

As a crow or raven feeds largely on putrid flesh, so those who revel in relating the unseemly conduct of others feed their souls on rotten food. Their desire to discuss the vileness of others can only be interpreted as a desire on the part of their unconscious minds to do these same things, if they but possessed the courage.

To the extent an individual talks about and thinks about that which is rotten, is this an expression of rottenness within himself. Those who are clean have a desire to keep away from filth. They do not revel in the sinfulness of others. Furthermore, just as the clerk who identifies himself with the hero, cultivates within himself a delight in valiant and honorable action; and just as the shopgirl who identifies herself with the sweet and admirable heroine, cultivates within herself pleasure in womanly conduct of the same high standard; so does the scandalmonger cultivate within himself an increasing relish for moral carrion.

Repressed desires, even though unrecognized objectively, can not be kept from finding some expression for their energy. And as the raven became black because he carried a black story, so that which is thought about adds its thought-images to the soul. The text thus follows: *Man Tends To Become That Which He Most Talks About and Most Thinks About.*

VIRGO   ♍   I Analyze

BOÖTES   ♍-♍   Achievement

CORONA BOREALIS ♏-☊   Renunciation

Chapter 7

Why Eve Was Tempted

THE Tree Which Grew In the Garden of Eden.
If we turn back the pages of the Bible to the time when man first appeared on earth we find him inhabiting a garden. One whole 30 degree section of the zodiac, where the Sun may be found from August 23 to September 23, was set aside by those who anciently studied the stars as representing just such a garden, and as having an influence over the fruit of the trees and the grain of the fields. It is the harvest sign, Virgo.

Were this not recognized to be the case, both in olden and in modern times, certain passages of Genesis would be astounding; such as where it relates that Adam and Eve heard the voice of the Lord God walking in the garden in the cool of the day.

Yet viewing this occurrence in the light of ancient stellar wisdom there is nothing obscure about it. It quite definitely locates the garden among the constellations, for, in the sense that there is yet more light than darkness, more heat than cold, all the time the Sun is in the garden sign, Virgo, it indicates that the Sun has not yet gone into the winter signs. Yet when the Sun moves out of this garden sign into Libra it will be in the cold half of the year, when the nights are longer than the days. As Virgo adjoins, but is not one of, the winter signs, when the Sun is in the harvest sign quite appropriately may be termed the cool of the day.

Virgo is an earthy sign; and out of the ground of this garden the Lord God made to grow every tree that is pleasant to the sight, and good for food, and also the tree of life as well as the tree of knowledge of good and evil. Yet because of certain actions on his part, man was not permitted to partake of the tree of life; and consequently to find it we must move across the zodiac to one of the decanates of the opposite sign. But man did partake of the tree of good and evil, through the advice of Eve; and thus the woman in the sky still holds the palm branch in her hand.

The sign Virgo, however, has rule not merely over gardens where dates grow on palm trees, but over labor and harvests of all kinds. Therefore, when Adam, and the woman who was called Eve because she was the mother of all living, were thrust from the parental environment to shift for themselves, it was said that in order to live they must till the fields and raise crops, not all of which would be wheat, as thorns and thistles also are mentioned. Furthermore, to keep warm they had to make clothing.

All of these things required just such labor as the zodiacal sign rules; and people still sweat to get the bread they eat; such bread as is signified by the ears of wheat held in celestial Virgo's hand.

It seems, from what is said in this third chapter of Genesis, that before man partook of the fruit which Eve offered him he was unable to distinguish good from evil. This same fruit is characteristic of this section of the sky, for Virgo, more than any other sign, confers the ability to discriminate. In fact, the Key-phrase for the sign is, I Analyze.

People born when the Sun is in Virgo are inveterate askers of questions, always wanting to know how things work. It was quite in character, therefore, that Eve should discuss the merits of the tree with the serpent, or with anyone else who would talk with her about it. She wanted to know all there was to know about the tree and about everything else. And after talking it over with the serpent she decided, after all, that the tree of knowledge was good for food, pleasant to the eyes, and to be desired as making one wise.

The implication is plain that she decided knowledge is worth all it costs. She paid the price, but she acquired that which Virgo most desires; for after they had eaten, the Lord God said, "Behold, the man is become as one of us, to know good and evil.

There are many things that man inherits, many things that come as gifts without cost, but knowledge is not one of them. No one can be given knowledge; it must be acquired. And the only method of acquiring it is through a process similar to that which Adam and Eve and their offspring followed after eating of the so-called forbidden fruit. That is, through a wide variety of contrasting experiences.

There is but one basis for consciousness, and that is the perception of relations. Whenever the mind, or soul, is unaware of relations it is in a state of coma.

In order for the soul to be aware of those relations which make it conscious, it must contact relative conditions. Such relative conditions are present only in association with substance. And to the extent the experiences have wide diversity in kind, and great range in intensity do they afford the materials out of which knowledge may be acquired.

We can know nothing whatever of coldness apart from our experiences with things which vary in degree of heat which they possess. We can know nothing of sweetness apart from our experiences with things which are less sweet and more sweet. If we have had some experience with that which is bitter and that which is sour, it gives us a better knowledge of the significance of sweetness when we contact it.

Our knowledge can be widened through reading books, or by hearing of the experiences of others. But this is only possible to the extent we have had experiences of our own, in contact with substance, with which to compare the experiences and information related to us.

The soul before its incarnation on the physical plane is depicted as Adam, without knowledge or responsibility, and, therefore, in a state bordering on unconsciousness. If it was to acquire that wisdom expressed in the Bible, "And the Lord God said, Behold, the man is become as one of us, to know good and evil," it had to have a broad basis of experience upon which to build. The entrance into physical conditions gave it the opportunity for such acquisition.

We have here, consequently, the answer to the so frequently asked question why man must undergo incarnation in physical form, must work and struggle, must have pain and hardship, and go through other experiences. Without such experiences he could not acquire the knowledge and power which enables him to participate in divine attributes. Such participation is clearly set forth in the Bible when it states that man was made in the image of God.

Everyone, of course, is quite familiar with the story of the immaculate conception, and how the Virgin Mother, warned of the enmity of Herod, fled for a time into the land of Egypt. And a somewhat similar mother was honored in various ancient lands long before the Christian era, and was pictured in the sky. In Egypt, for instance, where she was called Isis, there were yearly pageants in her honor, with processions of virgins who carried sistrums in their hands.

In America during ceremonies of similar purport certain of the Indians on the sidelines, all during the dance, shake white gourds filled with seeds. These rattles, identical in shape and significance with the sistrum, are used to signify the mother principle, which was held in highest esteem as indicated by Virgo being pictured with the wings of an angel.

Furthermore, the Hopi Indian girl of marriageable age wears her hair carefully dressed on either side of her head in a form to represent a squash blossom. Such a flower symbolizes both that she is a virgin and that she has potentialities for motherhood. She is not permitted to wear this distinctive headdress after she marries.

This use of a flower to symbolize the potentialities of motherhood, curiously enough, is still retained, along with a wide variety of other symbolisms of the primitive people of America, in our playing cards. On the Queen of Spades, which is the card corresponding to the zodiacal sign Virgo, in addition to the blossom held in one hand, which is common to the other queens, she bears in her other a lighted torch, to indicate that she has conceived by the solar power, or if you prefer, by the Holy Ghost.

Egypt was ever considered by Bible characters as the land of darkness. And as the seed of squash and bean and corn which the Indian placed in the ground had to remain in hiding for a period before the earth could bring forth, and as the Virgin persecuted by Herod sojourned for a time in the dark land of Egypt, so also the Sun, immediately after its station in the sky pictured by the Virgin, must pass across to the dark half of the year for a time, where the nights are longer than the days.

Virgo is an earthy sign, and to those who understand the stellar doctrine, the Sun's entrance into this sign symbolizes the descent of the soul into matter. Such traditions are among the oldest in Egypt and Chaldea. Quetzalcoatl of the Aztecs was also thus virgin born, as was Montezuma of the Pueblo, Mojave and Apache Indians. Thus was it taught that Mother Earth is the place of the soul's gestation; and that after the preparatory development which is supplied by the earth—after it has partaken of the fruit of the tree of good and evil which alone enables it to acquire knowledge—it will be born into a more glorious life.

Furthermore, because this is the harvest sign, in addition to revealing the necessity of the trials and tribulations of earth to teach us wisdom, and that after such necessary preparation there will be a passing from the physical to be born into a new and better life on a higher plane, it teaches that as we sow so shall we reap.

At all times we are sowing in the soil of our own consciousness. We are building thoughts into ourselves of various kinds. These thought-cells, in turn, when sufficient energy has been supplied them to give them strength, work to attract events of a similar quality into the life. The text therefore becomes: *If a Man Sows Discordant Thoughts He Will Reap Painful Experiences, But if He Sows Thoughts of Harmony He Will Garner Success and Happiness.*

Ariadne Gives Theseus a Clew of Thread

When viewing Bootes, the Husbandman in the sky, picturing the harvest-decanate of the harvest sign, through which the Sun passes each year from August 23 to September 2, one can not but wonder once again how much must be attributed to coincidence, and how much of ancient lore was actual knowledge. The chief star in the constellation is mentioned in Job 38:32, "Canst thou bring forth Mazzaroth in his season? or canst thou guide Arcturus with his sons?", as if, like turning the zodiac to bring any desired season, the control of Arcturus were an impossible task.

We are hardly warranted, I suppose, in believing that the ancients knew anything of the terrific speed with which a few of the stars travel. Yet Arcturus is classified as one of those "runaway stars" which have a speed so great, according to Simon Newcomb, the great astronomer, as to be beyond control of the other bodies in the firmament. Job might well ask about this swiftest of all the brighter stars, traveling 89 miles a second, or of the son, one of the stars of the Great Bear, which is smaller but moves at even greater speed, by what agency could they be guided.

Although Arcturus was chosen for another and quite as romantic reason to open the Century of Progress Exposition in Chicago in

1933, because this exposition was held in honor of, and to display, labor saving devices and scientific progress garnered during the previous hundred years, no better star could have been selected to symbolize the exposition than this chief star in the constellation picturing the mental and harvest decanate of the mental and harvest sign Virgo.

Its speed is typical of the new forms of locomotion displayed in the exhibits. And in addition to the sickle which the Husbandman carries to indicate the reaping of the harvest, the spear which he holds in the other hand indicates that the devices thus acquired have slain, let us hope forever, the sweatshop Minotaur nourished by Child labor.

The harvesting of the energy of Arcturus, rather than that of some rival in brilliancy, late in May, 1933, to close the switches that turned on the lights which formally opened the exposition, was prompted ostensibly by the circumstance that the light, which fell upon the photoelectric cells at the eye-end of the telescopes at four different observatories, left the Husbandman star at about the time the previous Chicago World's Fair was held in 1893.

From this miracle of modern science we can with advantage turn to the first miracle recorded by Saint John, the significance of which also, we may be sure, is revealed by its correspondence in the sky. Virgo, the sign of the mother, is adjacent to Libra, the sign of marriage. And it will be remembered that the mother of Jesus attended a marriage. Servants also are ruled by Virgo and His mother instructed the servants to do whatever He should ask of them.

In its annual circuit of the heavens, as indicated by Bootes, the keeper of the vineyard, it is when the Sun enters Virgo that the harvest ripens and the water drawn from the earth into the grapes swelling on the vine is converted into juice which is suitable for wine. The decanate thus pictured by the Vineyardist is the earthy-decanate of an earthy sign, and thus closely allied to stone. As Virgo also is the sixth sign of the zodiac, the six water pots of stone which Jesus commanded the servants to fill with water, and which He converted into wine of excellent flavor, indicate that this event, and those transformations within the character of man which correspond to it, are pictured by the constellation Bootes.

Thus the turning of water into wine by the Sun each fall, and the miracle performed by Jesus, both convey a spiritual teaching. Even steep hillsides and rocky soil may be utilized in raising grapes. So also, even when circumstances offer scant footing, and hard, rough obstacles are on every hand, it is possible to cultivate the finest traits of character.

Jesus did not ask the servants to go to the village and get some special materials out of which to make the wine. He used that which already was at hand. Nor is it necessary for those who develop the powers of their souls to seek special settings or unusual circumstances. All the materials necessary for the finest flavor of soul growth are everywhere present; and can be changed into spiritual qualities of the finest vintage.

In fact, even as the wine which Jesus formed out of what happened to be handy was of finer flavor than that which had been made under special conditions, so the spiritual qualities which can be derived from the proper attitude toward everyday experiences are of superior merit to those acquired through going into retirement or amid other surroundings which many consider most favorable to their development.

While the constellation Bootes thus explains the significance of the miracle of changing water into wine in six pots of stone, this miracle does not reveal the significance of the spear which the Vineyardist holds in one of his hands. Its meaning can better be comprehended through a story from the Greeks, a story in which also a woman, typical of celestial Virgo, takes a prominent part.

It seems that in the time of Minos, second king of Crete, there was a monster, half Bull and half Man, called the Minotaur, which was confined in a celebrated labyrinth. The Bull part, of course, refers to the rule of Taurus over money, and the Man part to the science and knowledge of Aquarius. In modern words, it was the monster of commercial exploitation.

To keep this monster pacified it was necessary each year to import some of the fairest youths and maidens from Athens for the Minotaur to devour. Among one such consignment of Athenian youths sent to the island was Theseus, who already had been successful in catching and killing, in his home land, a wild bull, called the Bull of Marathon. He had made up his mind to get rid of this Cretan monster also; and it was for this purpose that as Bootes he carries the spear which is pictured in the sky.

But just as at the present day the whole problem of money is involved in a maze of conflicting doctrines and opinions, from which the most skilled economists seem unable to free the world, so a problem of equal importance to vanquishing the greedy Minotaur was that of being able to find the way out of the labyrinth once the monster had been slain. It was a difficulty which gravely puzzled Theseus.

It so happened, however, that Minos, king of Crete, had a daughter, Ariadne, who fell in love with Theseus as soon as he landed on Cretan soil. Pictured as Virgo in the sky, she had the Virgo trait of keen analysis. And it was she who devised the means by which, should her sweetheart triumph in his conflict underground, he should not wander about in the maze of bewildering caverns until he starved, but would be able to find his way back into the light of day.

She furnished him with a clew of thread—an incident which to this day makes the term clue significant of a hint which followed leads to the solution of a mystery or an intricate problem—one end of which she fastened at the opening of the cave. As he descended the long and tortuous passage he unwound the thread. As was to be expected, after a time he encountered the vicious Minotaur, which rushed suddenly upon him. But he was armed with the spear, which still he carries in the sky, and after a terrific battle the monster was slain.

Then came the task of finding his way back to where his beloved Ariadne anxiously awaited him. Carefully, as he walked and as he climbed over jagged rocks and worked around corners where the network of passages interlaced, he reeled in the line, ever following it through the darkness, never losing the sense of its touch.

Great was the joy of Ariadne when at last he appeared again above the ground, and great was the joy of the Athenians, who no longer would be compelled to sacrifice the fairest youths of their land to the demands of this hideous creature.

But is not every individual faced with very much the same type of conflict which confronted Theseus? Very few, indeed, are free from the attack of economic necessity. Nor can one remain passive and expect to escape unscathed. Financial demands are not to be ignored; they must be met, and it is better to meet them courageously, as Theseus did, with the spear of critical analysis, which is a weapon specially designed for those born when the Sun is in this Bootes section of the sky.

Are we not all confined, as Theseus was, within a labyrinth of conflicting doctrines? Most of these are blind passages, leading nowhere through the dark. Theories abound, crisscrossing each other in a network so intricate that unless one has some clue to guide one to the light, about all that can be done is just to wander about amid darkness and confusion.

The Key-word for the decanate is Achievement; and the achievements of Theseus were great; but they were made possible only by that clew of thread which is the chief Virgo attribute, that is, by the power of discrimination. It is only through exercising the powers of discrimination to the utmost, only by following the thread thus discerned through careful analysis, that gradually one can extricate himself from the darkness and the confusion of false paths, to emerge into the full light of Truth.

It is this faculty which may be used to guide one through the intricate passages of life, which also can be used to determine the possibilities of the experiences encountered along the way.

Whatever the events that may be attracted into the life, it is possible to convert them into real values for the soul. The meeting of obstacles may be used to develop initiative and resourcefulness. The losses which occur may be used to build up fortitude. Difficulties when overcome teach how responsibilities can be carried. And thus each experience holds a lesson which can be used in later achievement.

Bearing upon these lessons the text associated with the constellation is: *From Every Event of Life the Soul May Extract Value, Even as the Verdant Vine Transforms Indifferent Waters into Rich and Sparkling Wine.*

The Twelve Labors of Hercules

One of the common tenets of astrology, ancient and modern, is that the influence of Saturn tends to attract work and heavy responsibilities. When, therefore, those of the olden time wished to comment in terms of universal symbolism upon the importance of labor, it is quite consistent that for the purpose they selected the

Saturn-decanate of the sign of labor. The Sun moves through this middle-decanate of Virgo from September 3 to September 13.

Following the method of universal symbolism still further, which demands that the big influences in life shall be portrayed by equally large pictures, they traced, to represent that labor is essential to all worthwhile accomplishment, a man of heroic proportions in the sky. Hercules, mightiest of all the laboring men, has a constellation of vast extent.

Like Samson, who toiled grinding the grain held in the hand of Virgo while he was in the prison house, Hercules was successful in a number of valorous exploits, and was led to ultimate disaster through an unfortunate love affair. Like Samson also, whose final triumph was aided by two pillars, against which he pushed, placing one hand on each; the two pillars of Hercules perform a function in the Greek version of the ancient story. But the chief claim to renown was the performance by Hercules of his twelve great, and self-imposed, labors.

No sign of the zodiac is bad, and no sign of the zodiac is good. No one sign can be singled out as better or worse than the rest. Each has its own special possibilities for good and its own special possibilities for evil. Every sign has its best qualities and its worst qualities, which are different than the best qualities and the worst qualities of other signs.

Thus is the work required of those born under the influence of each sign different than that required of those born under the other signs; but in all cases it consists of diverting the energies which might manifest through the less desirable qualities of the sign into channels which enable them to express through the better qualities of the sign.

The best quality and the worst quality of any sign express the same general type of energy; but express it through different avenues. It is almost, or quite, impossible to convert the type of energy or the character qualifications denoted by one sign into those of another sign. But it is not a difficult matter to divert the undesirable expression of the energy or character into the desirable expression of the energy or character of the same sign. This is the work which Hercules undertook, and accomplished.

As there are twelve different signs, representing the deep-seated characteristics of the twelve different types of people, and as Hercules undertook to demonstrate how the worst quality could be diverted into the best quality for each of these types, he thus had twelve different labors to perform before he had finished.

While these twelve great labors, which illustrate to the individual how to convert the weaknesses peculiar to his character into expressions of strength, are the most noteworthy tasks accomplished by Hercules, he had a wide variety of experiences in connection with other endeavors.

It is through experience that man learns how to do things. And as the experiences of Hercules in performing his numerous tasks were so extensive, the Key-word given to this section of the sky is Experience. Those born while the Sun is in this decanate usually have a wide range of happenings in their lives.

If a day were to be set aside from all the year to honor the sacredness of work, to be correct in its astrological correspondence, it would have to be one of those during which the Sun is in the Hercules section of the zodiac. If, instead, festivities were instituted to eulogize political personages, we should expect them to be observed on Sunday. If they were to encourage art, we should expect Friday to be selected. Thursday would be more fitting to celebrate the attainment of wealth.

But the Moon rules the common people; those who sweat and toil and hope for jobs; and thus Labor Day falls on Monday, the day of the Moon, while the Sun is in that section of the sky pictured by the greatest toiler of which we have tradition.

Although Samson slew a thousand men with the jawbone of an ass, perhaps the most remarkable of his works was his use of foxes to destroy the crops of those who had treated him unjustly. Foxes, of course, in ancient times as well as in those more modern, are universal symbols of shrewdness and cunning.

When the cunning of one nation is pitted against the cunning of another, or shrewdness against shrewdness, as often we have witnessed the efforts of people, each to gain an unfair advantage over the other, there is sure to be ultimate disaster. The inevitableness of the destruction of the fruits of human labor which follows such antagonisms, either among people or among the thought-groups within the finer body of man, is well illustrated in the story of Samson's foxes.

It seems that the Philistines were harvesting their grain; some of it still standing and some of it cut and placed in shocks. To avenge himself upon them Samson caught 300 foxes, paired them off, with the tails of each two united by a firebrand one end of which was tied to each of the tails.

The worst quality of the sign Virgo, of which Samson represents the middle decanate, is criticism. And the mental qualifications for keen criticism, as well as those for unfair bargaining, are well represented by a fox. Criticism, however, may be either constructive or destructive. It may point out a more advantageous way of doing something, a better line of conduct to be followed, in which case if the criticism is sound it may be helpful and constructive.

On the other hand, more frequently than not, pointing out weaknesses without indicating how they may be strengthened, and faultfinding in general. This type of criticism often is engaged in by political opponents, by factions within an organization, and by people in their domestic associations.

When people are subject to such destructive criticism they are likely to reply in kind, and the heat of the controversy may be like a burning brand between them; the final consequences, so far as destructive to the fruit of labor, being quite similar to that so vividly described in the Bible as the result when Samson lighted the firebrands between the tails of the foxes and turned them loose.

The foxes ran frantically through the standing grain setting it afire. They tried to find shelter in the shocks of grain that had been cut and awaited to be taken to the threshing floor. And when the fields were thus ablaze they fled to the vineyards and olive groves hoping to find refuge from their torture. Instead, these also were ignited, so that the crops of the year, of all kinds, went up in flames. Nothing was left to the Philistines to show for their toil.

Such is the observed result of destructive criticism. It kindles the fires of hatred and destroys whatever labor already has accomplished. It is a consuming influence which leaves nothing in its wake but bitter ashes. And it is just as destructive when directed against self as when applied to the endeavors of others.

The constant calling attention to the faults and imperfections of any person, including oneself, brings the image of the undesirable action or quality before the unconscious mind. When we think about a thing we are supplying it with thought-energy. Therefore, the more we think about an undesirable thing the stronger it becomes within our unconscious mind. Traits of character feed upon the attention given them.

This does not signify, of course, that we should ignore our weaknesses nor neglect to strengthen them. But finding fault, especially when such criticism arouses an emotional reaction, merely impresses the defect more strongly, through the power of suggestion, upon the unconscious mind, and makes it more difficult to overcome. Children who are continually criticised by their parents are receiving strong suggestions which increase the difficulty of adhering to a better line of conduct. And, likewise, the more we find fault with ourselves, the more we feel dissatisfied with ourselves, the more powerful becomes the thing within ourselves which causes the dissatisfaction. If it gains enough strength through such internal dissension a consuming fire is lighted within which, like Samson's foxes, destroys the fruit of effort.

Constructive criticism, on the other hand, while recognizing a weakness as such, or that a type of conduct is unworthy, does not dwell upon this aspect of the matter. Instead, it concentrates its attention and energy upon the correct line of conduct or the proper way to strengthen the observed weakness. The thought-energy thus flows into and feeds the action which is desired instead of its opposite. In this manner not only is the mental image of the thing desired strengthened, but the image of the undesired thing is weakened through lack of thought nourishment.

In self-culture it is quite as important to feel satisfaction when the best is done as to recognize when one is living below one's possibilities. If more is expected than lies within the powers to accomplish, there will be certain failure and accompanying dissatisfaction. This feeling, in turn, directs energy into channels which are destructive, and lessens the ability in the future.

On the other hand, it is quite as easy for some individuals to feel that they are living up to their possibilities when they are living far below them. Their appraisal of their abilities is too low, and they have a feeling of satisfaction from accomplishment which is much less than it should be. Yet even this does not signify that they should be critical of themselves in the destructive sense; but merely that they should recognize that they should strive for a more lofty goal.

Because we learn to do through effort directed at accomplishment the text is: *Perform Conscientiously Whatever Work Comes to Thy Hand, and Because of Thy Experience, Greater Things to Perform Will Be Given Thee.*

How Job Triumphed Over His Afflictions

Because illness and affliction so frequently burden the life of man we have a right to expect that those who formulated the spiritual doctrines of the past, which were intended to explain the significance of events and how to take advantage of them, should have commented on these tribulations in their symbolic writing in the sky.

It is true that the constellation Virgo, and the story of the punishment of Eve for partaking of the tree of experience which conferred knowledge set forth in sufficient detail the advantages of material incarnation with its variegated contacts, including labor and displeasures. But it would seem that trials and pain were sufficiently important in the lives of most that they should receive more explicit mention; and this they do, for the last decanate of the harvest sign gives them vivid portrayal.

Let us in imagination place ourselves in the position of those who drew the pictured figures in the heavens, and consider that it was their intention to symbolize in most fitting fashion the tribulations which beset most lives. First of all, the most appropriate section of the zodiac must be chosen, and in making this selection the tenets of practical astrology would be consulted.

Virgo in a natural birth-chart rules the house that governs not only work, but also illness and servitude, the most common afflictions of human life. When the Sun is in this sign it is moving toward the Autumnal Equinox where days and nights are equal, and after crossing which the forces of death prevail and the nights become longer than the days. The forces of Light are still triumphant while the Sun remains in any part of Virgo, but the closer the Sun draws to the next sign, Libra, the weaker becomes the power of Day, and the more is Night able to inflict its encroaching power of evil upon the solar waning strength.

The last decanate of Virgo, where the Sun may be found from September 13 to September 23, therefore, is the most appropriate place in all the zodiac to represent the afflictions to which man is heir, and his persecution at the hand of fate. The writer of Revelation

Spiritual Astrology 147

seems to have recognized this when he speaks of the pain accompanying birth, commencing the 12th chapter thus:

> And there appeared a great wonder in heaven; a woman clothed with the sun, and the moon under her feet, and upon her head a crown of twelve stars.

Having selected the place of tribulation in the zodiac, if it were desired to indicate that the proper attitude toward such afflictions would adequately be rewarded, the next step in starry portrayal would be the selection of some object significant of high honors attained. A crown is such an object, used throughout the ages as a reward for victory or as a mark of distinction. Thus was it used to denote the triumph over the afflictions symbolically associated with this last decanate of the summer signs.

Bearing in mind that the Sun takes just ten days to pass through this decanate of tribulations pictured by a crown, not of twelve stars, as poetically expressed by St. John the Divine, but of twelve iron spikes, it would be difficult to explain the significance of this section of the zodiac, or the ancient teachings regarding it, more concisely than he did in Revelation 2:10.

> Fear none of those things which thou shalt suffer; behold the devil shall cast some of you into prison, that ye may be tried; and ye shall have tribulation ten days: be thou faithful unto death, and I will give thee a crown of life.

It is unnecessary here more than merely to point out that the Sun each year dies on the Autumnal Cross of Libra, even as the Son of Man gave up His life on Calvary; or that preceding this far-reaching tragedy the gentle Nazarene was vilely persecuted and made to wear a crown of thorns, of similar purport to Corona Borealis placed by the ancients in the sky to mark the tribulations of the Sun before it temporarily succumbs each year to the forces of darkness.

The fruits of life, whether they be tares or wholesome grain, are harvested from experience. What that harvest shall be is not determined by the nature of the experiences, but by the mental and emotional reaction toward them; for both the physical conditions attracted in the future, and the spiritual values garnered, are dependent upon the seeds of thought thus sown and tended in the finer form and heading into character. In the final winnowing all except the golden grain of character is blown away as tares and chaff.

Constellated Virgo teaches the advantage of physical life if man is to acquire that variety of experience which enables him to gain wisdom. In addition to the character weaknesses of each sign, which Hercules shows how to overcome, each zodiacal sign also is associated with its own particular type of affliction.

The illness that one sign brings is not the same as that indicated by another. The loss attracted by one sign when it is discordant, is not the same type of loss which another sign brings when acting as an affliction. Thus are there twelve different sets of difficulties attracted from without which man should understand.

To represent these, the crown used to picture the reward of character triumphing over tribulations was given twelve spikes of hard, unyielding iron; one spike for each type of affliction. Such is the significance of Corona Borealis.

Because the call of duty so frequently when followed leads to the relinquishment of fond desires, and because those born while the Sun is in this last decanate of Virgo so frequently must hear this call, the Key-word appropriately is Renunciation.

One whole book within the Bible is devoted exclusively to a discussion of the spiritual teachings which those still more ancient sought to picture as the Northern Crown. In the Book of Job many wise sayings relative to life and its problems can be found; and the story of the afflicted hero is replete with sage advice.

Job was an unusually devout man who had prospered exceedingly in all ways and gave constant praise to God for his many blessings. But there came a day when the sons of God came before the Lord, and as so frequently happens on earth when good people gather together, Satan came among them

> And the Lord said unto Satan, Whence comest thou? Then Satan answered the Lord, and said, From going to and fro in the earth, and from walking up and down in it.

Thus was such an answer given as might be expected at this day.

In the course of the conversation which followed, the Lord pointed out to Satan what a fine, upstanding man Job had proved to be. But Satan, like some people, who glory in tearing apart the merits of all who receive commendation, was unwilling to admit the worthiness of anyone. He contended that Job was a good man because the Lord had taken care of him and given him everything he wanted; but that if these things were taken from him his holiness would soon depart. So it was arranged that a test be made, with Satan to have power over him in all ways except that he must not touch his body.

Thereupon, in one catastrophe after another, Job lost his property and his children, until he had nothing left. But with the wisdom of those conversant with Spiritual Alchemy he maintained that these things were merely given to him to use so long as it served the Lord's good purpose.

Satan was much chagrined at the outcome of the trial, and as might be expected of Satan, he whined around that it had not been a fair trial, that in any proper test the man's health also must be subject to affliction, for, after all, it was not much of a blow, no matter what a man lost, so long as he kept hearty and well.

Thus was it arranged for a second trial in which Satan should do anything he desired to Job so long only as he spared his life. Then it was that Job's friends turned against him, that he broke out from head to foot with boils, and that one misery after another came to afflict him, and in his wisdom he gave voice, among other things, to this oft' quoted thought:

> For the thing which I greatly feared is come upon me, and that which I was afraid of is come unto me.

In addition to the chemical reaction to the emotion of fear, which in Job's case seems to have depleted his adrenalin supply to a point where he was unable to resist infection, to fear a thing is to hold its image vividly in the mind and to feed that image mental energy. It thus creates a thought-form which has a certain power, acting from the four-dimensional plane, to attract into the life the thing thus thought about.

In his time of affliction Job's friends held forth the oriental doctrine that man's lot in this world is determined by his morality, and that the Lord must be punishing him thus for grievous sins. But Job held that even the afflictions he suffered were for some good purpose.

If individuals are undergoing training to fit them each for a different function in the cosmic organization, each will attract to himself just those experiences he needs to develop the required abilities. Accomplishment of any kind implies the ability to overcome difficulties. People who have never had hard problems to solve are unable to solve hard problems when suddenly presented.

Afflictions, therefore, as Job discerned, are not bestowed by heaven to punish man for sin, but to indicate that he has a lesson to learn. When he has learned this lesson he will be able to triumph over the affliction, as Job did in the end; for Job was healed, and the Lord gave him twice as much as he had before, and he lived a long and prosperous life. The text thus indicated is: *He Who Would Live the Life of the Spirit, Here and Now Upon this Earth, Seen and Known of Men Must Have Fortitude in Times of Adversity.*

Spiritual Astrology

LIBRA ♎ I Balance

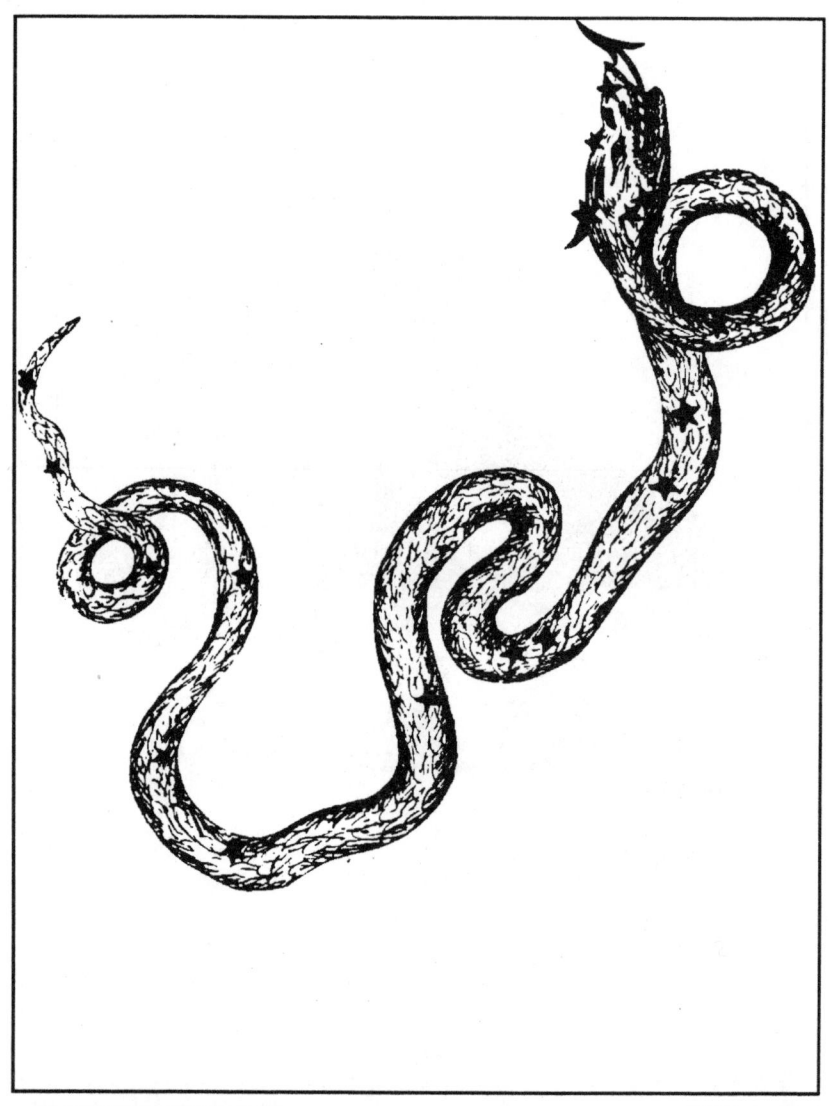

DRACO ♎–♒ Independence

Chapter 8

The Marriage in Heaven

ON THE Judgment Day.
Sacred literature from various lands makes us familiar with the idea of a day of judgment on which the kindlier deeds are weighed against those harsh to determine the rewards of the soul in the after-life. Almost every religion teaches that in proportion to man's adherence to its moral code shall his future be free from tribulation.

To picture in the sky this process of weighing the good against the evil, no more easily recognized symbol could be found than the Scales. But in addition to the purpose of their use, the Scales also present to view two dissimilar entities united by a common purpose; two spirits, as it were, represented by the circular pans, each dangling free to move in its independent orbit, yet both united by the beam to which they are attached. The Scales, therefore, is also a most fitting universal symbol of marriage.

Those who so carefully traced the constellated glories in the sky to make this universal symbolism still more obvious and complete, would also seek to place the picture in such relation to the zodiac that the position of the Sun at the point so designated, should both indicate a union representing marriage, and a balance of two nearly equal, but divergent forces.

The most familiar union, and the most familiar balance between contending forces are night and day. So common to our lives are they that they space and regulate the hours of our endeavor. We awaken and we sleep at their behest. Light becomes a symbol of life and activity, and darkness of sleep or death.

Those days in which the hours of darkness exceed the hours of light may well, therefore, be placed in one pan of the annual scales, and those in which the hours of light preponderate may fill the other. Thus day and night are weighed in Libra's Scales; and the Autumnal Equinox marks the point where summer and winter signs are married, one-half the zodiac balanced against the other.

The Sun thus moves out of the harvest sign where the grain was cut, into the place where it shall be valued. The produce of the fruitful period of the year is weighed, and the wholesome kernels are separated from the chaff. Such estimating of its worth, either of crops from the field or those from the span of life, most fittingly takes place when the vital forces, as symbolized by the Sun, have succumbed to those of cold and darkness.

The Jewish people, retaining the old time significance of this period of the year—although their calendar in modern times has been permitted somewhat to go astray—still honor the passing of the Sun each year into the sign of the Scales. This custom dates back to Leviticus 24, where it is commanded "Speak unto the Children of Israel, saying, In the seventh month, in the first day of the month, shall ye have a sabbath, a memorial of blowing of trumpets, and holy convocation." The year, of course, began with the Vernal Equinox, and Rosh-ha-Shanah is thus held the first of Tishri, or Libra.

As the day is still religiously observed, a quotation from the Jewish Encyclopedia in reference to its significance will not be amiss:

> Rosh-ha-Shanah is the most important judgment day, in which all the inhabitants of the world pass for judgment before the creator as sheep pass for examination before the shepherd. Three books of accounts are opened on Rosh-ha-Shanah wherein the fate of the wicked, the righteous, and those of the intermediate class are recorded. The names of the righteous are immediately inscribed, and are sealed 'to live.' The middle class are allowed a respite of ten days till Yom Kippur to repent and become righteous; the wicked are 'blotted out of the book of the living.'

One of the most important qualities of the human mind is the ability to weigh evidence and from a comparison of diverse factors to pass sound judgment. Every day of our lives we are called upon to make minor decisions, if of no greater importance than the amount and kind of food to be eaten, and on rare occasions to pass judgment which affects the fate of human lives.

Spiritual Astrology

In racial tradition, one man above all others stands out as the symbol of unusual wisdom. As wise as Solomon, has come to express the very essence of discrimination; and while this Jewish king exhibited the keenness of his mind on many another occasion, it was a certain decision he rendered which first proclaimed that the wisdom of God was in him. It related to two contending women who stood before him for judgment. Without doubt this is the most famous trial in the whole of human history.

To understand its celestial significance it must be recalled that the sign of the harvest, Virgo, pictures an unmarried woman, and that she stands in the sky immediately before the Scales where judgment must be passed. Where the Sun passes from Virgo into the sign of the Scales, as previously indicated, is where the wheat is separated from the chaff and the value of the harvest ascertained.

Thus were there brought before Solomon two unmarried women, each of whom, nevertheless, had had a child. Yet as in threshing there is both sound wheat and worthless chaff, so was the harvest, or child, of one woman alive, and the child of the other woman dead.

According to the story related to Solomon, the two women lived together in one house—which certainly must have been the case if both were phases of Virgo—and a child was born to each, the difference in the children's ages being but a matter of three days. Through the carelessness of one woman, the life of her child was crushed out in the darkness. This also is significant; for it is at this point that the Sun each year dies through the increasing weight of night.

One woman claimed it was the other woman's child who died, and that the other woman arose at midnight and finding her child dead, had stealthily removed the living child from the first woman's bosom, and replaced it with the child that had died. But when the light came in the morning, the woman who had remained asleep, finding the child in her arms dead, also perceived that it was not her own, but the child of her companion in the house.

This story and this accusation the other woman stoutly denied; and both women loudly proclaimed the living harvest as her own. Thus stood they before King Solomon, each disputing the right of the other to the infant.

Summer and winter are divided, one from the other, not only at

Libra, but also at Aries; an invisible line, called a colure, cutting the sky between the Vernal Equinox and the Equinox of Fall. The first of Aries marks the place where days and nights are equal in the spring, and the Scales marks where they are equal in the fall. And the sword held in the hand of Perseus has its tip almost on the line right across the sky from the judgment seat.

This militant sword of Aries often is used as the symbol of cutting asunder of the celestial circle in spring, just as the cross as frequently is used to signify the waning strength of the Sun in fall; and, after all, even as summer and winter are but inversions of the relation of night to day, so also in its form does a sword present the inversion of a cross.

Solomon, therefore, called for a sword to be brought to him and commanded, after the manner in which the equinoctial colure divides the zodiac at the point marked by the Scales, that the living child should be divided in two, one half to be given to one woman and the other half to the other.

To this procedure one woman readily agreed, but the other would not consent. Virgo, in human anatomy, rules the bowels, and the Bible states: "Then spake the woman whose the living child was unto the king, for her bowels yearned upon her son, and she said, O my lord, give her the living child, and in no wise slay it."

When she had said this, Solomon at once perceived that she was the real mother of the child, and the child was not slain, but awarded to her.

Libra is the home sign of Venus, the planet of love; and in his wisdom, Solomon weighed the love of the women who came before him, and, convinced that love seeks to preserve the object of its affection and not destroy, passed judgment accordingly. A life was not sacrificed but delivered to its rightful owner.

It was this same doctrine that love lies at the foundation of life, here and hereafter, and that the harvest of years must eventually be judged on the basis of kindness and compassion, that in later days was set forth by the Nazarene as the commandment to his followers to love one another.

Turning now from the teaching in reference to judgment, it should be noted that in the marriage of summer and winter the forces are not exactly equal; for each year there are seven more days of preponderating light than of preponderating darkness. Evil certainly is present in the world, but if the celestial correspondence holds true, it is not of equal strength with the good. Like summer and winter, they may be closely balanced in power, but if we could look close enough we should find that in the long run the good has a little advantage, and that consequently the world does make spiritual progress.

And followed far enough, this doctrine set forth in the starry symbolism of the Scales, where the Sun may be found each year from September 23 to October 23, reveals the use of evil, as well as signifying the paramount importance of love in human life.

The Key-phrase of this section of the sky is, I Balance. Those then born find a harmonious partnership especially important; and because in such a marriage spiritual qualities are engendered it gives this text: *Not By One Alone May the Highest of All Be Reached, But By Two United Souls Who Are Exalted By the Sweet Reverberations of Holy Love.*

Wisdom and the Serpent Fire

At the side of Virgo, the celestial Eve, the wise men of the east pictured the serpent, which is reputed to have tempted her. Virgo joins Libra, the sign of marriage, and Serpens portrays the marriage-decanate of this marriage sign, through which the Sun moves each year from September 23 to October 3. It therefore represents, with a more precise significance, that point in the heavenly circle where summer and winter signs are joined in marriage.

When positive and negative forces thus fuse and blend, yet at the same time their opposite pull is not exactly balanced, action results which takes the spiral form. Because such a spiral does not return upon itself, as does a circle, it is the typical motion of evolution.

Thus it is that when the 179 days of winter darkness are married to the 186 days of summer light, the result is not a perfect equilibrium between ignorance and knowledge, but a spiral which ever rises, even though slowly, away from darkness and toward more light, much as the front spiral formed by Serpens in the sky lifts its head to a plane above its body.

Because of its wave-like motion of travel, its coiling, and its phallic significance, the snake has been used throughout the world as the symbol of virile power and creative action. Hence it came to be the emblem of the Sun, the source of such creative energy. Instead of using the head of a lion for the sign Leo, therefore, its accepted astronomical hieroglyphic is simply a conventionalized snake.

This serpent of the first decanate of the marriage sign, however, expresses something more than virility and desire; for near its head, and another near its tail, may be seen loops which present to view the spiral. It is indicated, therefore, that the creative powers have been used, or enter into a combination, to produce a form which tends to progress, or is retrogressive.

At all times the surface of the earth presents a marriage of light and shadow, one half being in the sunshine and the other half in night. Yet these areas of light and shadow are not constant, but move as the earth turns on its axis. Furthermore, due to the inclination of the earth's equator to the apparent path of the Sun, the lighted half of the surface of the earth moves to the northward half the year, and to the southward the other half, the perpendicular Sun tracing the outline of that spiral to which we owe the seasons.

Sun and Moon among the orbs are typical of the Father and Mother principle. While the Moon revolves around the earth, the earth revolves around the Sun, making the Moon's path not a circle, but a wavy line in form like that of Serpens in the sky. At New Moon the Sun and Moon are united, and from thence on things of earth expand and grow, the united Solar-Lunar energies working in the direction of progress, as indicated by the higher plane held by the Serpent's head. From Full Moon to New, having reached the region of divorce, things diminish and weaken, as indicated by the tail of the snake crossing a higher level than its body.

That which happens in the sky also must happen on the earth; and the two halves of the Moon's cycle in reference to her spouse, the Sun, represent two things common in marriage. The product of the union may be a force, or evolutionary movement, which carries the pair higher and higher in their spiritual aspirations and practical endeavors. Such is pictured in the constellation by the loop near the Serpent's head, which lifts it well above the body, where it is adjacent to the signs of light, the signs which mark the warmth of summer. Or it may result disintegratively, in a movement which carries them ever down to lower depths, as clearly shown by the loop far down in winter, which gives supremacy to the Serpent's tail.

The Far East brings us a doctrine of the serpent fire, and it is to be regretted that it has so greatly permeated our West, as many have suffered damage in trying to follow it. In reality, it is one of the questionable oriental temple practices. But when in Numbers 21, reference it made to fiery serpents, the obvious inference to be drawn is that the people Moses led likewise had contacted this serpent fire doctrine, which then as now was a common portion of the perverse temple practices of oriental priests.

The Israelites had journeyed from Mount Hor by way of the Red Sea, to make a detour around the land of Edom, and were bitterly discouraged. The manna on which they fed while wandering in this wilderness, because it fell from heaven, is symbol of spiritual nutriment. As such it well represents the spiritual food husband and wife feed each other in the form of loving thoughts and high ideals. It is thus in direct contrast to the selfish purposes for which the oriental priests arouse and use the serpent fire.

It would seem, therefore, as the story is given in the Bible, those led by Moses turned away from love and kindness and adopted the perverse notions of another race.

> And the people spake against God, and against Moses, Wherefore have ye brought us up out of Egypt to die in the wilderness? for there is no bread, neither is there any water; and our soul loatheth this light bread.
>
> And the Lord sent fiery serpents among the people, and they bit the people; and much people of Israel died.

Then in their dire extremity, they turned once again to Moses and begged his help.

> And Moses made a serpent of brass, and put it upon a pole, and it came to pass, that if a serpent had bitten any man, when he beheld the serpent of brass, he lived.

Because brass is a marriage, or fusion between copper, ruled by Venus, and another metal, the universal symbolism of many ancient lands made use of it to signify a union based on love. The brazen serpent, therefore, which Moses raised upon a pole, has the same significance as that other more precise scriptural passage; "Be ye therefore wise as serpents, and harmless as doves."

It denotes that Moses taught his followers true wisdom in the use of the energies generated in marriage, and made them aware of the importance of love as the guiding principle, even as both doves and copper are under Venus' rule.

So long as they sought to rouse and use the serpent fire for the attainment of selfish ambitions, they tuned in on the spiral loop pictured near the Serpent's tail; and it carried them down to destruction and death. But when in wisdom they learned to utilize the powers engendered by holy love for the attainment of lofty aspirations and human betterment, they tuned in on the spiral loop pictured near the Serpent's head, and it lifted them up, higher and ever higher, into those regions of spiritual life denoted by the adjacent signs of summer.

The utilization of this love principle for the advancement of the race was an important part of the Stellar Religion handed down from Atlantis and Mu which found its way to various peoples. But perhaps no others gave it the supreme importance as did the Maya of Mexico and Central America. As a dominant note of architecture, to be found on bas relief and balustrade wherever jungle permits the unearthing of a temple, there is to be found some representation of the feathered serpent.

Because birds fly above the earth, their feathers became the symbol of that which belonged to the spiritual plane. Therefore to portray the thought expressed in the sky by the loop near Serpent's head, the Maya adorned a snake with feathers. In such a manner, even as did the brazen serpent raised on a pole above the sordid earth of the wilderness, did they symbolize that the energies of marriage were to be devoted to the development of spiritual powers and nobler characters; to indicate, that is, that the Serpent moves in a higher, more idealistic realm.

In any marriage which is real, the closeness of companionship adjusts the vibratory rates of each quite completely to the other. A condition is maintained which commonly is called rapport, each, that is, tuned in upon the other. Thus do the thoughts and desires flow freely back and forth, each feeding the mate with spiritual food or spiritual poison.

In any form of mental treatment, the image held in the mind of the person sending the thought is impressed upon the person receiving, and tends to make changes in the pattern of his life and actions according to its design. This is the fundamental principle in all forms of absent or other mental healing.

If, therefore, the image held in the mind of the mate is an ideal, embodying nobler, more spiritual attributes, and this image is constantly vitalized by the emotional energy of a tender and adoring love, it becomes the most powerful influence known to develop, in the one thus treated, the spiritual attributes of character. And when each, in marriage, thus holds the image of the other in higher states than this, the spiritual evolution of both is vastly hastened and a high development of character assured. This was the teaching of the feathered serpent.

But on the other hand, when married partners live in an attitude of finding fault, each with the other: when bitterness and strife creep in, and their thoughts go forth in resentment and discord, the one receiving the image thus vitalized is powerfully influenced toward developing the obnoxious traits thus mirrored, and the inharmonious forces injected into his finer form tend to disrupt and lead to failure and moral dissolution.

As picturing the balance-decanate of the sign of the balances, Serpens relates to marriage of opinions as well as to the marriage of people. Usually in any vital issue the views of opposite factions are extreme. Usually also, where there is strong contention, a compromise is more satisfactory than the triumph of either. This gives to the decanate its Key-word, Policy, and leads to the text: *In Matters of Philosophy and in Matters of Action the True Course Usually Lies Somewhere Between Advocated Extremes.*

The Battle With the Dragon

Krishna of India, according to the legends of that land, sought out and slew a noisome dragon whose poisonous breath withered the crops, bred famine, and whose movements through the countryside left death and destruction in its wake. In legendary Christendom it was St. George who played the role of valiant hero, and after long and violent battle, succeeded in leaping on the back of the scaly monster and driving his great two-handed sword straight through its wicked heart.

As Draco, this vicious creature from out the vastness of the past still is pictured in the northern sky, winding its slimy length with a turn about the Pole Star as if to strangle Truth, and with another turn about the ecliptic pole, in a mighty endeavor, it would seem, to wrench the Sun from its more accustomed path. So fearsome is it to the sight that nothing else is needed to convince it symbolizes nothing good; and this first impression is further verified by the explanation set forth in Revelation, 20:

> And I saw an angel come down from heaven and having the key of the bottomless pit and a great chain in his hand. And he laid hold on the dragon, that old serpent, which is the Devil, and Satan, and bound him a thousand years, And cast him into the bottomless pit, and shut him up, and set a seal upon him, that he should deceive the nations no more, till the thousand years should be fulfilled: and after that he must be loosed a little season.

This word, Satan, is derived from Saturn, the planet having special affinity for loss and sorrow, for evil and selfishness, for despair and desolation. It has its exaltation in the Libra sign, of which the middle decanate is pictured by the starry Dragon, and olden people held that his home domain was the bottomless pit, where his victims stewed amid the smoke and heat of a never-ceasing fire of smoldering brimstone.

As it is a decanate of the sign of marriage which the Dragon pictures, it is quite obvious that universal symbolism points to some destructive union, both in the sky and on the earth, as the influence which the pictured reptile thus explains. Nor is its heavenly significance far to seek; as not only in ancient times, but at the present day, the ephemeris gives the positions of the Nodes of the Moon, which still more commonly are called, the Dragon's Head and the Dragon's Tail.

The Moon in its orbit around the earth does not follow the same path which apparently is taken by the Sun. This apparent path of the Sun is called the ecliptic. The orbit of the Moon is at an angle of a little more than 5 degrees to the ecliptic, so that even when the Sun and Moon are exactly in the same zodiacal degree, the same east-west position, they may still be several degrees apart in a north-south direction. As the diameter of the Sun or Moon is only about half a degree, the effect, so far as a shadow is concerned, is as if an object were slightly west of a house in the morning, but ten times the width

Spiritual Astrology

of the house to the north or south of it.

The two points, or nodes, where the orbit of the Moon cuts the apparent orbit of the Sun are called the Dragon's Head and the Dragon's Tail. When the Sun in the zodiac is farther from the Dragon's Head or the Dragon's Tail than 13 degrees at the time of Full Moon, the Moon can not be eclipsed; but when it is within 9 degrees of either of these two places, a Lunar Eclipse must take place.

When the Sun at New Moon, that is, when Sun and Moon are married, is farther than 19 degrees from the Dragon's Head or the Dragon's Tail, no eclipse can take place; but when this union of Sun and Moon occurs within 15 degrees of either of these Nodes, a Solar Eclipse is always present.

Thus it is that the relation of the Sun to the Dragon's Head or Tail determines whether or not an eclipse takes place. And an eclipse, particularly an eclipse of the Sun, indicates some disaster in the region where it is visible. Symbolically, the Sun is then being devoured by the Dragon, or in case of a partial Eclipse, the Dragon gnaws at the disc of the Sun; a symbolism that is still taken literally by, and produces terror in, the more ignorant peoples of eastern lands.

In China, where the populace spend far more energy in ceremonies to prevent misfortune than in observances to attract the good, the most dramatic spectacle of the year is the pageant and play wherein the Dragon is met and finally vanquished. This oriental version of the St. George episode is a gorgeous affair, rich in setting, artistically presented.

As a precedent for the most approved of western plots, a fair damsel in distress arouses the sympathy of the gathered throng. This meek and virtuous maiden arrayed in lovelist silk, wears also decorations which proclaim her to be the goddess of the Moon, and as such the spectators give her welcome.

Not long is her lovely presence upon the stage, however, before disaster threatens. From his lurking place within the shadows, a huge and scaly monster writhes out; a Dragon, exhaling fire. The smell of burning sulphur fills the air. The Moon goddess flees in terror, but finds her retreat cut off. She is hemmed in, crowded into a corner, and the vile reptile's jaws have opened to seize her, when, with a shout and a rush, the hero comes upon the scene.

In raiment resplendent with glittering gems, he is dressed to take the part of the refulgent Sun. The Sun god dashes to the rescue, and the monster thus attacked turns its attention to him. The fumes stifle the hero, the smoke from the creature's nostrils blind him, the fire scorches his cheeks and the hair on his head. Terror grips the hearts of the spectators; for if the monster wins, the world is lost.

This demon from the pits of hell almost gets the hero down. The Moon goddess, from the corner where in dread she crouches, utters an awful scream, and holds her out-turned hand before her eyes to shut the too terrifying spectacle from her gaze! The fate of the universe is weighed in the balance!

But no! The hero only slipped, he is not completely down. He recovers himself, and with a mighty sidestep avoids the crushing weight, then vaults upon the scaly back and drives home his great two-handed sword.

The Dragon is dead. The Sun god is triumphant. He gathers to himself the lovely goddess of the Moon, marries her then and there, and they live happily ever after.

No less seriously do the Hopi Indians of Arizona consider the influence of the celestial Dragon. In their legends also, an eclipse is attributed to the Dragon devouring Sun or Moon. And their snake dance is the traditional ritual by which, among other things, the effect of a possible eclipse upon their crops can be avoided. They believe, as astrologers do, that where the shadow of a solar eclipse falls, is apt to be a region visited by pestilence, by catastrophe or by famine. And as their most frequent calamity is crop failure due to drought, their chief ceremony is staged particularly to prevent this evil.

A picture of the Hopi snake dance reveals that the reptile carried in the dancers' mouth is in form the same as the symbol commonly used for the Dragon's Head or Dragon's Tail. He does not hold it in his mouth while he dances to prove his bravery; but to symbolize the eating of the Sun or Moon by the Dragon.

The agriculture tribe who further south in Arizona built that famed house of many rooms, the pueblo of Casa Grande, also had a careful respect for the Dragon in the sky. The Sun is in the Independence-decanate of Libra, pictured by this monster, from October 3 to October 13. And a hole was bored, by this people, through the

Spiritual Astrology 167

many walls to the interior of the vast dwelling, so aligned that the rising Sun on October 7, when in the Draco decanate, and again on March 7, when in the Andromeda decanate, would shine through and cast its beams upon the central sanctuary.

The union of Sun and Moon to ancient peoples was the symbol of the union of the Ego and the Soul, that is, of mind and spirit. The Moon has ever been the symbol of the indwelling soul. The Dragon, on the other hand, represents the environmental forces which tend to develop the reptilian traits of character, the cruel instincts and ruthless selfishness which shut out the light of spirit, and thus eclipse the soul. To the extent, therefore, an eclipse is total does it present a spectacle representing the soul or spirit devoured and destroyed by the powers of darkness associated with the struggle with physical environment.

We perceive now why Yom Kippur, which is ten days after Rosh-ha-Shanah, and thus when the Sun enters the Draco-decanate, is the most sacred of Jewish observances. Kippur means the atonement, the setting at one, the reconciliation of two parties, just as Sun and Moon are reconciled and united as one at New Moon, unless an eclipse is present. When there is an eclipse the light, or good, is devoured by darkness, or evil. This signifies the destruction of the soul, unless the powers of darkness and of evil, symbolized by the Dragon, are vanquished and the final atonement made.

The whole purpose of evolution, up to the state of man, is through combat with environmental conditions and the struggle for physical survival, to develop the selfish instincts and the animal qualities of the soul. Difficulties are not overcome by weakness, nor is accomplishment made without aggression and courage. Those who permit the competitors for food, for mate and for shelter to force them to one side are not fulfilling the highest purpose of physical destiny.

But when, and to such extent as, the abilities and possibilities developed in the fierce struggle of its animal past are turned to purposes which have for interest the welfare of all, does that soul cease to function on the plane of brute, and rise to something which we term divine. It has thus triumphed over the Dragon, and its atonement is complete.

When it thus has reunited with its Ego, and the dark peril is past, it can find no joy in the pain or discomfort of any living thing. The text thus emerges: *Deal Justly, Even With Thy Enemies; For it is Better to Suffer Evil than to Retaliate With Vengeance.*

Little Red Ridinghood

When the masters of an ancient day traced a wolf in the sky it is quite certain they had in mind those qualities which then and now this creature most commonly is known to express. A wolf is a cunning beast, using its mind, as the mental-decanate of the partnership sign would indicate. It is aggressive and cruel, runs in packs when that is an advantage, and hesitates not to kill and devour such a partner when it becomes so weakened or crippled as to be unable to defend itself. Thus does a wolf stand as the universal symbol of ruthlessness.

Picturing that section of the celestial circle where the Sun may be found each year from October 13 to October 23, the Wolf, Lupus, is directly across the zodiac in antagonism to the Ram. Sheep thus constitute its natural prey, and to stalk them the predacious beast resorts to many a cunning device. At the time of year so designated the days are shorter than the hours of darkness, and wolves chiefly do their depredations under cover of the night. Although they are the terror of the shepherds, seldom are they to be seen in light of day, or do their killing in the open. Instead, they resort to subterfuge, which makes the passage of St. Matthew clear:

> Beware of false prophets, which come to you in sheep's clothing, but inwardly they are ravening wolves.

The best commentary which has come down to us perhaps, as to the full significance of this Wolf of heaven, and what its teachings are, is to be found in the wide-spread and symbolical story of Little Red Ridinghood.

From your nursery days you will remember, I am sure, that the grandmother of this nice little girl was ill. As a dutiful granddaughter should, Little Red Ridinghood went to pay the old lady a visit, taking with her some cookies which she felt her ill relative would enjoy.

Little Red Ridinghood, quite unmistakably, as the hero of the tale, must represent the human soul. The grandmother who was ill, and whose house was by the road at the other side of the wood, represents those people in the world who suffer afflictions of various sorts, and who are too weak and helpless to be able to defend themselves. They thus are symbolized by a helpless woman because the Moon is the ruler of women and of the Domestic Urges, those impulses which incline not merely to the care of home and children, but also to the care of the helpless old, and to ministering to such others as misfortune makes it impossible for them to care for themselves.

The road along which Red Ridinghood went. with her basket of cookies on her arm, ran through the forest of human contacts which flanks the path of every life. There were flowers and butterflies and beautiful birds to give interest and pleasure to her self-appointed task, and so full of joy was she with it all, that she sang a merry little melody as she danced along toward her work of mercy.

Then all at once, out from behind the bole of a giant tree where he had been hiding, stepped a wolf. Red Ridinghood was badly frightened, but she knew there was no use to run, as the wolf could easily overtake her. So she said, "Good morning Mister Wolf, what a fine day it is!"

And the Wolf, although very hungry, thought to himself: "Before I eat her, I will find out where she is going and what she intends to do, as this may lead me to something else I want."

So the Wolf said, "Good morning, and where are you going so happily, and what do you carry in that fine basket on your arm?"

He spoke so pleasantly, as people are wont to do when they seek to gain the confidence of others, later to despoil them, that Red Ridinghood was quite disarmed, and thought she had misjudged him in her first impression that he was intent on evil. So she told the Wolf all about her grandmother, where she lived, and that there were cookies in the basket, which she was taking in the hope to give the dear old lady a better appetite.

The Wolf then thought to himself, as predatory people do, that it were better not to act too hastily, but to lay a cunning plan by which he might gain for himself every possible advantage, even though it meant more loss and misery to others.

The old lady, according to Red Ridinghood's account, was ill in bed and quite helpless. It would be an easy matter to make a meal from her, in the manner customary to his pack to kill and devour such members as became too weak to defend themselves. After that, he could wait for the little girl, get the cookies, and devour her too.

In this manner, he would be able to gorge himself with food and more completely satisfy his lust for blood.

He therefore smiled at Red Ridinghood, bade her good day pleasantly, and started down the road in the opposite direction from which she was going, so that she should have no suspicion he had any thought of her harm. But as soon as he was out of her sight, he made a wide, swift detour through the forest back to the road ahead of her, and ran swiftly to the house, where he made the expected meal from the ill old lady.

It was not literally a case of a wolf in sheep's clothing, but figuratively it became so; for no sooner did he finish with grandmother and lick his bloody chops, than he donned her garments and climbed into bed to doze, all prepared to look as much like the late departed as possible.

When Little Red Ridinghood came to her grandmother's house, she knocked lightly on the door. This awakened the Wolf from his after dinner nap, and as soon as he had adjusted the white cap as nicely as possible on his head, he called, "Come in."

Said Little Red Ridinghood, as she entered the room, "My! Grandma, what a deep voice you have."

Replied the Wolf from the bed, "All the better to call you in."

Walking toward the bed, to deliver the basket of cookies, the little girl noticed how unusual her grandmother appeared, and said, "But, Grandma, what bright eyes you have."

Said the Wolf from where he lay, "All the better to see you with."

Then the child noticed the ears, where they stuck out from under the white nightcap, "And, Grandma, what big ears you have!"

Answered the Wolf, growing quite excited by now, "All the better to hear you with."

In his excitement he had opened his mouth quite wide, displaying its red cruelty, and Red Ridinghood, by now thoroughly alarmed, exclaimed, "Grandma, Grandma, what great teeth you have!"

"All the better to eat you with," shouted the Wolf, as he threw off his disguise and leaped from the bed.

In another bound he would have had the terror-stricken little girl by the throat; but some passing woodsmen had overheard the hoarse voice of the Wolf, and had stopped to listen further, and now dashed into the house, axes in hand.

Even as he made the leap for the child's white throat an axe cut the Wolf down, and shortly nothing was left of him but the pieces.

Predatory interests, cruel and ruthless, still speak to the public through the press, pulpit and radio, in a voice they endeavor to disguise as that of general welfare, but which in reality has for its purpose the influencing of all who will listen to come closer that they may more easily be despoiled.

Their eyes are bright with avarice and greed, quick to note the slightest opportunity by which others can be placed at a disadvantage.

They listen with big wolfish ears to the trend of popular interest, that they may utilize it for the benefit of their own self-seeking and human-destroying schemes.

Their rapacious mouths are armed with teeth of war, pillage and destruction. Blood lust is upon them, and the suffering of sweatshop, of child labor, and of armed strife brings forth no thought of sympathy.

But after a time the woodsman's axe always cuts them down. Those who live through deceit and cunning, who exploit their fellowman, are inexorably doomed to final expiation.

The Wolf as pictured in the sky no longer takes his toll of blood. No longer is he able to hide his wickedness behind the cloak of lawful practice and social respectability. He has met, not the woodsman's axe, but the spear thrust of Centaurus. His tail and ears are drooped, his legs are crumpled under him, tongue protrudes, and the blood of death drips from his mouth. He has reached the certain fate of those who prey on others.

Little Red Ridinghood escaped destruction; for she was on an errand of mercy. She was building thoughts of peace and joy, of good will, and of compassion for others, into her finer self. The human soul thus fortified may be despoiled of earthly things, but nothing can destroy its spiritual life, or filch its spiritual treasures.

It should not be thought that those who are born when the Sun is in the Lupus decanate are more given to cunning exploitation of others in the interests of themselves. But it does seem that those then born, when they do turn their energies to such despoiling, more quickly are called upon to pay dreadful penalty. It is the observation of this that gives the decanate its Key-word, Expiation.

But aside from astrological considerations, anyone who cultivates within himself the ruthless cunning and heartless cruelty of the Wolf, can not but attract disaster to himself in time. The thought-cells of his finer body, given practice in cruelty and despoliation, sooner or later receive such stimulation as is necessary to cause them to work quite as energetically from the four dimensional realm, to attract similar misfortunes into the life of the one who gave them birth.

Where the thoughts and desires find no sympathy and no consideration for the well being of others, even though the intelligence and body are human, the soul is that of the Wolf. All should understand this text: *It is Impossible for a Man to Injure Another Without Himself Being Injured, or for a Man to Benefit Another Without Himself Being Truly Benefited.*

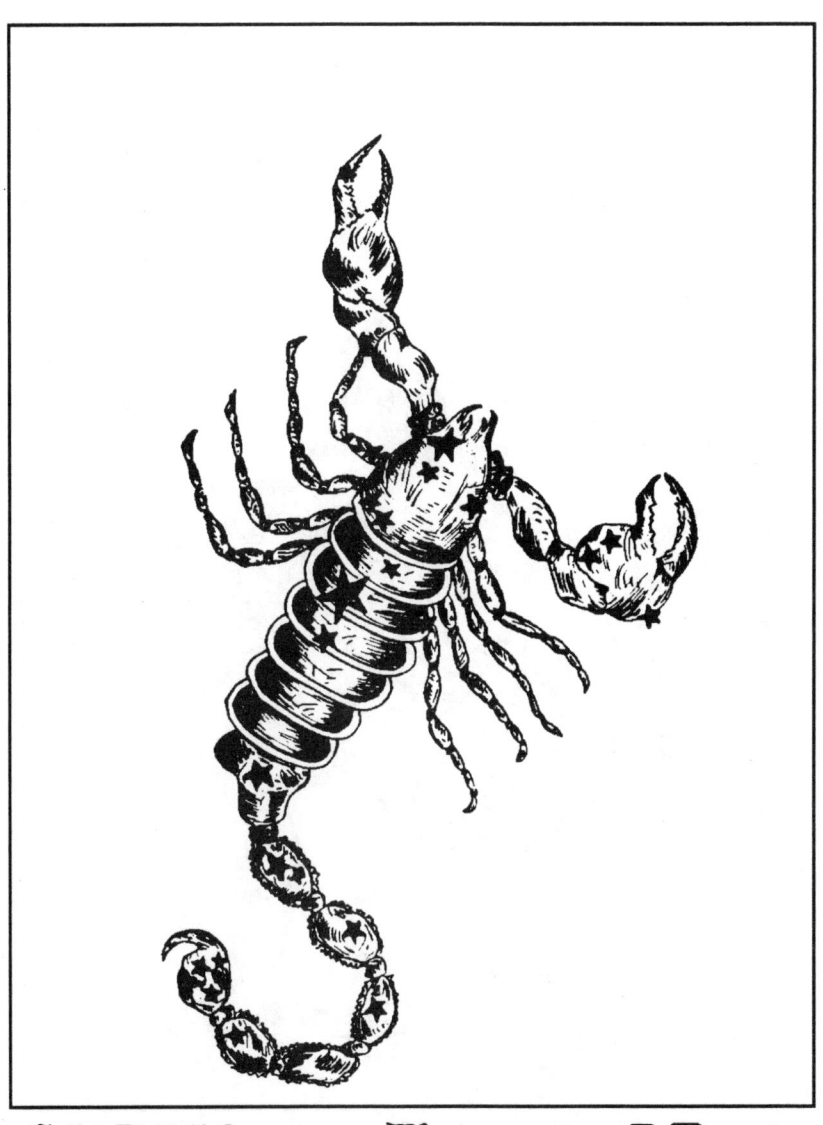

SCORPIO ♏ *I Desire*

ARA   ♏♓   Responsibility

CORONA AUSTRALIS ♏︎   Attainment

Chapter 9 _____

The Scorpion and the Eagle
_____

WHEN the Scorpion Grows Wings.
There is a creature of the desert which lives in the arid dust, hiding from the light of day under sticks and stones, preying upon other living things. It has claws with which to grasp, a cruel mouth with which to bite, and in addition, a deadly weapon where least to be expected, a venomous sting at the end of its tail. This creature is the treacherous Scorpion.

No other animal, perhaps, exhibits such intensity in its love making, and none is more jealous and cruel once its desires are satisfied. The male and female Scorpion, preceding the nuptial union, clasp hands in ecstasy, and each in rapt admiration of the other stands immobile for as much as a night and day. The enthrallment of the other's touch seems, for the time being, to lift them to such heights of bliss that they are oblivious of the world and passing time. They are entranced by the wonder of it all. Desire so permeates their bodies as to render them motionless.

Yet when finally the spell is broken, and fertilization has taken place, a monstrous change in attitude occurs. In members of this and allied tribes, such as the spiders, the female is the larger. And it is as if, satiated by the long embrace, she were consumed with jealousy of a future rival, driven to frenzy by the thought her mate might desert her for another. This, at any cost, and at any cruelty, she is determined to prevent. She, therefore grasps her erstwhile lover, and despite his frenzied struggles, his mute entreaties, and his attempts to recall to her the beauties of their recent honeymoon, she tears him limb from limb and devours him completely.

Those, therefore, in the ancient past, who wished to portray in the sky the intensity, the power, the cruelty and the vileness of the destructive side of sex, could have selected no more fitting universal symbol than the Scorpion. The oldest seals and boundary stones of Mesopotamia bear the picture of this constellation; and it is one of the symbols to be seen on the Arkansas Astrological Stone, reproduction of which is to be found in chapter 1.

All energy, wherever manifest, is the result of the interaction of positive and negative potencies, and broadly speaking can thus be considered as an expression of sex. That is, mental action and spiritual aspiration, as well as physical movement, are dependent upon desire; upon the utilization of energies on a higher vibratory level which if permitted to express on the Scorpion plane would manifest as cruelty and lust. Religion also is the sublimation of the love impulse, and all art and appreciation of beauty are its manifestations in a realm above that of the brute.

Because creative ability can express on an infinite variety of levels, it would not be feasible to represent each separate plane of its manifestation. Yet it would not convey the correct information if its expression were portrayed merely on the cruel, lustful and destructive level so well represented by the dastardly Scorpion.

Religion being a sublimation of the impulse which on a lower stratum leads the individual to seek a mate, the only Eagle among the constellations portrays the second-decanate of the religious sign, Sagittarius. Yet tradition maintains that the Eagle is also the symbol for the higher side of Scorpio; and in symbolizing the four quadrants of heaven, instead of the Scorpion being used to represent the Scorpio quadrant, the Eagle invariably has been employed. That is, the four fixed signs of the zodiac, as representing the whole celestial circle, are always pictured as a Man, a Bull, a Lion and an Eagle; the Scorpion never being shown.

The Eagle is the bird which it was believed flew higher than any other creature. At least, in its upward soaring it ascends until completely out of sight. Moving thus upward into heaven, it came, quite naturally, to be considered the universal symbol of the highest spirituality. Thus in the Scorpion the ancients sought to convey the idea of the lowest and most vile; while in the Eagle they saw the symbol of those most exalted spiritual heights to which it was possible for man to attain.

This creative energy, manifesting on innumerable planes and

permeating both the highest and the lowest in the universe, was expressed by the Mound Builders who left the Arkansas Astrological Stone as the zigzag bolt of lightning. They pictured it as coming from out the Scorpion constellation in the sky, descending to vivify the productive powers of man.

The Hopi Indians of our Southwest, however, living in a region where lightning is a constant source of danger, where trees and dwellings are frequently struck during the numerous summer thunder-storms, where life is forfeited to this menace from the sky, regarded the lightning not so much as the symbol of the sexual power, as the manifestation of its destructive use. Instead of picturing the Scorpion, they pictured the lightning. And to indicate the constructive trend of the sexual force they used, as Old World peoples did, the Eagle.

Strangely enough, their ceremonies in which the destructive lightning is used to indicate the lower Scorpio attribute, and the Thunderbird, which is an Eagle, is used to portray the higher side, coincide most perfectly with our knowledge of the co-ruler of Scorpio, knowledge which we have gained only since the discovery of the Planet Pluto, early in 1930.

This most remote member of our planetary family not only has an affinity for the Scorpio sign, but in a violently marked manner it expresses, in its observed influence upon human life, both extreme characteristics of the sign. It may partake of the highest or the lowest, belong to the light or the shadow, produce glorious life or ignoble death.

In such Hopi ceremonies, therefore, as have for their object the over-coming of evil and the prevention of destruction, the Thunderbird commonly plays the leading part. It is he who at the winter solstice, for instance, after a struggle, dispels the darkness, brings back the Sun, and gives to earth the light.

These ceremonies, in which the Thunderbird takes part, are held in a kiva, or chamber beneath the ground; for Pluto, the planet of Scorpio, rules the underworld. This underworld, however, is not merely the ignoble region of the desert Scorpion, but also the high empyrean of blue in which the upward soaring Eagle is lost to sight. That is, it is the invisible world, the realm of the after life, divided into a realm of light and a realm of darkness, into heaven and hell, into the abode of the good and the dwelling place of the wicked.

The kiva, therefore, into which the Indians go to hold communion with the dead, to get in touch with their ancestors and to perform their more sacred rites, is built underground to symbolize that region where the spirits of the departed dwell. That is, such constitutes an appropriate surrounding for the Thunderbird to express his peculiar powers; for in all lands Scorpio is recognized not merely as the sign of sex, but also as the abode of Death.

In Central Asia the constellation still is known as the Grave Digger of Caravans; and Greek mythology tells us that invincible as Orion seemed, he was finally vanquished by a Scorpion. Juno presided over marriage and was the patron of women distinguished for their virtue. It was she who sent the Scorpion to bring the downfall of Orion, who had incurred her displeasure. True to its nature, it lay concealed in the ground, and stung him in the foot as he passed. As the foot represents understanding, and as nothing defeats understanding more quickly than passion. the significance of this story is obvious; that he was vanquished through unwise devotion to sex.

Orion sets in the west, goes down to defeat, just as Scorpio rises triumphant in the east. And it will be remembered that Phaeton also met grief through his encounter with the Scorpion, which sank its sting into the flank of one of his steeds as he strove to guide them through the heavens.

From the commencement of this sign, to the first of Aries, where the Sun is released from the signs of winter is a distance of five months. This circumstance, together with the knowledge that on its inversive side Scorpio rules those forces and entities which most torment mankind, makes Revelation 9:3-5, understandable:

> And there came out of the smoke locusts upon the earth: and unto them was given power, as the scorpions of the earth have power. And it was commanded them that they should not hurt the grass of the earth, neither any green thing, neither any tree; but only those men which have not the seal of God in their foreheads. And to them it was given that they should not kill them, but that they should be tormented five months: and their torment was as the torment of a scorpion, when he striketh a man.

Because, as psychologists have discovered, the sex impulse is the seat of most of those insistent desires which when suppressed lead to a wide variety of nervous and mental complaints, and because the mating urge is so strong a force wherever life manifests, the Keyphrase given Scorpio, where the Sun may be found each year from October 23 to November 22, is, I Desire.

Its energy is either creative or destructive, light or darkness, and can express in any field. Creative writing calls it into use, all art is its expression, the orator can sway his audience little without it. Yet whether it takes the upward trend, carrying its user on the back of the Eagle into rarer atmospheres, or sinks him in the mire of grossness and dissipation, depends upon his Desires. These give the trend which the energy must take, and the energy carries him along wherever it goes. If Desire is in the direction of refinement, charged with aspiration to something better, his progress is assured. If it is toward the sensual it pulls him down.

Desires become surcharged with emotion, and emotion tunes the nerves and etheric body in on invisible energies of a similar vibratory rate. This leads to the text: *Through Sex Man Contacts the Inner Planes, Drawing into Himself According to His Mood, the Finest Energies that Vivify the Spaces or the Grossest Forces from the Fetid Border Spheres.*

The Man Whom Jacob Wrestled With

When the ancient wise ones traced the spiritual teachings regarding the sex-decanate of the sex-sign Scorpio in the sky, they selected a man, Ophiuchus, and represented him as engaged in a life-or-death struggle with Serpens, symbol of that energy generated through the union of polar opposites, which pictures the marriage-decanate of the marriage-sign Libra. Thus intimately united in the sky, an interlocking and inseparable pair, are pictured sex and marriage.

Man's likes and dislikes, and therefore his habitual actions, are conditioned by his experiences; but back of any experience in human form are certain irrepressible drives, such as the desire to live, the desire for significance, and the desire for reproduction. These fundamental drives are inherent in all life, providing the force which impels it to struggle and to attempt to move forward. They can not be obliterated in any living thing; for they are essential constituents of life itself. But their expression, in their attempt to seek satisfaction, is conditioned by experience.

As furnishing energy which can be used not merely to satisfy the urge of sex, but also to secure significance, which in human life becomes self esteem, and to secure food and other advantages, the reproductive drive is of great importance in the life of every human being. So important is it that the ills resulting from its suppression have given rise to a whole literature. The Freudian doctrines of the unconscious mind and the practices of psychoanalysis revolve almost entirely around the struggle of man to adjust himself to the demands of sex.

While not the only struggle man is called upon to make—for does not Orion engage his environment in mortal combat?—yet the proper conditioning of his sexual impulses is so important a matter to every living person, that the ancients felt the need of picturing it in association with the sex-decanate of the sex-sign, where the Sun may be found from October 23 to November 2. Ophiuchus wrestles with the generative snake.

Not always are we fortunate enough to possess a story from the ancient times which reveals the triumph over difficulty, and another which as well imparts the cause and result of defeat. But relating to Ophiuchus we have both, one a story from the Bible, and another a legend from the Greeks.

Genesis 32, relates that Jacob, after sending his wives and sons over a brook was left alone:

> And there wrestled a man with him until the breaking of day. And when he saw that he prevailed not against him, he touched the hollow of his thigh; and the hollow of Jacob's thigh was out of joint as he wrestled with him.

Ophiuchus does not wrestle with a man, but with the serpent of generation; and in all the old star atlases he is pictured as somewhat crippled in the struggle, his thigh being out of joint.

The thigh is ruled by Sagittarius, the sign of religion, one decanate of which is pictured by an eagle, indicating the sublimation of sex energy. Thus, as the story is told, we are led to infer that there was a maladjustment due to religious views. But to go on with the Bible story:

> And he said, let me go for the day breaketh. And he said, I will not let thee go, except thou bless me. And he said unto him, What is thy name? And he said Jacob. And he said, thy name shall be called

no more Jacob, but Israel: for as a prince hast thou power with God and with men, and hast prevailed. And Jacob asked him, and said, Tell me, I pray thee, thy name. And he said, Wherefore is it that thou dost ask after my name? And he blessed him there.

And Jacob called the name of the place Penial: for I have seen God face to face, and my life is preserved. And as he passed over Penial the sun rose high upon him, and he halted upon his thigh. Therefore the children of Israel eat not of the sinew which shrank, which is upon the hollow of the thigh, unto this day: because he touched the hollow of Jacob's thigh in the sinew which shrank.

The only man in the sky who wrestles is Ophiuchus, and he is likewise the only man among the stars whose thigh is shown to be out of joint. It is the creative energy with which he struggles.

As the thigh is so specifically mentioned, and as Serpens is pictured crossing it, it would appear that religion, which is ruled by Sagittarius, and which corresponds to the thigh, has suffered a misadjustment in its relation to the problem of sex.

In various oriental lands, and among the priests and devotees of certain occidental religions, those who turn to a religious life are required to take a vow of celibacy. Likewise, it seemed to Paul, that great leader in establishing Christian institutions, that married life and religion were in deadly opposition. He seems to have been a woman-hater who was successful in imposing his own private views as to the degrading effect of marriage upon a multitude of followers. As a consequence nunneries and monasteries flourished, and the priesthood were not permitted to form family ties.

We do not need to agree with the views of the Freudian school of psychiatry, but merely to read the history of the mystical manias and mass obsessions which so persistently have pervaded nunneries and monasteries, to become convinced that enforced celibacy is a source of danger to the mind. And practically all schools of psychology of the present day agree that some maladjustment in the sex life is back of the majority of cases of neurosis, and back of much psychosis.

The urge for reproduction is one of the most insistent drives of every form of life. Nature has taken every pains to make this urge so strong as to be irresistible. That is, she has provided in each organism for the generation of a specific kind of energy in a volume sufficiently great that it can not be prevented from expressing. This insures the perpetuation of the race. The effort, in the manner advocated by St. Paul, to keep it from expressing has never been successful. The energy is never merely stored up within the human body. It invariably finds an outlet.

Suggestion is powerful, and under certain religions the suggestion is repeatedly given the child that sexual desire is iniquitous and that only those ignoble and depraved have such intense feelings.

The child thus indoctrinated also must satisfy another fundamental drive which is equally strong. The desire for self esteem. Yet if he admits, as he enters adolescence, that he has insistent sex desires, because of false training this implies to him that he is a degraded creature, that God disapproves of him, and that he probably will ultimately simmer in hell.

These thoughts are so repugnant to him that he is unwilling to believe he has such iniquitous impulses. His constant suggestion to himself, and also frequently the suggestions of those in his environment, is that he could not possibly have such disgraceful urges. And the unconscious mind, accepting the suggestion of his spotless purity, builds up an evasive mechanism which will satisfy him that this is true. He is as unaware that he has sexual impulses as a hypnotized subject, told a stick is a cigar, is unaware that he is not smoking tobacco.

The unconscious mind, with all its resources, is powerless to obliterate any of the fundamental drives of life. The most it can do is to divert them from one channel into another.

Yet the sex urge can express fully and with complete satisfaction, while maintaining physical and mental health, on a wide variety of levels and through diverse creative channels. The love-life, for instance, can be elevated to the plane of regeneration in which the physical no longer feels a need, that need being replaced by a fusion and interchange of finer forces Or the sex urge can be diverted completely into the creation of literature, art, music, or social service work.

It is only when the creative energy is not expressed through some creative channel that, under the implied suggestion that it has no existence, it expresses itself under disguise as some of the numerous symptoms of neurosis, psychosis, or erratic behavior, with which psychoanalytic literature has made the public familiar.

Jacob seemed to have the difficulty that many people have in adjusting his reproductive desires to the demands of his religion. He wrestled with the problem, as Ophiuchus is yet observed to be doing until he solved it. This caused him some affliction, and he never succeeded in adjusting it to his early religious convictions, as implied by the shrunken sinew in the hollow of his thigh. Yet that he finally did make a satisfactory adjustment, even from the standpoint of his later religious convictions, is to be inferred from the statement that the Sun, which is symbol of virility and vitality, halted upon the part of his body having religious significance, that is, upon his thigh.

And as always is the case, when he had made the proper adjustment, so that he was able to divert his creative energies into channels of accomplishment which were socially acceptable and beneficial, this adjustment blessed him. He then had at his disposal to use for a worthy purpose a volume of energy not possessed by less fortunate men.

Laocoon, in the Greek story, was not so fortunate in making the adjustment. It was at the siege of Troy, and the enterprise required that a wooden horse—symbol of religion, just as was Jacob's thigh—should be moved into the beleaguered city. Laocoon, who was a priest of Apollo (Sun) opposed the admission of this horse. As a punishment for this attitude two enormous serpents were sent to attack him while he with his two sons was offering a sacrifice to Neptune. Coiling around the men, the serpents crushed all three to death.

Of the two roads, one of which is demanded by Neptune, octave of Venus, the planet of love, instead of sublimation, Laocoon chose suppression. He was unable to adjust his creative desires to his religious views, as symbolized by the wooden horse. Instead, therefore, of being blessed, as was Jacob who defeated the serpent and sublimated his desires to a higher plane of expression, he was crushed and strangled by them in an attempt at their annihilation.

Resourcefulness, which is the Key-word of the decanate, follows the ability to divert the sex-energy into proper channels. As a constructive and acceptable outlet for the energy must be found, we have this text: *Continual Kindness Between the Sexes Generates a Power by Which the Heights may be Scaled.*

The Altar of Cain and Abel

The Altar upon which sacrifice is made by priest and devotee is repeatedly mentioned in the symbolical stories current in various lands. In religious observances of the past it has ever held a position of importance, particularly in those religions in which the propitiation of astral entities forms an essential part of the ceremonies.

The departed friends and ancestors come under the astrological rule of the eighth house, pictured by Scorpio; but elementals and various other astral entities, particularly those which attempt to deceive or enslave their votaries, come under the rule of the twelfth house, pictured by Pisces. To have significance where both the house of death and the house of astral entities are concerned, in selecting the appropriate place for Ara, the Altar in the sky, the ancients allotted it, therefore, to the Pisces-decanate of Scorpio.

To reveal its true significance, it could picture a decanate of no other sign than Scorpio; for sacrifices are made either to the light or to the darkness, to true religion as represented by Sagittarius, or to blind and erroneous belief as indicated by Pisces, the other sign which Jupiter, the religious planet, rules. Or to state it more precisely, sacrifices are made to the beast in man, pictured by the vile and treacherous Scorpion, or to the angel in man, pictured by the high-soaring Eagle.

Pluto, the co-ruler of Scorpio, has dominion over the invisible world, over both the spiritual heavens and the astral hells. One side of its influence enables the individual to contact the highest realm of all, and the other brings the individual into touch with the most degraded and terrifying wickedness. Scorpio, according to tradition, is the Great Deceiver. Consequently, when opportunity offers for the inversive influence of Pluto to get in its work, true religion and spiritual aspirations are given such a twist as to lead the devotee into folly and wickedness under the belief he is practicing that which is good in the sight of God.

It was customary, for instance, among the ancient peoples of Mexico, at prescribed times astrologically ascertained, to bring to the priests for sacrifice upon the Altar, fruits and flowers. Flowers, of course, are the reproductive parts of plants, and thus ruled by Scorpio; and the fruits are the issue, containing the seeds which permit of a new generation. This ceremony, from which is derived the custom of hanging May Baskets, signified the knowledge that the purpose of incarnation on earth is to develop the seeds of spirituality., that the experiences of earth can be used to unfold the beauties of the soul, even as blooms the flower; and that the desires of the devotee to devote all his resources, as symbolized by his offering, to the development of those qualities which make him a better citizen of the universe, lead to the highest happiness.

Whatever the sacrifice on the Altar might be, if it were burnt, the smoke ascending, and the aromas permeating the air, symbolically conveyed the idea that the motives and desires were carried into the invisible world, attracting intelligences of a quality corresponding to the nature of the sacrifice, who, it was believed, would assist the individual in attaining that for which the sacrifice was offered.

For instance, as related in Numbers 22 and 23, Balak desired to employ Balaam to bring a curse upon the Israelites, and sent word to him: "For I will promote thee unto very great honor, and I will do whatever thou sayest unto me: come therefore, I pray thee, curse me this people."

When finally Balaam was persuaded to come to Balak, he was taken to a high place where he could see all the people, that he might bring a curse upon them: "And Balaam said unto Balak, Build me here seven altars, and prepare me here seven oxen and seven rams. And Balak did as Balaam had spoken; and Balak and Balaam offered on every altar a bullock and a ram."

Here we have an effort typical of the inversive side of Pluto, showing that the employment of a magician to bring a curse upon those it was desired to destroy was not uncommon in Bible times. But in this instance the effort failed, Balaam at the last instant refusing to pronounce the curse, and saying: "Surely there is no enchantment against Jacob, neither is there any divination against Israel."

In ancient Mexico, as the above incident from the Bible indicates was the case among the Semites, there were those who worked under the inversive side of Pluto, who attracted to themselves not the eighth house influence so much as the twelfth house denizens, and used them, and were used by them, to do injustice and to work evil.

Gradually, and subtly, as such underhanded forces always work, these Priests of the Shadow gained dominion over the religious observances of the land. After a battle, with the blood lust still upon them, it seemed to the populace quite the fitting thing that prisoners of war should be offered as a sacrifice upon the Altar, instead of the customary fruits and flowers. Especially so, as the priests told them that thus would the strength of the victims be inherited so it could be used against future enemies.

Once the custom was established of making human sacrifices, it was easily extended to imply a demand by the gods for more and more victims. If prisoners of war were not forthcoming, individuals from the populace must be selected, otherwise the anger of the gods would be visited upon the nation. And in time of national crisis, still more victims must be had, in order to avert the threatened peril.

Mass murder, such as that practiced by modern racketeers with machine guns, is typical of the lower influence of Pluto, co-ruler of the sign of Death. The more cruel and bloodthirsty a killing is, the better it corresponds to this ruthless side of Scorpio. The Aztec Priests of Darkness, therefore, when they gained supremacy, devised a particularly horrifying method of human sacrifice. The victim was spread-eagled, face up, on the Altar, each hand and leg held by a priest. Another priest, after appropriate magical invocation to the gods (bloodthirsty elementals of the twelfth house), with a single slash of a stone knife ripped open the victim's breast, and with the other hand tore the living, palpitating heart from the shrieking man or woman; then held the bloody trophy aloft as an offering to invisible beings and for the assembled populace to see. If the victim died before his heart was jerked from his agonized body the sacrifice was considered ineffectual.

To go still deeper into the teachings of the Altar in the sky, let us consider the story of the first two children born on earth. Genesis 4, relates that Cain was a tiller of the ground; by which is probably meant that his interests were material. Abel, on the other hand, was a keeper of sheep. Instead of being earth-earthy in his inclinations, it is implied that, like Aries, the fiery exaltation of the Sun, his zeal and enthusiasm were for immaterial things.

Cain, with his purely physical outlook on life, offered as his sacrifice to the Lord, the fruits of the ground. That is, he seemed to think, like certain men at the present day, that he could buy spirituality. Instead of turning the creative energies within himself into channels which would develop refinement of feeling, and ener-

Spiritual Astrology

gize action which was above the plane of brute, he merely worked hard to acquire material possessions, and turned a portion of these over as a religious tithing.

Sheep are symbols of creative energy. This energy is of animal origin. When Abel, therefore, brought in the firstlings of his flock and the fat thereof, and offered them as a sacrifice, the implication is that he sacrificed the animal part of himself, and turned his creative energies into channels which would not express the gross, but would develop refinement and conduce to those actions which prove spirituality.

In other words, Cain was quite willing to sacrifice his material possessions; but he made no effort to change the brute within himself into something more acceptable. That this is the correct interpretation subsequent events seem to prove; for jealousy is one of those destructive emotions which are fed by the energy of unregenerate Scorpio. When he was reproved for his manner of living, instead of taking it in good part, he became angry that his brother should have had better fortune than himself.

The Altar pictures a decanate in the sign of Death. Yet even though Abel was slain, he had contacted the Eagle side of Pluto. Cain, however, in his anger, contacted the Scorpion side, and his energies, flowing into destructive channels, wrought the death of Abel. Truly, the energies of Scorpio go aloft like the Eagle, or sink into the earth. To the extent they are present they must express.

The entire teaching which the ancients sought to convey by Ara, where the Sun may be found each year from November 2 to November 12, is condensed in Cain's reply when the Lord asked him where was his brother, Abel: "And he said, I know not: Am I my brother's keeper?"

Responsibility is the Key-word for the Ara decanate, and the Cains of earth always disclaim responsibility for that which befalls their fellowman. Although they occupy human forms they still function on the brute plane where fang and claw, and a total disregard for the welfare of others are dominant factors. But every Brother of the Light must forever renounce such an attitude, which attracts the twelfth house astral entities. Those who would attract help and guidance from the truly spiritual must assume Responsibility for contributing all within their power to the welfare of others.

Like Abraham, as related in Genesis 22, instead of killing after the manner of the Aztec Priests, when his own son was tied a victim on the wood of the altar, he must sacrifice the animal within himself, the creative Ram, turning its energies to the service of God. In no other way can spirituality be attained. Hence the text follows: *By Sacrificing His Animal Thoughts, Desires and Pleasures Upon the Altar of Aspiration to Higher Things Man Comes into Possession of Intellectual and Spiritual Pleasures that Yield a far Keener Delight.*

The Adept's Laurel Crown

It was the custom of the ancient Greeks to crown the victors in the Pythian games with a wreath of laurel. It was also used by them as a mark of distinction for certain high offices; and later came to be employed to denote academic honors, from which the European custom arose of calling the poet or artist who won the highest place, the laureate, such as the poet laureate; that is, the poet who by his excellence had merited the crown of laurel. It is such a crown, Corona Australis, which pictures the attainment-decanate of Scorpio.

Scorpio is ruler not merely of the energy of sex, but also of death; and the placing of the universal symbol of highest attainment where it represents the Cancer-decanate of Scorpio implies that the victor thus designated is the master of the energies of his creative functions, and that the scope of his powers is not confined to the material world, but extends into the realm where reside those commonly denoted dead. He has, while still in the flesh, attained immortality, and is able to work both on the external plane and in the realms of disembodied life.

The Sun is in the decanate of the Southern Crown from November 12 to November 22, and the adjoining sign into which it moves when it leaves this decanate is Sagittarius, the religious sign, the sign of benevolent Jupiter. To pass through the section of the zodiac pictured by the Crown takes the Sun ten days, and while so doing it is still in the sign of Death, Scorpio, and thus subject to the influence, not merely of the spiritual side of Pluto, the co-ruler of the sign, but also to the dark afflictions of its inversive side. The victory over these Brethren of the Shadow, the period of the Sun's passage through this decanate, the significance of it as belonging to the sign of Death, and the nature of the Crown which is gained as a reward for the victory, all are mentioned in Revelation 2:10:

> Fear none of these things which thou shalt suffer; behold, the devil shall cast some of you into prison, that ye may be tried; and ye shall have tribulation ten days: be thou faithful unto death, and I will give thee a crown of life.

It is also mentioned in I Peter in a manner which makes its significance obvious: "Feed the flock of God which is among you, taking the oversight thereof, not by constraint, but willingly; not for filthy lucre, but of a ready mind; Neither be lords over God's heritage, but being examples to the flock. And when the chief Shepherd shall appear, ye shall receive a crown of glory that fadeth not away."

These two Bible commentaries on the nature of the work by which the Southern Crown can be gained make it quite clear that force and compulsion, which are typical of the inversive side of Pluto, are to be avoided. Neither is fear to be countenanced, even when danger threatens. The individual, by his thoughts, feelings and actions must serve as an example of correct living, that other men may observe and do likewise. The energies must be devoted to helping others to the utmost extent, to feeding the flock as Peter states it; but not because of expected recompense—filthy lucre—but of a ready mind, that is, because there is a deep and abiding desire to benefit to the utmost all with whom there is contact.

Those, therefore, who undertake the winning of this Southern Crown, token of the highest attainment which is possible to life on earth, must adopt as the pattern of their lives the effort to contribute their utmost to universal welfare. They must realize that they are workmen in the cosmic organization, with a responsibility to universal society; that the universe does not run itself, but depends upon the wisdom and initiative of its various intelligent cells; and that they each have a definite function to perform in furthering the fulfillment of the Divine Plan.

Any aspirant to the universal Laurel Crown must make this conception of his responsibility to all other life-forms so completely a part of his character that every decision he is called upon to make will habitually be weighed, and every thought, emotion and action decided, by considering which contributes most to cosmic welfare.

When, after due thought and analysis, he has decided that a

particular line of endeavor, or a specific attitude toward events, or some accomplishment, is in the direction of the universal good, he must then not merely have the skill, but also the energy, courage, and fixity of purpose to carry his decision into action, and to make its end a reality. That is, if he is to make any real attainment, he must possess will power.

It is here that the energy denoted by Scorpio plays an important part, particularly when the individual reaches that state in his progress where he is able to work not merely on the physical plane, but on the inner plane as well. The habit of not making a decision until it is ascertained if the object sought is within the scope of the abilities and if it is worth the effort, and then, once having made a decision never permitting anything to prevent it being carried out, develops that fixity of purpose which is essential to the exercise of a powerful will. But a powerful will, in addition to fixity of purpose, must have available an abundant energy which can be brought to bear in the carrying out of any decided upon course of action.

If, therefore, the individual has advanced far enough along the path toward adeptship that he is able not to suppress, but actually to sublimate and transmute the energies of Scorpio, so that they may be directed into channels which are decided upon, this gives him a reserve energy supply which it is possible to use on any plane for any purpose.

Needless to say, the use of such surplus energy to the disadvantage of others immediately attracts the Legions of Darkness, ruled by the inversive side of Scorpio, and ultimately brings the enslavement and downfall of the one so using it. But its use as an energy to support the will in undertakings which have for object the advancement of the race, enables work to be accomplished that would be impossible without it, and tend toward true spirituality.

Yet with or without this additional energy supply, which is available to the adept who has attained the Laurel Crown, the benefit any individual can be to cosmic society is limited by his knowledge, and his abilities at the time. Those, therefore, who strive for the Crown of Adeptship, seek also to increase their knowledge; for unless they understand the purpose of the Divine Plan they are in no position to aid in its realization; and unless they know how to help people, their efforts in that direction are fruitless. They also strive at all times to develop their abilities; for to the extent abilities

Spiritual Astrology

are present can that which is known to be desirable accomplishment be realized.

The world of material science offers a certain type of information which can not be neglected. A knowledge of physical laws is a great advantage to anyone who undertakes important work. But such knowledge quite neglects the action of those invisible forces and the existence of invisible realms which have an even more important bearing upon human life and destiny, both here and hereafter.

The one who seeks the Crown of Life, therefore, undertakes to make himself as completely familiar as possible with all the occult forces of nature. In addition to the type of information which the common educated person is expected to possess, he makes himself thoroughly familiar with the occult sciences.

He finds in astrology a method of gauging and determining the trend of invisible forces as they exist at any given time; and this gives him the best possible information as to when and how to direct his energies to attain the best results. The manner in which thoughts unite to form the thought-cells of which his astral body is formed gives him the key to character building, and enables him to convert energies received from the planets into channels that attract to him the desired conditions. The invisible vibrations of selected environments also, when understood, can be utilized to make his life far more effective than otherwise it would be.

But aside from the acquisition of knowledge of the operation of all these invisible energies which commonly are called occult, and the utilization of this knowledge for human betterment, the one seeking the supreme Crown of earthly life also develops certain capacities and abilities within himself which relate to the use of the psychic senses and the development of higher states of consciousness.

If he is to adapt his life on earth to maximum usefulness, he must also be familiar with the conditions and requirements of that life in which he and others must function after the change called Death. He recognizes that earthly life in human form is but one link in an endless chain of existences; and that if it is to perform its highest function, it must fit the individual for the succeeding phases of existence. To know what will be advantageous in that after life, and also to contact those of greater wisdom than himself who there dwell, it becomes advantageous to him to be able to explore it and to contact its conditions and intelligences.

He does not attempt to do this through the unreliable channels of irresponsible mediumship, which tend to break down the will; but through developing the senses of the astral body so that he can see and hear and feel, and even travel, on the astral plane much the same as he does on the physical. In this manner, as he makes progress, he in time becomes as familiar with the conditions and people of the next plane of life as he is with the conditions and people of the physical world. Pluto, ruler of Scorpio, relates to both planes, and those who attain the Crown live consciously and function on both planes at will.

Holding to the pattern of life which calls for maximum service for the common good, they acquire knowledge of occult laws, and develop their abilities to use occult forces, in a constant endeavor to increase the scope of usefulness. Their attitude and efforts lead to the text: *Men Should be Esteemed Not Because of their Race, Color, Sex, or Ancestry, but for What they have Accomplished for the Common Good. The True Monarch is He Who Renders Greatest Service to His Fellow Man.*

SAGITTARIUS ♐   I See

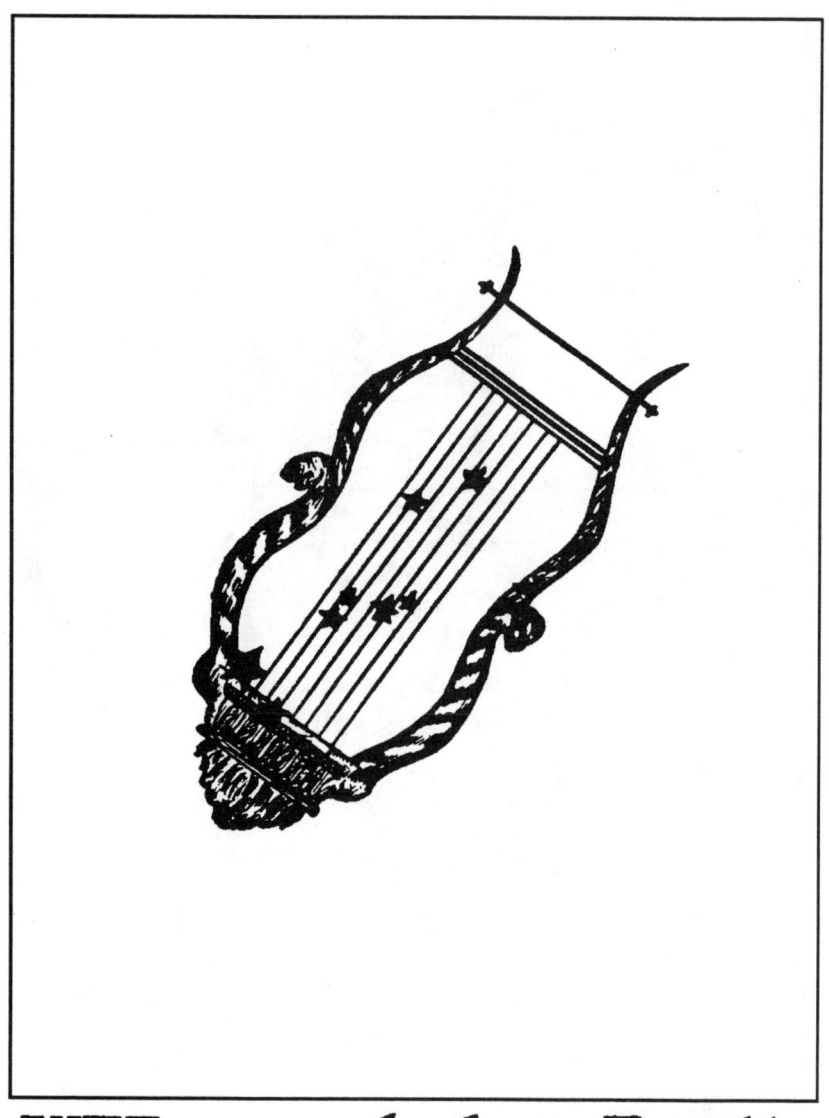

LYRA ↗ - ↗ Devotion

Spiritual Astrology

AQUILA ♐-♈ Exploration

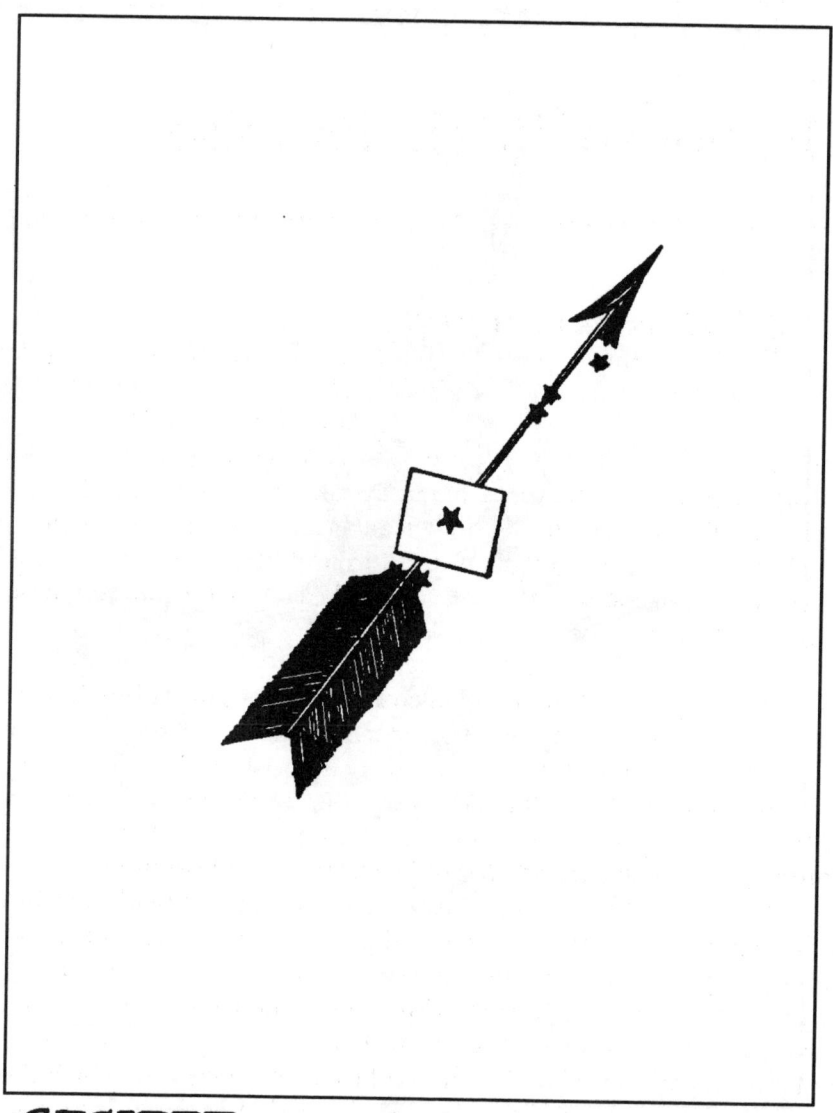

Chapter 10

The Bow of Bright Promise

THE Luck of the Horseshoe.

In northern Arizona, over rough country to the east of Grand Canyon National Park, is a great arch of stone, carved by the forces of erosion, known to the world as Rainbow Bridge. To it for centuries past the Indians have made pilgrimage, holding it to be a symbol given to them by the Great Spirit, a religious token to which in reverence they pay homage. It is the bow of bright promise, wrought in imperishable rock, a crystallized replica of the many-hued bow to be seen after rain when once more the Sun is shining.

The Archer, Sagittarius, where the Sun may be found from November 22 to December 22, also holds a bow, and aims its arrow straight at the treacherous Scorpion's heart, ready to prevent further depredations, and guarding humanity against its inversive legions. This Bowman of the sky pictures the sign of Religion, the so-called sign of the Higher Mind, which has rule also over teaching, long journeys, publishing and all public expression of opinions.

The Bow was known as a beneficent religious symbol early in the Bible days. Jupiter, the planet of religion, known in astrology as the greater benefic, having chief power to protect from danger, is the ruler of the sign Sagittarius. Therefore, when the earth had been ravaged by flood and all flesh destroyed, except that which had entered the ark with Noah, and a token was desired by which those whose religious devotion had saved them, that no more would such destruction take place on earth, the most appropriate symbol of divine protection that could have been selected would pertain to

Sagittarius. The Bow is such a universal symbol:

> I do set my bow in the cloud, and it shall be for a token of a covenant between me and the earth.

The protection and good luck which Sagittarius, the hunting Horseman, is able to bring to those whom he favors is also indicated in the present-day custom of hanging a horseshoe over the door. A horseshoe in form is a Bow. But because it is used on the foot of a horse it takes on the significance of understanding as well as Jupiterian good fortune. That is, symbolically it denotes the sound judgment which the activities of the Higher Mind promote, in addition to the benevolent influence of the major benefic.

This matter of the Higher Mind and the Lower Mind, because it so frequently is referred to in occult literature needs some explaining. As a matter of fact there are not two minds, but only one. Nor does this refer to objective consciousness and subjective consciousness, as do Castor and Pollux. Instead, it refers to the motives and aims of the mind, or soul. There is really no distinction between the term soul, mind and character. They are the same thing, and embrace all the experiences, including those derived from mental activities, which are retained and organized within the finer forms.

The motives which prompt the thoughts and the actions which they direct, however, can be divided into two categories quite as much in opposition as are the signs Gemini and Sagittarius. The motive may be self-centered, having no concern as to how others will be affected. This need not impair the intelligence. And frequently work done solely from this motive in the end proves a boon to humanity.

Thus an inventor may have no thought of whether his invention will conduce to human good, such as a labor-saving machine, or to human destruction, such as a more effective type of gun. His sole aim may be to produce something which will bring him a lot of money; and he may care not one whit how it affects the human race. Such an attitude betokens a dominance of the Lower Mind. But in spite of his indifference to the welfare of others, he may find it more easy and profitable to invent something which will benefit humanity.

The healer may have no interest in getting the patient well. He may be interested merely in moneymaking. He is dominated by the Lower Mind. But if his great desire is to alleviate suffering and to benefit his patients; if he looks upon the financial rewards of his profession as affording him a livelihood through which he can be of greater benefit to others than he could be if he were without money, this indicates that the Higher Mind is dominant.

Even a priest or preacher may be actuated in the choice of profession chiefly by the dictates of his Lower Mind. He may view the matter from the selfish standpoint, not of the occupation in which he can be of most service to his flock, but as the avenue through which, with his special talents, he can do the utmost for himself.

Almost anything or any ability that can be used for the benefit of the world, can also be used for the benefit of its possessor at the expense of others. The findings of material science, for instance, give the knowledge and facilities for making the world a better place in which to live. But often they are not used for the benefit of the race, but as a means by which the few can oppress and exploit the many.

Research, study, and thought are ruled astrologically by the third house, and thus are related to Gemini, the sign of the Lower Mind. But when the results of research, study and thought are given to the world through publishing, preaching or teaching, this public expression is ruled by the ninth house, and is related to Sagittarius, the sign of the Higher Mind. The implication is that the wide dissemination of information is advantageous to the race.

Yet while Sagittarius rules the Higher Mind, or Divine soul, it is only the human part of the sign that has this significance. Chiron, one of these half-man, half-horse characters of Greek mythology was famous for his knowledge of music, medicine, and shooting; and taught mankind the use of plants and medicinal herbs. He was a great instructor, and taught such heroes as Jason, Medeus, Hercules, Aesculapius and Achilles.

He also, as a fitting end to a completely noble career, took the place of Prometheus, and underwent the agony of having his liver devoured daily that the hero who had conferred the greatest possible boon on mankind might be free. Prometheus, who in the sky is pictured as Andromeda of the middle-decanate of Pisces, in his zeal to serve mankind had stolen the divine fire from heaven. That is, he had enabled mankind to attain spiritual illumination.

The great discernment when the Higher Mind is developed gives to this sign the Key-phase, I See. But the sporting, animal side, which nourishes the Animal Soul, shuts its eyes to everything that interferes with its desires. It is heedless and impulsive, as is illustrated by the Greek story of Eurytion, who was one of the Sagittarians.

Being invited to the marriage of Pirithous, he became intoxicated with wine, and, although when sober, a jolly good fellow, such as Sagittarians usually are, under the influence of wine he attempted violence to the bride. The other Centaurs who had gone to the wedding party with him, and who also were drunk, thought that a good idea, and each grabbed a woman. In the resulting brawl a number of them were slain.

Across the zodiac from north to south is a wall, or colure, which divides the signs in which the days continue to grow shorter, as they do from June 22 to December 22, from the signs in which the days continue to grow longer, as they do from December 22 to June 22. This wall, or chimney as it is sometimes called because it runs from Capricorn down to the sign of the house, Cancer, touches the horse sign Sagittarius on one side.

It seems, as related in II Kings 9, that Jezebel, for the time being no longer practicing witchcraft, had come under the influence of the sporting side of Sagittarius. When Jehu entered the city she, "Painted her face, and tired her head, and looked out at a window.

It is evident she was attempting to make a feminine conquest, but the religious convictions, the human side of Jehu was too strong; and as inevitably happens to those who exalt their own pleasures above the pain and suffering they cause others, these lower Sagittarian expressions, as symbolized by horses, destroyed her:

> And he said, Throw her down. So they threw her down: and some of the blood was sprinkled on the wall, and on the horses: and he trode her under foot.

Science, which observes how nature acts, and classifies these observations in formulas which are called laws, is under Gemini. But when these sciences which have classified knowledge are used as a basis for a pattern of life, the resulting design is called a philosophy, or religion, and then comes under the dominion of Sagittarius.

The Higher Mind then perceives, as the result of correlating the sciences and bringing to bear upon them the inner vision which it customarily uses, that the universe is not an insensate machine, but a living organism, the various entities comprising it constituting the cells, each cell and each group of cells, with its own particular function to perform. Furthermore, it perceives that the cosmic whole is moving in a definite direction, developing constantly a more complex structure, with a specific, although ever expanding accomplishment as its aim. There is Divine Plan.

The Higher Mind endeavors, in as great detail as possible, to grasp the significance of this Divine Plan. And then it strives to understand where, to the best possible advantage, it can fit into this Plan as a constructive factor. It assays its various abilities and possibilities to discover how these may be used to forward the movement of universal progression. And having determined the line of effort it should follow to be of greatest use, it sets to work to render that service.

Thus the expression of true religion is perfect or imperfect according to the abilities, and according to the correctness of the insight into what needs to be accomplished in the furtherance of the universal scheme. This conception is set forth in the text: *True Religion is the Discernment of the Divine Plan and a Conscious Cooperation in its Fulfillment.*

The Harp on Which the Angels Play

It was by no accident that the Crown which implies the Great White Throne and the Harp on which the angels play are so located in heaven that they picture adjoining decanates of the celestial circle. And if we consider Sagittarius as ruling not only far travel, but also the highways on which such travel is made, then the Sun, ruler of gold, in this sign gives rise to the thought of golden streets. Thus do we have a zodiacal origin of an after life and a Crown or throne relating to the last of Scorpio, to streets paved with gold, and to angels playing eternally on harps before the throne, as indicated by the next decanate, by Lyra, picturing the Sagittarius-section of the sign of religion.

The intimate relation existing between both religion and the underworld of Pluto, co-ruler of Scorpio, and between harmony and this invisible realm, is set forth in the Greek story of Orpheus and his lost bride Euridice. Pluto, ruler of the sign of sex, on its higher, or Eagle side, relates to perfect union, to regenerate marriage, and to the union of true soul mates. On its inversive, or Scorpion side, it relates to separation, to antagonism and to dissolution.

The harmonies within ourselves are chiefly set in motion by our thoughts, and as the Harp pictures a section of the sign ruling the Higher Mind, and as thoughts are ruled by Mercury, Greek legend quite appropriately held that the famous Harp on which Orpheus could play so sweetly that rivers ceased to flow and savage beasts forgot their wildness, was given to him by Mercury.

Orpheus, the master harpist of all time, married his ideal, his soul mate, Euridice, to whom he was tenderly devoted. Apparently, however, their adjustment was not so successful as that which the Biblical Jacob made; for the serpent with which Ophiuchus still wrestles bit Euridice. Instead of attaining the Crown, which pictures triumph over the sign of Death, she was bitten by the serpent, died, and passed to the realm of Pluto.

Orpheus was disconsolate. He could not reconcile himself to the loss of his beloved mate. Therefore, to recover her, he made a visit to the infernal regions. Taking his Lyre along, he played so sweetly that the wheel of Ixion stopped, the stone of Sysyphus stood still, Tantalus forgot his burning thirst, and even the Furies relented. More important still, so enraptured did Pluto become with the music, and so moved by the depth of Orpheus' sorrow, that finally he agreed to restore Euridice to him. This reunion of Orpheus and his lost Euridice is one of the most touching incidents of legendary lore.

In the story, first of all we have set forth that the abuse of sex is destructive, even when those married are ideally suited each to the other. It led to the death of Euridice.

Then there is set forth the power of harmonious thoughts engendered by love to find the object of its affection, even across the border line of death. The invisible realm of Pluto can be contacted and controlled through the harmonies engendered by pleasant emotional states and loving thoughts more successfully than in any other way.

Ixion was tied to a wheel in hell, that continually whirled around, keeping him in perpetual torture. Sysyphus, in the infernal regions, was condemned to roll a stone to the summit of a hill; but the stone always rolled back, thus making his punishment eternal. Tantalus, in the underworld was in a pool of water which flowed from him whenever he attempted to take a drink, causing him perpetual thirst. But the music of Orpheus had so powerful an influence in the region where these condemned souls were undergoing punishment that their torture ceased.

Those who have attained the Laurel Crown of adeptship not only work upon the physical plane, but often also use their abilities to release from suffering those who have passed to the after life in a state of mind which keeps them in torture. The suicide, for instance, often, like Ixion, is tied to the wheel of the mental images which caused him thus to try to flee from reality. By taking his own life he hoped to free himself from a distress which seemed too great for him to bear. But he merely transferred his suffering to another region. Round and round he goes with the images of the awful conditions from which vainly he hoped to escape.

Pluto, as the story goes, in permitting the reunion of Orpheus with his long lost soul mate, imposed one condition, that the musician was not to look behind him until he was out of Pluto's realm. Orpheus promised to obey this instruction. But as he was traveling upward and neared the region of the upper world, Euridice following at his heels, he forgot his promise, and looked back at his cherished bride, whereupon she vanished, never more to be seen.

This looking back, of course, as in the story of Lot's wife who turned to a pillar of salt, is the turning of the thoughts to a contemplation of the conditions and experiences of the past. This tunes the individual in on the old desires, sets in motion the vibrations of the past, and again attracts to him the external conditions from which he is fleeing. If we are to enjoy a condition of greater harmony and bliss, and if we are to prevent separations similar to those which have occurred in the past, we must avoid thinking the thoughts, and thus entering the vibratory conditions, that in the past have resulted in discord and separation. But Orpheus, in spite of the admonition of Pluto, could not refrain from again contemplating Euridice in the same manner he had considered her in bygone times; he looked back at her, and again she left him, this time gone forever.

The result of this separation, of contacting the disintegrating or antagonistic side of Pluto, is dramatically set forth in the tragic ending of Orpheus. The female Scorpion, symbol of the inversive side of Pluto, when her lust is satisfied, tears her mate to pieces and devours him. Orpheus, after the loss of Euridice, separated himself from the rest of mankind. This offended the Thracian women, and during the celebration of the orgies of Bacchus, enraged at his coldness, they set upon him, tore his body to pieces and threw his head into the Hebrus. Having, lost love, and with no desire left to cooperate, which desire Pluto rules, the disintegration of Orpheus was to be expected. Love is the one great integrating force.

In Bible times, Saul was accustomed to be troubled by obsessions. Morbid thoughts would occupy his mind, and these would so tune him in on the discordant side of Pluto that astral entities would take possession. I Samuel, 16, relates:

> But the spirit of the Lord departed from Saul, and an evil spirit from the Lord troubled him. And Saul's servants said unto him, Behold now, an evil spirit from God troubleth thee. Let our Lord now command thy servants, which are before thee, to seek out a man, who is a cunning player on an harp: and it shall come to pass, when the evil spirit from God is upon thee, that he shall play with his hand, and thou shalt be well.

Thus was the Crown, as represented by the King, and as indicating a decanate of the sign ruling those in Pluto's realm, brought into association with the Devotion-decanate of Sagittarius, where the Sun each year may be found from November 22 to December 2, pictured by the Harp.

> And it came to pass, when the evil spirit from God was upon Saul, that David took an harp, and played with his hand: so Saul was refreshed, and was well, and the evil spirit departed from him.

David, among the constellations, is pictured with his harp as one of the Twins, which rule the hands; but the Harp itself, as a separate constellation, quite appropriately depicts the most religious decanate of the whole zodiac. Of this harp a master wrote:

> Harp divine, whose strings the angels tune and set in motion sweet waves of music that vibrate round the spheres, and bring to man the tidings of his once celestial state, that says in tones of heavenly sweetness to faint and struggling souls; Look up and onward, thy spirit calls thee home. God Jehovah is, and thou must be.

But in the case of Saul his thoughts were so morose and savage that the inspiration, or vibratory level of intelligence, he often tuned in on was discordant. Instead of tuning in with prayer and devotion he tuned in with anger and revenge. And following the law which governs contacting the invisible realm, he thus came into rapport with entities of the same general vibratory level as his thoughts, and of the same desires. They were malignant, and finding the avenue thus open to them, they took possession of the king.

The one way to cure a condition of this kind is to stimulate thoughts of an entirely different character. When the dominant thoughts are harmonies this immediately cuts off all approach of unseen entities whose essential nature is discord. When the thoughts are elevated, as sweet music has an influence to raise them, to noble aspiration, it tunes the consciousness in on a corresponding invisible plane, and automatically cuts off any association with evil spirits.

When thus understood, the method which was applied by David to sooth the troubled spirit of Saul, and thus cure his obsession, is the most approved and successful method that can be applied to such cases today.

It also explains much of the value to be derived from devotional exercises and prayer. Devotional exercises accompanied by appropriate music are a great help to tune the feelings and emotions in on the plane of intelligence corresponding to such high emotional states. If they perform their office properly, this raises the consciousness to a much higher plane than is its customary vibratory rate. It brings the consciousness into touch with invisible entities on the inner plane who are higher in spirituality and in wisdom than the devotee, and enlists their help.

Discouragement and feelings of self disapproval keep the mind tuned in on the lower states of Pluto's realm. But faith and devotion tend to enable the individual to rise above all such sordid and discordant feelings, so that they, for the time being are no longer troublesome, no longer attract discordant intelligences from the invisible. Like the music of David's Harp, faith and devotion sooth and lift the thoughts. For as the text states: *On Every Plane Harmony is Life and Discord is Death.*

The Eagle Takes a Trip to Heaven

Of all creatures it was believed that the Eagle flew highest, and thus was the explorer of heaven. He was the bird of Jove, the bearer of his Thunder, the one who, when a cup bearer was needed for the king of the gods, was sent forth and brought back the youthful

Ganymede. Quite appropriately, therefore, was he placed in the sky where he would picture the Exploration-decanate of Sagittarius, in which each year the Sun may be found from December 2 to December 12.

When Jupiter, ruler of Sagittarius, lay concealed in the cave at Crete, to avoid the fury of his father, Saturn, Aquila brought him nectar that his hunger might be satisfied. And the Rig-Veda states that it was this Eagle which brought the Soma juice to India.

The cup in which Aquila carried the spiritualizing juice to India, and which it was the duty of Ganymede to keep handy that Jove might quaff and assuage his thirst, relates to the first-decanate of the pleasure-loving sign Leo. It thus pictures the love-affair decanate of the love-affair sign; the region of the sky where desire burns with its hottest flame. Both wine and soma juice are intoxicating. They are stimulants, even as desire is stimulating and causes action to flow spontaneously and without hindrance toward those things in which most pleasure is found. The more intense the pleasure, the more readily does action take the direction of its fulfillment.

The Eagle now pictures the middle-decanate of Sagittarius. But tradition also associates it with the sex-sign Scorpio. When sex takes wings and soars on the pinions of regeneration to the utmost heights, it moves from the house of Death, from Scorpio, over into the house of Religion. In fact, it is only under the influence of religion, of the desire to spiritualize sex, that this transmutation takes place. Yet the religious aspirations expressed by Sagittarius, in turn are due to the sublimation of the love impulse. The Thunderbird of our Southwest Indians expresses this not less than the classical bird of Jove.

Love or desire is the motive power behind every action. It also stimulates every thought. Activity takes, therefore, the direction of the strongest desire; that desire so well symbolized by Crater, which is Jove's cup of wine and the goblet which carried the oriental soma juice.

The wine or soma is the stimulant; the desire which gives rise to action. Yet whether that action be powerful or weak depends not merely upon the stimulant, upon the desire, but also upon the amount of energy which is available. A weakened swimmer may intensely desire to save his life; but unless there is sufficient energy available, he will be unable to make the shore. Desire alone is not sufficient for accomplishment; otherwise there would be more successful men and women. Desire can only direct such energy as is available into a definite channel of activity.

Scorpio is the great energy reservoir. It contains an energy which must be expressed through some channel. Since life began on earth those who have yielded to the mating impulse have left offspring, and those who have resisted the impulse to mate have been sterile. That condition remains today. Nuns and celibate priests seal the death warrant on the perpetuation of their strain. Those who successfully resist reproduction leave no biological heritage; they die out. Thus do only those racial strains survive in which the impulse to mate overcomes any artificial prejudice to remain barren.

Natural selection has thus, since life on earth began, been building up the power of the reproducing energy until it has gained such strength in every normal human being that it will not be denied expression. Yet nature has dictated no rigid channel through which alone this creative energy must flow. The extent to which it can be sublimated and made successfully to flow through more spiritual channels is an individual problem. All creative work, however, tends to afford it some expression; and many find it possible so fully to transmute into more spiritual endeavors that other expression is unnecessary to a completely satisfactory life adjustment.

Such spiritualizing of the Scorpio energy, expressing it on the higher side of Pluto, is pictured by the Eagle. The cup of Desire is the stimulant, but the Thunderbird, which is associated with Jove's lightning, affords the energy which is thus carried to the place where Religion dwells.

Nectar, ruled by Venus, the planet of love, symbolized the spiritualized essence of love. Saturn, the cold and crystallizing influence of selfishness is, quite naturally, bitterly opposed to the generous, free-hearted and benevolent Jupiter. To the extent this self-seeking influence of Saturn is present are the unselfish impulses of Jupiter in danger. The best way to escape such danger is for the benevolent tendencies to keep away from those seeking only the interest of the material self. So doing, the Higher Mind and Religious Life are fed with the nectar of a spiritualizing love, carried to them by the energy of the Eagle.

As portraying an ideal sex influence, the Eagle is uncommon among birds. With a few exceptions our feathered friends are either polygamous, like the barnyard fowls, or mate only for a single season. But the Eagle, used by the ancients to represent the most spiritual influence of sex, such as conforms to the true Religious Ideal, mates for life. It thus represents that higher side of Pluto in which not only are the energies sublimated to a higher plane of expression, but in which those who are ideally suited one to the other, true soul mates, are united.

In their hunting habits, so strong of wing are they that they go, like the soul in dreams, exploring in far distant places, but always returning to their home, to which they are singularly attached. And the house which Sagittarius rules, the ninth mansion of the birthchart, has dominion over dreams, and over all forms of astral travel. It is the house of long journeys, not merely of the body, but also of the mind.

When the mind explores the universe, even as Sagittarius is a dual sign, so also are the reports which it brings back into the region of objective consciousness of two distinct types. The one type reports the reality of the condition actually contacted. It holds itself strictly to an accurate account of what has been seen and heard, and what has happened. Yet life would sadly miss one of its most alluring phases if it had no power to create, no power to visualize something not yet a reality of substance, but which, under suitable circumstances might become so. In addition to reporting reality the artist, the composer, the writer, the inventor, and all who bring to life its highest joys, must have imagination.

Without imagination the mental life is sterile. But through its use the individual is able mentally to picture the condition or action which finds fulfillment for some desire. The first step in the objective realization of some wish is the formulation of that which is to be sought.

This image making power of the mind not only aids us to the concrete realization of our desires, but plays an important role in enabling us also to obtain some emotional satisfaction merely through associating with the mental images of the thing desired. People read fiction to enjoy vicariously the adventures of the hero and heroine, that is, to find satisfaction for impulses and desires which the practical requirements of objective life forbid. The thrills they long for, but dare not gain through action in the world of reality, they are able to indulge sufficiently to feel satisfied by going to the movies.

According to the dictum of scenario land, if you would produce a picture of unusual success, you must enable the audience to experience, through the screen actors, that which is most lacking in their own lives and which at the same time they most desire.

These images of things desired and of the things to be avoided permit an easier emotional response when seen upon the stage or screen, or presented from the pages of a book. The author has performed the labor of creating visual images, and of skillfully arranging them in a sequence that will arouse the desired emotional response. But each individual possesses and exercises, in some degree, this ability to form phantasies within his own mind.

This building of mental images through which the individual has experiences and feels emotions is carried over into the time of sleep. Such experiences are called dreams. All people have dreams.

In the waking state the mind travels from one series of experiences to another, constantly receiving new impressions or comparing those already received. And in the state of sleep it is no less active, moving from experience to experience, from sensation to sensation, without cessation.

Because the impact of physical environment, and the necessity of perceiving it correctly if the organism is not to suffer injury, tends to a habit of mind in the waking state in which commonly it concerns itself more with reality than with images of its own creation, most people in their waking hours do only a small amount of day dreaming. Within limits, however, it is optional whether the mind is engaged with phantasies or with realities.

In the sleeping state, because there is no such imperative necessity to keep the mind alert to realities, the common habit is chiefly to permit it to wander in phantasies. Nearly all people do, however, at times, direct their attention in sleep to actual happenings. Their dreams then give them warnings, or apprise them of conditions that later are recognized. The extent to which in sleep the mind becomes absorbed in images of its own creation is largely a matter of habit and training. That is, there is no necessity for the mind to engage in phantasy thinking during sleep, no more so than in the waking state. Either waking or in sleep both types of mental activities are open to it.

More difficult than perceiving realities while asleep is the work of bringing them into the memory of everyday consciousness. Yet through training the individual can bring back the reports of his explorations on the inner plane. This leads to the text: *In Sleep the Soul Wanders on the Wings of its Desires to the Region Most Attractive to it; Let that Region, therefore, Be the Highest.*

The Arrow that Slew the Cyclopes

Sagittarius is the constellation of the Higher Mind and of Religion. Lyra depicts the method by which this mind tunes in on higher planes of existence and responds to inspirational harmonies from such upper spheres; while Aquila represents the power of the soul to free itself from the limitations of physical environment and travel to inner worlds, there to search for information. We may expect the third decanate of the sign, therefore, where the Sun may be found from December 12 to December 22, to portray still another high mental activity; and this it does; for Sagitta relates to Illumination.

This constellation is represented by an arrow, apparently let fly by the celestial Archer. Swifter than the horse of the Bowman, swifter even than the Great Dog of the middle-decanate of the Lower Mind, Gemini, the Arrow symbolizes the speed of thought, its unswerving aim, and its ability to strike the mark. As shafts of light penetrate the darkness, so do the higher powers of the soul pierce the clouds of illusion.

While the Sun is in this Arrow-decanate, the hours of darkness so increase that we have the shortest days of the year just at its end. Directly across the zodiac, where Gemini and Cancer join, is the decanate of the Giant Bear, typifying various other ancient giants such as the Cyclopes. These were the sons of Coelus and Terra, that is, of heaven and earth. They were three in number, Arges, Brontes and Steropes, and they occupied themselves in Vulcan's workshop, where they forged the thunderbolts used by the king of the gods, who benevolently rules the Sagittarian sign.

These thunderbolts, which thus they manufactured, represented, as yet they do to the Indians of our Southwest, the destructive use of the Scorpion's power, instead of its constructive use, such as is denoted by the Eagle or Thunderbird. And the Cyclopes who forged them represent Reason, which is the Key-word of the decanate where the Sun climbs highest, the place in the zodiac pictured by the enormous Bear.

These Cyclopes each had but a single eye, located in the middle of the forehead. They were several because Reason is employed in all the various material sciences. Yet in such work but one viewpoint is tolerated, the single eye which can perceive only the happenings and relations of the physical world. The Reason of material science is totally blind to the still more important factors and influences of the inner plane. It takes no account of them, and scoffs at their very existence.

Instead, therefore, of constructing a plan of human life which takes into account the persistence of the soul after the dissolution of the physical body, and the responsibility of each soul for the welfare of other souls in an eternally progressive scheme of existence, it forges doctrines of soul annihilation, thunderbolts which destroy all hope of life on other planes than this. One after another, physical facts are cited to prove all religion is superstition, that there can be no world other than the one which can be seen with the Cyclops eye, that great eye of physical discernment which materialism maintains is the only source of valid information.

Even as at the time of winter solstice, when the Sun has reached the end of the Sagitta-decanate, the nights are longest, so do the positive utterances of those who reason from the viewpoint of materialism cast a pall of darkest gloom over the struggling soul. For three days the Sun remains at this same darkest declination before starting back toward the north with its illuminating promise of life for another year; and of Cyclopes, therefore, there are three. But they were exterminated, according to Greek mythology, these three single-eyed giants, by Sagitta, the arrow sped from the bow of Apollo, god of the Sun.

Not force, not physical movement or physical action, dissipates darkness; but it is exterminated by the presence of light. Such light, the beams of which pierce the blackness of physical night, is represented by the celestial Arrow.

Wisdom alone, such as the speeding Arrow brings, however, is not all sufficient to the progress of the soul. Light it must have as a guide to action if that action is to lead to progression; but the action itself which permits the perpetual unfolding of its powers, requires another factor. As a companion to Wisdom, as its polar opposite, both of which in cooperation make evolution possible, there is Love. Love and Wisdom are the avenues through which alone the advancement of the soul is made.

Therefore, while Sagitta stresses the importance of Wisdom, in the traditions of this heavenly arrow Love has not been overlooked. Mythology holds, not only that it is the arrow of the Sun, but also the one shot from Dan Cupid's bow. By this is implied that in true Illumination feeling, as well as knowledge, plays an important part; that it is more than an intellectual perception, that Love joins hands with Wisdom.

In the Hopi Indian ceremony of calling back the Sun, a ceremony held at the winter solstice just when the Sun has reached the end of the Sagitta-decanate, arrows which are violently thrown into a mound of earth by the Thunderbird man play an important part. And when Elisha lay dying, and Joash asked help of him before he departed, that their enemies might be defeated, mention is made of the horseman, that is, of Sagittarius, of the three—before the light begins to triumph over darkness after the Sun has reached the solstice—and of the arrows. II Kings 13, relates:

> And Joash the king of Israel came down unto him, and wept over his face, and said, O my father, my father, the chariot of Israel, and the horsemen thereof. And Elisha said unto him, Take bow and arrows. And he took unto him bow and arrows. And he said to the king of Israel, put thine hand upon the bow. And he put his hand upon it: and Elisha put his hands upon the king's hands.
>
> And he said, Open the window eastward. And he opened it. Then Elisha said, Shoot. And he shot. And he said, the arrow of the Lord's deliverance, and the arrow of deliverance from Syria. For thou shalt smite the Syrians in Aphek, till thou have consumed them. And he said, Take the arrows. And he took them. And he said unto the king of Israel, Smite upon the ground. And he smote thrice, and stayed.

That from which men seek deliverance, as Joash sought deliverance from the Syrians, is the darkness of misconception. When the arrow of the soul pierces the illusions imposed by physical limitations, it then perceives the road it must follow to reach the desired spiritual attainment. But unaided Reason is quite inadequate to furnish this illumination. If sufficient light is to be had to see the way clearly an inner faculty of understanding must be brought into play.

When Reason, the one-eyed Cyclops, intrudes its presence, it quite effectually prevents that which spiritual men of all ages have referred to as Illumination. This state of consciousness is an identification of the individual with the knowledge sought. Instead of thinking about it, he feels the truth within himself. Yet such inner feeling can not gain recognition so long as ordinary mental processes are active. They must be routed, laid to rest, or otherwise vanquished, before the inner contact with the desired information can be felt.

In the use of any of the senses, even those of physical sight and hearing, we tune in on some particular aspect of a thing. That is, our eyes tune in on the light reflected from a surface, or our ears tune in on certain molecular vibrations. In this manner we recognize certain phases of physical existence. But when Illumination takes place, we tune in on the thing quite completely, on its inner character and its qualities. Identifying ourselves for the time with it, we know it from the inside and the outside in all its essential vibrations, and this gives rise to a knowledge of certainty about it.

The astral body has various senses, such as clairvoyance, clairaudience and psychometry, with which to perceive objects and occurrences from the four-dimensional plane. Yet the employment of these inner senses is not Illumination, it is merely the use of more effective organs of perception to get impressions about things. Such impressions, while more comprehensive than those gained through the use of the physical sense organs, only include certain aspects of the thing under consideration.

When, however, the individual can completely tune himself in on the subject of his attention, he so identifies himself with it that there is no sense of separateness; he seems to be that thing and to know all there is to know about it, both inside and outside. This information, or knowledge, instead of coming through the inner sense organs, is felt as if it were a light flooding the utmost recesses of the soul; hence its name of Illumination.

One should not conclude from this that those who experience true Illumination are never in error. Like all other information, to reach objective consciousness it must pass from the unconscious to the conscious mind. Therefore, whether the information comes through the physical senses, through Reason, through the astral senses, or through Illumination, it is always subject to the influence of any opinions or emotions that have a dominant power within the unconscious mind. These control the avenues through which the information must pass to reach objective consciousness.

If the information, however correctly received and true, does not meet the approval of these dominant unconscious factors—providing such are present—they act as censors. The information can not pass them and reach the conscious mind until it conforms to their standards. For this reason information received through any channel should be checked as to accuracy in as many ways as possible.

Nevertheless, whether it is permitted to pass from the unconscious to the conscious without censorship or not, Illumination is the most satisfactory and comprehensive way of securing knowledge. To thus tune in on the desired information requires great concentration, hence the text: *Concentration is the Arrow that Pierces the Illusions of Matter and Makes Possible High Accomplishment.*

CAPRICORN ♑ I Use

CYGNUS ♍-♍ Organization

DELPHINUS ♑-♉ Martyrdom

Chapter 11

News From the Summerland

AND JACOB Stole From Esau. The solstices are those points in the zodiacal circle where, for a short time, the Sun stands, or stops moving in declination, and soon turns back to move by declination in the opposite direction. That is, on June 22 the Sun has reached its highest northern declination and the days consequently are longest; and on December 22 the Sun has reached its lowest declination and the days are shortest.

These days are much more easily ascertained than are the equinoxes, where the days and nights are equal; for on the longest day of the year the shadow cast by a stake at noon is shortest, while on the shortest day of the year the shadow cast by a stake at noon is longest.

The difference in the angles cast by the shadow on the longest day and by the shadow cast on the shortest day is, of course, the angular distance the Sun moves from its farthest south declination to its farthest north declination; and this divided by two gives the inclination of the ecliptic, or Sun's path, to the equator. By such shadows recorded at noon on the longest day and shortest day of the year the Chinese, in 1100 B. C., ascertained the inclination of the equator to the ecliptic.

Slightly more than two hundred years before the Christian era, Eratosthenes, who had been brought from Upper Egypt to act as custodian of the Alexandrian Library, recorded similar measurements from the top of the library building at Alexandria. There he found the angle of the shadow at the summer solstice to be 7 degrees, 12 minutes. Six months later, at the winter solstice, the shadow showed an angle of 54 degrees, 54 minutes, 39 seconds. The difference, 47 degrees, 42 minutes, 39 seconds divided by two, gave the inclination of the ecliptic to the equator as 23 degrees, 51 minutes.

Then to the distance, 7 degrees, 12 minutes, that the Sun was south of Alexandria at the summer solstice, he added the distance thus found that the Sun was north of the equator at the solstice—23 degrees, 51 minutes, and some seconds—which gave him the latitude of Alexandria as 31 degrees and a little more than 3 minutes. Present day refined instruments give it as 31 degrees, 12 minutes, which is a difference of less than 12 miles from that obtained by Eratosthenes through the use of shadows.

It was because the day of the solstice could so easily be ascertained merely by watching the shadow of a stake, that the Aztecs, and those who possessed the same calendar system, began their year, not at the equinox, but at the winter solstice. The winter solstice, rather than the solstice of summer, was chosen because it was then that the days commenced to lengthen, the Sun having reached its lowest station, and a new period of increasing light was born.

Capricorn, which the Sun enters at the winter solstice, is an earthy sign; and as the Sun is then lowest in declination, this position often is referred to symbolically as a tomb or cave. Thus it is that Mithra, the Persian god of light, is held to have been born in a cave; and Jesus remained three days in the tomb before the stone was rolled away and he emerged. Pawnbrokers, who follow the footsteps of Jacob in taking advantage of the weaknesses and misfortunes of others, also display the three golden suns as the emblem of their trade; pledges being entombed until redeemed.

When the Sun has remained three days at its lowest declination, it then starts climbing, and continues to climb during the next six months until it reaches the pinnacle. This persistent tendency to climb, the ambition to mount higher and higher, is one of the chief characteristics of people born while the Sun is in Capricorn, from December 22 to January 20; therefore, the ancients who traced the starry figures in the firmament, to portray this attribute of both Sun and people born in the sign, employed the picture of a Goat, an animal which customarily moves to the mountain tops.

In addition to vaunting ambition, however, the natives of Capricorn also possess a flair for diplomacy. They are able to employ whatever is at hand to the best advantage, which gives to the sign its

Spiritual Astrology

Key-phrase, I Use. And they are equally at home, and can adapt themselves to, any environment. Therefore, the ancient constellation represents not a common Goat, such as travels merely on the land; but one with the tail of a fish, which enables it, when occasion requires, also to live in the water.

The Greeks called the constellation Pan. And the legend is that one day Pan, with some other deities, was feasting near the bank of the Nile, when suddenly the dreadful giant Typhon came upon them. In order to escape they all were compelled to assume a different shape. In this camouflage Pan took the lead, Capricorn like, and plunged into the river, the part of his body under water becoming the tail of a fish and that part remaining in the air retaining the form of the Goat.

Typhon is the Egyptian conception of Saturn, the planet governing Capricorn. It is the planet of fear; and the fright which Pan experienced upon the appearance of Typhon, that is, the fright of Capricorn at Saturn, has been associated with a name which perpetuates the legend of the obsessing terror of those who fled a danger which was largely imaginary, on the bank of the Nile; for from this occurrence is derived the word Panic.

Astrologers hold that the best quality of Capricorn is Diplomacy, such as symbolized by the half fish half goat; but when this ability is abused it becomes the worst quality of the sign, which is Deceitfulness. This use of false pretense to aid the ambition to climb to wealth and power is set forth quite clearly in Genesis 27.

Already had Jacob taken advantage of his brother's necessity to deprive him of his birthright; for in this story he represents the Capricorn influence and Esau represents the Sagittarius type:

> And the Lord said unto her, Two nations are in thy womb, and two manner of people shall be separated from thy bowels and the one people shall be stronger than the other people; and the elder shall serve the younger.

When the Sun is at the winter solstice the days of increasing darkness are thus separated from the days of increasing light, and Sagittarius is older than Capricorn in the sense that the Sun passes through it first; yet in worldly matters Capricorn is more shrewd and thus gains the advantage. Furthermore, "Esau was a cunning hunter, a man of the field," a typical outdoor Sagittarian; while, "Jacob was a plain man, dwelling in tents," with the Capricorn flair for trading and the desire to advance himself among people.

Isaac, the father of both young men, loved the generous spirit of his elder son, Esau, and when he was about to die called him: "And he said, Behold now, I am old, I know not the day of my death: Now, therefore take, I pray thee, thy weapons, thy quiver and thy bow, and go out into the field, and take me some venison."

But word came to Jacob, the Capricorn brother, that his father was about to bestow his blessings upon Esau; and advised by his mother, he sought by some cunning means to gain the blessings that rightfully belonged to Esau, as he by other artifice had acquired his brother's birthright. Instead of using venison, such as the Huntsman had gone to secure, he brought to his mother two good kids of Goats, ruled by Capricorn, from which to make the savory meat to please his father.

To still further deceive his parent, who was blind, when he brought the savory meat to him:

> Rebekah took goodly raiment of her eldest son Esau, which were with her in the house, and put them upon Jacob her youngest son: And she put skins of kids of the goats upon his hands, and upon the smooth of his neck.
>
> And he came unto his father, and said, My father, I am Esau thy firstborn; I have done according as thou badest me: arise, I pray thee, sit and eat of my venison that thy soul may bless me. And Isaac said unto his son, How is it that thou hast found it so quickly, my son? And he said, Because the Lord thy God brought it to me. And Isaac said unto Jacob, Come near, I pray thee, that I may feel thee, my son, whether thou be my very son Esau or not. And Jacob went near unto Isaac his father; and he felt him, and said, The voice is Jacob's voice, but the hands are the hands of Esau. And he discerned not, because his hands were hairy, as his brother Esau's hands: so he blessed him.

When, therefore, Esau returned with the venison which he had been sent to get, his father was compelled to say: "Thy brother came with subtlety, and hath taken away thy blessing."

The sign of selfish Saturn is divided from the sign of benevolent Jupiter only by a thin line called the solstitial colure. The one sign relates to business and the acquisition of worldly goods and honor, the other to religion and the spread of useful information. We meet both types of people every day; the Esaus who are more than willing to work hard merely to please, who joy in the happiness of others; and the Jacobs, sly, cunning, scheming, caring nothing for the pleasure or welfare of others, but only by fair means or foul to gain an advantage and to further selfish ambition.

Such injustice will prevail so long as it is permitted. Therefore it is the task of those who have the interests of humanity at heart to devise means by which these selfish interests which grind down the poor and prey upon the helpless shall be prevented from their depredations. With such a significance the story ends with a prophecy concerning Esau:

> And it shall come to pass when thou shalt have the dominion, that thou shalt break the yoke from off thy neck.

Only at its worst does Capricorn relate to deceit. On its better side it relates to beneficial use. The text, therefore, is: *Every Environment Offers Opportunities for Spiritual Advancement, and He who Makes Good Use of His Present Circumstances for Spiritual Ends Will Attract New Opportunities.*

News From the Summerland

If Jesus was born at Christmas, as popular tradition holds, the Sun in His birth-chart was in the first-decanate of Capricorn, pictured by the migrating Swan. It had then just passed the colure where the days are shortest, and having had the three days at its lowest declination, had started back north again, bringing, as does the Swan, the promise of a new cycle of light and warmth.

At the opposite end of the colure is the point where the Sun six months previously had entered the watery sign Cancer, turning back from its northward journey as it entered the water. This going down, or decrease of declination, into the water at the summer solstice is typical of the ministration of John the Baptist. According to Luke I, John the Baptist was six months older than Jesus, and therefore must have been born in the Cancer sign.

Furthermore, from the birth-sign Cancer on the length of daylight decreases, while from the birthsign Capricorn, where Jesus was born, the length of daylight increases; a condition recognized and made use of by John in the symbolism of his prophecy as recorded in John 3:30, "He must increase, but I must decrease."

As the Nazarene brought the glad tidings, "Peace on earth, good will to men," so the graceful Swan is first of the migratory birds to return in spring, when its appearance indicates, to those who know the way of nature, that ere long the tender shoots of grass will thrust through the soil, that verdant leaves will adorn the trees, and scarcity which marked the winter cold will give place to a more abundant season.

Swans are reared from downy youngsters in the icy regions of the north. But grown to adult size, at the approach of winter they take their departure from that region which so well, with its bleak hardness and cruel perils, symbolizes the environment which we call the earth.

Like some friends we have known, loved ones who already have passed, they leave the scenes of their early hardships, and wing their way to sunnier skies. As the stone was rolled away from the sepulchre, or lo,west point of the Sun's descent, giving the promise of a future life, so also at their appointed time, do the Swans again return. Snow white in purity, the most graceful of all that fly, with wide expanse of wing, nothing so readily suggests angels. Message bearers, coming from a brighter realm than this, bringing news of loved ones, and telling something of the surroundings there, where we too will live before many cycles of the Sun.

After all, in basic essentials, the conditions of the after life, which are promised by Cygnus, the flying Swan, are similar to those of this. There we shall live and work and love, not just as we do here, but with added abilities and with vastly greater facilities of expression. To the properties of existence with which we have become familiar, there is added another dimension. And this immensely increases the range of movement, thought and feeling. Everything is speeded up, given an intensity not known on earth, and instead of the slow process of physical adjustment, by which things here are brought to pass, in that realm the dynamic force is thought.

To build anything on the physical plane we require the application of energy to slowly moving physical substance. It takes considerable time, usually, to collect the various materials and properly to assemble them in the desired form. But, due to the peculiarities of a four-dimensional plane, the substance of the astral world can instantly be molded into any desired shape through the application of the energy of thought. A house thus built on the astral plane through visualizing and imparting thought-energy to it, is there quite as solid, perhaps more durable, and as useful for a home or office, as a similar building of concrete or brick on the three-dimensional plane.

The immediate responsiveness of the environment to the power of thought is probably the most striking feature of life in the realm where the soul finds Itself immediately after it passes through the tomb.

By this same process can be built a private heaven or hell. Not that the wicked person can get away from the thought-cells which he has built into himself, and which attract him to an environment corresponding to their nature. But if certain images are so energetically impressed on the individual in his life that they dominate his consciousness, these images will surround him after death until he awakens to a realization of their true nature and origin.

The reports of those who have been in the after life only a short time are seldom very enlightening. One must live on the physical plane many years to know much about it. Even in the course of a lifetime the ordinary individual is acquainted intimately with only a small section of the globe, with only a little scientific knowledge, and with only a few of the happenings here. And while on the astral plane the reports of the astral senses may be consulted, which have a wide range, yet the regions of that four-dimensional world are so immense and varied that any comprehensive, even though general, knowledge of them can be gained only at the expense of considerable time and energy.

Yet those who have been on the inner plane for many years, who are investigative by temperament, and who apply themselves diligently to obtaining precise information about conditions as they there exist, do occasionally, like the migrating swans, come back as messengers to enlighten us.

Their reports, and the investigations of those still attached to the flesh who have journeyed to that realm, advise us that money is of no value there. Neither is false pretense nor sham. Everyone is known and esteemed for his real character and abilities, not for their semblance. And the only currency of any value there is that of service to the common good. Those who by their efforts contribute to the welfare of others, by that token possess a wealth reserve which they can draw upon. This they display in their characters, and perceiving which, others are pleased to render them willing assistance.

Having pointed out the two conditions that seem most strange from an earthly standpoint—that thought does things directly, rather than merely acting as a guiding force, as here; and that money has no value—it should, perhaps, be indicated in what way the after life is most strikingly like the one with which we are most familiar.

On the earth plane action is always in the direction of the strongest desire. That is, what we do is determined by those desires which are stronger than the combined influence of other desires which tend to prevent it, or tend to move us in other directions. Furthermore, even while on earth, the thought-cells of the astral body which have been built by experiences and thoughts, attract to us environmental conditions and events which have a corresponding nature and corresponding harmony or discord.

It is this power of desire, and the influence of the thought composition of the body, which seems to be the most striking similarity between life on earth and life in the four-dimensional world. In that world, of course, all action being speeded up, the result of desire is more quickly apparent.

On the physical, one desires strongly to go some place, and after considerable time spent with some physical form of transportation—walking or riding—one arrives at the designated spot. But on the astral one desires strongly to be in the place and one is instantly there, provided its vibratory rate is not without the range of that which one is able to develop within himself. That is, one can thus immediately move to any location or environment on the plane where he is able to function.

In the after life when an individual's desires are too low to find expression on the plane or level where commonly he functions, if they are maintained, the individual drops to a lower world where such thoughts can find expression. If they are vicious and evil enough, he may find himself in the so-called astral hells. But if they are higher than the plane on which normally he functions, if they are maintained, they ultimately will raise him to a higher world, a heaven, as it were, where their full expression is possible.

Whether from the standpoint of the physical world, or from that of the after-life worlds, the most important things of life are man's thoughts, desires and ambitions; for here and hereafter they are the factors determining his destiny.

To many people the after life seems a vague and nebulous region. Not because it really is so; for it is more vivid and intense and real than earthly existence; but because that which we personally have had little contact with tends to seem less concrete than those things with which we are familiar.

Had you endeavored to describe to the people of 100 years ago the world as it appears today you would have been met both by incredulity and by a total inability to comprehend what you were talking about. Moving and talking pictures would have seemed as amazing to them as the thought-created environment of the astral world seems to those who have had no experience with it. Automobile and airplane travel would have startled them as greatly as the across the planes travel of those in the four-dimensional realm. The radio and television would have seemed as improbable as the thought-transference method which is common to the astral plane.

Far places and unusual conditions, even those of Mongolia or the South Sea Islands, always seem hazy and unreal to those who have never visited them. So also, to most, does the scenery of the astral region seem bizarre and unbelievable. Yet it is not a weird region. It is a place where, with certain marked improvements, life is lived very much as it is lived on earth.

The Swans, returning from the south, like messengers bringing information from this after life, do not fly in loose flocks, but in well defined V-formation. The Key-word for the decanate represented by the Swan, where the Sun may be found from December 22 to January 1, therefore, is Organization. And the text is: *Under Certain Conditions the Stone is Rolled From the Entrance to the Tomb and Man Consciously Exchanges Ideas with Those Who Have Entered the Chamber of Death.*

The Dolphin Makes a Rescue

Not only does Saturn, the planet of Capricorn, rule the grave, but it is when the Sun is in this earthy sign of Capricorn that it reaches its lowest point in the annual cycle, representative of the tomb. All three decanates, therefore, quite consistently, give some teaching in reference to the condition encountered after the stone has been rolled from the entrance of the tomb at the winter solstice, and the soul has left its tenement of clay and passed to more congenial realms. While, therefore, the constellation picturing the middle decanate of the sign, where the Sun may be found each year from January 1 to January 10, represents a Dolphin, it is not surprising that in various lands it is also known as a coffin. Among nations familiar with the Bible it is more commonly referred to as Job's Coffin.

The Dolphin, which is the picture of the constellation in the sky, is always represented as a beneficent sea dweller which performs good deeds and rescues from death those who are persecuted, especially those who are martyrs to some just cause. It is due to these legends. and to the observation that those born when the Sun is in this decanate often take up some worthy cause and work ardently for it in spite of its unpopularity, that the Key-word of the constellation is Martyrdom.

There are three Greek legends which give the outstanding teachings which the Dolphin was placed in the sky to reveal. One relates to the administration of strict justice in the after life; one pertains to the reunion of loved ones in that realm; and the other to the importance of harmonious thoughts as a means of attracting those who on the other side of life will assist the one who has passed from earth life to make a quick and satisfactory adjustment to the new conditions.

It is related that the famous poet Hesiod was slain and his assassins, in order to escape retribution, threw the body into the sea. They supposed this would be the end of the matter; but the Dolphins, who are the friends of poets and all who are benefactors to the human race, recovered the body and brought it to the shore, where it was found by Hesiod's friends. These then gathered together, and using the poet's own dogs trailed the murderers until they were captured; then threw them into the sea so that they should receive as punishment exactly the same kind of death they had caused the famous poet.

It is not always possible, in the after life, to make complete restitution to the person who has been wronged. But before much advancement can be made in that realm, injuries to others must be paid for, if not directly to them, at least by rendering some commensurate service to society. Unless we are willing to pay for our transgressions, their persistence as factors in our finer bodies weights us

Spiritual Astrology

down, Saturn-like, so that we drop to lower vibratory spheres. As progress consists in moving to higher levels, and such movement is accomplished through refinement, these self-centered, destructive, and therefore downward pulling vibrations must be sublimated into those which are constructive and uplifting.

Repentance, like most other activities, can be approached from either a negative or a positive direction. All make mistakes, all take actions which later they regret. Under these conditions the negative approach is to feel sad and despondent, to dwell on the effect of the mistake and to feel miserable because it was made. Yet this sackcloth and ashes method of repentance is disastrous to the individual, and because it unfits him for constructive work in the universal scheme, still further injures society. The discords he thus cultivates attract to him misfortunes, and these hamper him and make him less effective in that which he should do.

The true way of repentance, either here or hereafter, is the positive approach in which the error is acknowledged, but is not dwelt upon in thought, nor permitted to cause mental anguish. Instead, the individual recognizes he has injured someone, or retarded the progress of society. He therefore focuses his attention, desires and efforts on paying this debt to society through doing something for the individual injured, or at least for society, which will be of as much benefit as he has caused harm.

Another Greek legend narrates that Neptune was very much in love with the goddess Amphitrite and greatly desired to marry her. This goddess, however, had taken a vow of perpetual celibacy, and consequently refused his proposal. Neptune, after pursuing his courtship in vain, finally called to him the Dolphin and told him his difficulties. Acting as a mediator, the Dolphin succeeded in persuading the goddess to marry the Sea-god, and as a reward was placed in the sky as one of the constellations.

Neptune in astrology is the octave expression of Venus, the planet of love. The love he rules is not the ordinary Venus type, but an expression which is devoid of the physical element; an ideal love which, rather than express in physical marriage turns to celibacy. Yet when those who thus love are able to sublimate their affections, so that they express as a complete circuit of energy which flows between the two, blending completely their thoughts and feelings, as pictured by the ribbon binding the two fish which Neptune rules, they are more truly married, in the inner sense, than those who enter merely physical matrimony.

Life in its various expressions tends to move from lower levels of expression to higher levels of expression. This is not merely true of the aims of action and the acquisition of ideas, but is equally true in emotional expression.

According to the findings of psychology the normal love life passes through well defined evolutionary stages, moving from an expression which is suited to the infant's capacity, to such heights and complexity as the individual is capable. These successive levels are now so well recognized that they each have been given definite names by which they commonly are recognized in psychological literature.

The infant's affectional interest, quite naturally, centers about himself. This level of the emotional life is called the Narcissus stage. As the infant develops there is a transference of his love from himself to a parent. This level is called the Oedipus stage. The third level is when the growing child transfers his affections from members of the family circle to some person of the same sex outside the family. This stage usually just precedes the change at the end of adolescence. The fourth transference, which normally occurs as the youth approaches maturity, is toward some member of the opposite sex. This stage is the level of marriage. The fifth transfer should not be from husband or wife, but merely a widening of the affectional interests to include the children, which normally are now a part of the family.

Neptune, however, when its influence is powerful in the birth-chart, is never content with this fifth level, or state of affectional expression. Up to this point Venus has dominated the love life; but it is here, if progress is to continue, that Neptune exerts his power.

The children grow up, marry, and have homes of their own. Thus the sixth level of expression of the love life expands the affectional interest to embrace humanity at large, and causes the individual to work as if he were responsible for its welfare. And if the proper transference is made, husband and wife are not less in love, but more so. Yet the physical aspect of union has been left behind, and instead, an inner exchange of energies takes place. This is the regenerate union, which is excluded by physical union.

Therefore, when the Dolphin persuades the goddess who has taken a vow of perpetual celibacy to unite with Neptune, it is indicated that after man has passed through the tomb he can rejoin his mate; but that, unless he remains in the lower spheres of the astral world, his affectional expression will not be similar to physical marriage, but will be that complete blending of finer forces which is even more satisfying, and which when accomplished on earth is termed regenerate marriage.

It seems, according to still another Greek story, that Arion, the famous lyric poet and musician, who was a native of the island of Lesbos, went to Italy with Periander, tyrant of Corinth. There he attained both high honor and great riches through following his profession.

After making such a success, it was quite natural that he should desire to return to his old home for a visit, and he embarked on a ship to make the journey. The sailors on the ship, learning of his wealth, determined to murder him and get possession of it. But just before they put him to death they granted him a last request; that he might play on his lute. The music attracted a number of Dolphins, and as soon as he was sure these were present, Arion jumped from the vessel into the sea, and one of the Dolphins immediately took him upon its back and carried him safely to land.

Paralleling this, there are those of the invisible world who, if we will but tune our thoughts to them, will be ready to help us make the adjustment to the after death life. Those who die in terror, those who with no preparation meet sudden death, and those who are unduly attached to physical things, often are difficult to help for some time after their passing.

Commonly the individual after leaving the physical body falls asleep. This may be a long sleep, as in the case of an earth-bound soul, or it may be but a moment's lapse of consciousness. But during it the individual moves in his astral form to the level and place where his new birth takes place. This is not the environment where later he will find himself, but a transitional region. It is here he awakens into a knowledge that he has entered a new life.

His home on the inner plane is the type of environment which he has built for himself by his thoughts and desires while on earth. It may be a place of great beauty and harmony. On the other hand, if his thoughts have been filthy, so will his astral home reflect filth. If he has been cold and heartless, squalor will mark his after-life home, until he gets a more expansive attitude.

The text associated with Delphinus therefore is: *Man, by His Thoughts, His Emotions, and His Actions on Earth, Builds for Himself a Home in a Higher Realm where He Will Dwell After Passing From the Physical Plane.*

When Venus Met Typhon

In ancient Sumeria the plots of land on which produce was raised were laid out, much after the manner of farming land today, in rectangles. The corners of these areas, to provide means of identifying ownership, were marked with boundary stones. These boundary stones, among other things, commonly bore an astrological symbol.

Thus it was, following the still more ancient custom of regarding that which is on earth as a replica of that which is in the sky, that they also sought to plot the heavens in a somewhat similar manner. While recognizing its spherical shape, they established corners, each corner marked by a first magnitude star, so that it was laid out as a great rectangle. The spring corner of the sky was marked by Aldebaren, the summer corner by Regulus, the fall corner by Antares, and the winter corner by Fomalhaut, a lonesome star rising far to the southeast, to be seen only close to the southern horizon. These four markers were later known as the four Royal Stars.

Fomalhaut marks the head of the Fish, Pisces Australis, which is pictured drinking, and swimming in, the water which flows down from the urn of Aquarius. Aquarius is the Man of the sky. Not only does he pour down an influence upon the earth, which is eagerly absorbed by Pisces Australis, but with one hand he measures the place and power of the heavenly bodies. That is, he represents not only the intelligence of those who have passed beyond the tomb, but also the energies of the signs and planets which descend from above to influence the life and destiny of man on earth.

The joining of the sign of the one who Knows, Aquarius, to the stream of planetary energy pouring down upon man, indicates not only that, like the Fish, man on earth is subject to this invisible flood, but that he should use his intelligence to take advantage of it. How this may be done is set forth in the universal symbolism of the Greek legend of Typhon and Venus.

Typhon is the Egyptian portrayal of Saturn, the planet of selfishness which rules Capricorn, one decanate of which is pictured by the

Southern Fish. Venus is the planet of love, the influence of which is the natural antidote for the influence of Saturn. According to the legend, Typhon made horrible advances to the beautiful goddess of love, and to escape him she transformed herself into a Fish which now may be seen in the southern autumn skies.

A fish lives in the water, symbol of the emotions, and love must have an emotional environment to thrive. There is but one manner in which we can escape the Typhon of selfishness, and that is through love. Whenever and wherever there is absence of love of someone other than the Self, to that extent does love of Self take charge, with all its terrible implications. If, therefore, we are to escape Selfishness it is imperative that we acquire love of others, such as is symbolized by the Fish immersed in the humanitarian stream.

Yet there is a still more technical significance to this transformation which took place when Saturn and Venus met. Thought trends and planetary vibrations both utilize astral vibrations, and are quite similar in their power to affect the finer body of man. That is, certain groups of thought-cells are given additional energy, and therefore can perform additional work, whether the energy supplied them comes from the planetary vibrations of Saturn or the thought-vibrations of Saturn quality. The same thing is true of the influence of all the other nine planets.

Astrologers find, therefore, that the most effective manner of counteracting the undesirable influence of any planet is to cultivate a type of thinking which forms a natural antidote to it, that is, the vibrations of which either cancel out the influence of the planet, or combine harmoniously with it to form beneficial thought-cells which attract favorable events instead of the misfortunes which would have been attracted if the planetary influence had gone unnoticed.

To be more specific, the ancient initiates, as well as modern astrologers of the more enlightened class, looked upon planetary influences not as indicating inevitable events in the life of the individual, but as astral weather conditions which if not recognized tended to cause the individual to be attracted to the indicated event. If the invisible environment, such as the Southern Fish is seen to be swimming in, was harmonious, a knowledge of the direction of its flow would enable the individual to move with the fortunate tide and attain a success that otherwise would be impossible. But if the stream were adverse, if it represented a period of stormy astral weather, proper preparation usually would enable the individual to pass through the period uninjured.

There were three methods advocated by which planetary energies could thus be brought under control These embraced the use of Rallying Forces, the employment of Conversion, and the application of Mental Antidotes. It is this latter method, which has the widest range of application, and can be used by the untrained individual as well as by those of special skill, which is indicated in the story of Venus and Typhon.

When there is an adverse influence from the planet Saturn, the best thing that the individual can do to counteract it is to cultivate a line of thinking and activity which is ruled by Venus. The thought energies having the Venus vibratory rate are of such a nature that when they unite with the Saturn vibrations they tend to produce a compound within the thought-cells of the astral body which has no inimical influence. Furthermore, the Saturn thought-element and the Venus thought-element quite readily enter into a very beneficial mental compound if they are thought about in association in a pleasant manner.

Venus and Saturn are only one pair of Mental Antidotes; for each planet is naturally related to some other planet in such a way that the vibrations of the two, or the thoughts which they rule, tend to unite in a harmonious compound very readily. Neptune, the octave of Venus, is also a mental antidote of Saturn. That is, not only does harmonious thinking of the Venus or Neptune type overcome the inimical influence of Saturn; but when the planetary influences of Venus or Neptune are discordant, this discord, and the misfortune otherwise attracted, can most readily be counteracted through cultivating harmonious Saturn thinking.

In the same manner thoughts of the Mars type most readily enter into harmonious compounds with those of the Moon or Pluto type. The Jupiter discords may most readily be annulled by cultivating thinking of the Mercury or Uranus type. This signifies also that when the Moon is afflicted the best type of thinking is that of a harmonious but aggressive nature; and that when Mercury is afflicted the best antidote is to cultivate the hail-fellow-well-met attitude, and the benevolence of Jupiter.

There is also a Bible story which revolves around the Southern Fish. It relates that Peter at one time was hard pressed for money with which to pay taxes. Relying upon the higher powers, he cast a hook into the water and drew forth a Fish which held a piece of money in its mouth, of sufficient value to meet the urgent need.

Those who take up some worthy work, especially if it be of a type which is encouraged by the better individuals of the inner plane, always find that they are under a somewhat similar protective influence. This does not mean that they will always escape danger, for the conditions may be such at times that those on the inner plane can not make their influence properly felt. This is not due to lack of desire on their part; but to the mental attitude of the one they wish to help, or to environmental conditions, which shut them off from him. It is then as if the Southern Fish were to desert the stream in which he normally lives, and be for the time being stranded.

Almost, or quite, every person who has become devoted to carrying out some noble work on the physical plane which has the support of invisible brethren, can relate experiences in which, when a crisis arose, he has been helped in a manner no less startling than was Peter when he so badly needed money. And it is significant that, as related in Matthew 17:27, the coin was not for the purchase of food, but for a purpose which comes under the same astrological rulership as friends on the inner plane; for both the dead and taxes are ruled by the eighth house of a birth-chart.

Yet even when the conditions for exchanging ideas with such friends on the inner plane are perfect, the amount of information that can thus be acquired by one on earth is dependent upon his mental capacity. Should an equation in differential calculus, for instance, be given to an individual not well versed in mathematics, it would be so meaningless to him that he probably would pay no attention to it. To bring things from the unconscious, which is necessary in such communication, there must be a bond of association between them and things already known and in the objective consciousness.

Those on the inner plane who have advanced in character and in wisdom band together in societies and groups, formulate better methods of living and higher standards of conduct, and make the endeavor to project these ideals to people yet on earth. The ideals of earth are thus received by those who are advanced enough here to receive them, from minds on the inner planes. For this reason, and because those born from January 10 to January 20, while the Sun is in the third-decanate of Capricorn, are particularly receptive to such exalted ideas, the Keyword of the Pisces Australis section of the zodiac is Idealism.

While such ideals, and valuable information, may be broadcast from the inner planes to all the earth for anyone who is receptive to pick them up; usually some one individual on the earth becomes the one through whom they are given to the world. This individual, through his basic character vibrations and intellectual interests, has an affinity for the ideals and knowledge given. His subsequent thinking about them and teaching them, keep him in the stream of vibratory influence flowing from those on higher levels, much as the Southern Fish lives in and absorbs the stream from the Aquarian urn. Thus the text becomes: *From the Inner Planes it is Possible For Man to Attract Any Information Whatsoever He is Capable of Utilizing.*

AQUARUIS ♒ I Know

EQUULEUS ≈-≈ Originality

CETUS 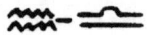 *Repression*

Chapter 12

In the Reign of Aquarius

MAN **Comes of Age.**
To picture the eleventh sign of the zodiac, which in a natural birth-chart rules the house of friends, the ancients used the figure of a Man. This man, with his left, or receptive, hand measures the influence of the heavens by means of a 24 hour gauge; while his right, or executive, hand is engaged in pouring down upon the earth, from an urn, the flood of wisdom thus acquired. Because Aquarius expresses the highest type of intelligence developed on the earth the Key-phrase of this section of the zodiac where the Sun may be found each year from January 20 to February 20 is, I Know.

It was long believed, and is now in process of being verified, that when the Equinox, which is the pointer of the Great Cycle of 25,868 years, just as the Sun is the pointer in the annual cycle of 365¼ days; when the Equinox should enter Aquarius, the sign of Knowledge, that the human race under that influence would make tremendous strides in science, in philosophy and in practical living. The Equinox moves backward through the circle of zodiacal constellations, not due to any movement of the Sun, but due to a wobble of the earth which causes the pole of the equator to move in a small circle about the pole of the ecliptic.

The earth is known to have five major motions. It rotates on its axis, bringing night and day. It revolves in an annual orbit around the Sun, producing the seasons. The Sun, accompanied by the earth, is moving at the rate of twelve and one-half miles a second toward the dividing line between Hercules and Lyra. The fourth major motion is that of the whole Milky Way System, or galaxy, which is turning, like a pinwheel, about its center in Sagittarius. By this motion the Sun and earth. traveling at the rate of 150 miles a second, take 240 million years to complete one orbit about the galactic center. The rate of travel of the fifth major motion, by which the earth, Sun and all the billions of stars of the galactic system are carried along. is as yet unknown.

It will be seen that while the Sun. along with other suns. moves around a center in 240 million years, that this has nothing to do with the precession of the equinoxes. The precession is caused by the pull of the Sun and Moon on the bulging equator of the earth, which is not in the same plane as that in which the members of our solar system perform their revolutions. The gyration of the earth's pole as the result of the pull on the equator causes the point where the Sun each year crosses the equator to move backward through the circle of stars.

Signs of the zodiac are always just 30 degrees in extent. The constellations which picture the signs may be more or less than 30 degrees in extent, Cancer, for instance, covering only about 15 degrees, while Virgo covers about 50 degrees. Furthermore, there being no exact record of the boundaries of these constellations, they are not well defined, but only approximate.

When, therefore, the Equinox is said to have backed into the sign Aquarius, that does not mean that it has moved back to a point where some of the stars in the constellation Aquarius are located; because no one knows within a degree or two what stars should be included in the outline of the constellation. Instead, it means that the Vernal Equinox has moved back 30 degrees from the correspondence of the First of Aries among the constellations; because the sign Pisces (not the constellation Pisces), through which it has moved, by its very definition of being a sign, must contain 30 degrees along the ecliptic.

As the whole cycle by which the equinox moves through the 12 signs takes 25,868 years, the date when the Equinox entered Aquarius by the back door and the Aquarian Age started could be determined precisely by adding one-twelfth of 25,868 years, or 2,156 years, to the date when the First of Aries among the constellations coincided with the First of Aries among the signs.

Unfortunately, there is no undisputed record of the date when the First of Aries among the constellations thus coincided with the First of Aries among the zodiacal signs. We can not, for this purpose, select the western boundary of the constellation Aries, because no one knows precisely where that boundary should be, or whether the picture as it appears on the maps of today is of the same size and contour as it anciently was. Thus there is no precise astronomical observation by which can be determined when the Aquarian Age began.

It would appear, however, that the First of Aries among the constellations must lie very close to the most brilliant and conspicuous star in the constellation Aries. This star, Alpha Arietis, now has a Right Ascension of 2 hours, 3 minutes. That is, the Vernal Equinox has moved back not quite 31 degrees since it was on the meridian occupied by this bright star in the head of the Ram. Calculating at the rate of precession by Right Ascension, in 1881 the Vernal Equinox was just about 30 degrees along the ecliptic west of the meridian of Alpha Arietis, so that if this star be used as a starting point for the circle of constellations, the Equinox backed into Aquarius just about 1881.

In determining the time of the commencement of the Aquarian Age, as it is mere assumption that Alpha Arietis is the starting point in the circle of stars, we are faced with a problem similar to that of determining the hour of birth of a person when the precise time has not been recorded. It is essentially a problem of rectification, such as all astrologers are familiar with in their natal astrology practice.

Within the time limits which for other considerations seem reasonable, the most satisfactory method of rectifying a birth-chart is through the comparison of the events which have happened in the life with the positions found in the chart, and with the progressed aspects. And by the same token, rather than make calculations from Alpha Arietis, or from other equally uncertain starting points, it seems better to ascertain the commencement of the Aquarian Age from a consideration of events which clearly are not of the type which are characteristic of Pisces, through which for more than 2,000 years the Equinox moved by precession.

Aquarius is a scientific sign, and during the past 50 years science has made greater advances than during the 2,000 Piscean years. Its ruler, Uranus, governs invention, psychology. electricity and the study of the stars. It has been within the past 50 years that the world has adopted electricity as an important source of power, that inventions have revolutionized industry, that astronomy has extended its boundaries from our solar system to the measurement of stars and other universes, and that psychology has come to be recognized as a subject that should be taught in our schools.

There is traditional basis also for considering that the Aquarian influence over world affairs started in 1881, but, as anyone familiar with Aquarius can hardly believe that present-day activities are actuated by the mere Belief of Pisces rather than by the Knowledge of Aquarius, to present other evidence would be to use space that can better be utilized in pointing to the most important developments which, now we are in the Aquarian Age, shortly will be with us.

Because Religion forms the pattern of human conduct, its significance is even greater than that of the industrial and scientific advancement now to be seen under way. Science, which is classified information, gives power to accomplish. But whether that power will be used for the benefit of the race or will enable the few to subjugate and exploit the many, is a religious consideration. It depends upon the attitude toward life whether selfishness shall rule, or the humanitarian spirit which characterizes the finer side of Aquarius.

Whether we like it or not, now that the world has moved into the astral current of Aquarius all institutions resting on a foundation of mere Belief will disintegrate. The orthodoxies of the Piscean Age are irrevocably doomed. Energy spent tearing them down is wasted, because their falsities already are disappearing, dissolving like the morning mists, faster than those who are enlightened can disseminate true knowledge to take their place.

All the facts that material science has to offer must fit snugly into the religion of the Aquarian Age. Not that the unsubstantiated theories of materialists should be included; for fashions in scientific theories change as often as do the styles in women's clothes. But all those things which have been proved a part of physical reality must be included.

Yet in addition to the facts accepted by the materially minded there is a vast field of carefully verified truths relating to planetary influence, relating to the development and use of other than physical sense organs, relating to the conditions that are present after the dissolution of the physical body, and having to do with the basic purpose of life itself. This information also, however wide its range

Spiritual Astrology 247

and varied its character, and regardless of its conflict with preconceived ideas, must fit smoothly into the Aquarian religion.

All obtainable information must be organized into a single consistent structure and made practical in application. And as the zodiacal sign pictures a Man, this religion must provide man with the best possible method of meeting every contingency of his life. There is a best way to act under every circumstance wherein the individual finds himself, and this religion should be so comprehensive and yet so explicit that those who adopt it will have no difficulty in determining what is the best course of action under the conditions that confront them at any particular time.

Because knowledge of astrology is essential as a guide to such best course of action, and because astrological relations, through their correspondence with things on the earth and within the mind are the avenues to the more comprehensive Knowledge required by the Aquarian religion, the religion thus formulated should be called The Religion of the Stars. And as this religion is based on that wisdom which expresses the Aquarian spirit of altruism, the text associated with the constellation is: *Do and Think Unto Others as You Would Have Them Do and Think Unto You.*

The Significance of Horse Sense

A horse immediately suggests two things, speed of travel and ability to carry a rider. The head of a horse, the animal's body missing, conveys the thought that the intelligence factor is to be considered rather than the physical propensities. To have Horse Sense is phraseology with which most people are familiar, even though it is not a refined expression. It indicates such a correct appraisal of circumstances that action of practical value can be based upon it. Yet the full significance of the Horse Head, Equuleus, as a universal symbol employed by the ancients to convey information, is not apparent until it is remembered that the sign Aquarius rules astrology, and that Equuleus pictures the astrology-decanate of the sign.

To be more explicit, the planet Uranus rules astrology, and the Aquarius-decanate of Aquarius is specially under his dominion and thus has an unusually close affinity for the starry science. Furthermore, individuality and inventive ability, wherever found in marked degree, denote the Uranus or Aquarius influence. Hence the Key-word for this section of the sky where the Sun may be found each year from January 20 to January 30 is Originality.

Those who feel that they have so complete a grasp of the laws and principles through which nature operates that nothing can transpire not explained by the text-books used in formal education, jump to the conclusion that astrology is "exploded" merely because they do not perceive how it works, and because their teachers have so informed them. Yet such as so glibly proclaim there is nothing to astrology are free to admit—at least our foremost astronomers have thus admitted—that they have never tested the science out experimentally, and, in fact, would not know how to go about it to set up and read a birth-chart. Utterly unfamiliar with the rules, and often attributing to astrologers claims to omniscience which no well versed astrologer ever makes, they merely echo what happens to be academic fashion.

Horse Sense, which the general populace often possesses in greater degree than those who are bound by the tenets of formal schooling, demands that before condemning anything as untrue it should be tested out in actual experience. Theories are very fine, but the man in the street who has had numerous practical contacts with life, has come to realize that the accepted theories of the schools often fail signally in actual practice. He, therefore, is much less willing than the college professor to discountenance something just because he has no ready explanation for it. Following the dictates of experience, his Horse Sense informs him that the best way to find out if a thing works is not to theorize as to its possibility, or probability, but to actually test it out in practice.

Thus we find a peculiar situation in our land; the so-called learned schoolmasters denouncing the public because, more and more, that public is coming to lean on astrology for help. And the public, in spite of the condemnation of the schoolmasters who depend merely upon theories in such matters, gaining more and more confidence in astrology; because they have had the opportunity to test it out through actual experience. If a thing actually works and is decidedly helpful, the man in the street is not unduly concerned whether or not it breaks the conventional traditions of scholastic opinion.

Such gain in the popularity of astrology is made in the face of the unusually severe handicap that those who know almost nothing of the science, who are really astrological quacks, through their flamboyant advertising are able to draw people into their clutches and give them misinformation under the astrological banner.

Because the public has had so little opportunity, in the face of academic condemnation, to become informed as to what can and what can not be done with astrology and as to what constitutes a correct birth-chart, or even that it should be progressed if the time and nature of events likely to be attracted are to be given, it is easy for rank charlatans to flourish under the pretense they are astrologers, and to fleece the public of money

This also makes it very easy for the academic upholder of conventional tradition apparently to disprove the claims of astrology. All he has to do is to answer the advertisements of those who for a dime will tell your fortune from the cradle to the grave. To these he gives his birth day and birth year, such seldom even asking for the precise data necessary to erect a correct birth-chart. Then when he has collected a series of readings from these ten cent advertisers, he has all the evidence he needs that astrology is false.

He does have, it is true, plenty of evidence that those who advertise to give something of immense value for almost nothing are charlatans. But he need not go to the get-rich-quick pretenders to astrology to prove this. He could learn it from a dozen other types of get-rich-quick advertisements found in the same periodicals from which he obtains the addresses of the fake astrologers.

But even with an array of such evidence he does not convince the man in the street, because that man already has learned that if he goes to a doctor, a dentist, or to any other professional man who makes exaggerated claims, and whose omnipotent services can be procured for a mere pittance, that he will be defrauded. He has learned not to expect something for nothing; and that in employing professional services of any kind it is necessary to consider reliability; and that those who have established themselves through merit do not advertise in the P. T. Barnum manner.

Primarily the birth-chart is a map of the astral body of the person then born. As a photographic negative bears the impress of light-waves reflected from the thing photographed, so the birth-chart pictures what the astral body of the individual then born contains.

This astral body holds within its organization all the experiences and mental states that the soul has had up to the time of human birth;

these organized into stellar cells and stellar structures which form the character. The astral body, which the birth-chart maps, is thus a form built by mental and emotional states; and it is the function of the birth-chart to convey to the astrologer precise information regarding these mental factors and their relation one to the other as affecting the abilities and character, and therefore the destiny.

The relation existing between the most active, or dynamic, thought-built structures in the finer body, are mapped by aspects between the planets in the birth-chart. Relationships that are thus so constant and powerful build a line across the astral form, from one group of mental factors to another, and this line, which is mapped by an aspect, acts as an aerial to pick up energies which are broadcast from each of the planets involved in the aspect. Thus are those more pronounced factors of the character supplied with additional energy from their four-dimensional environment. Whether that energy when received adds harmony to the astral body, or adds discord, is determined by the way the mental factors were organized, which is mapped by the aspect.

Thus from a consideration of the character, which is mapped by the birth-chart, it is possible to determine the natural abilities, and the normal trend of the events attracted; for these are shown by the organization of the character. This does not mean that the individual can not develop abilities other than those shown in his birth-chart; but that experiences before human birth already have developed certain types of ability, and he can utilize these natural talents with great ease. To develop qualities which are not shown in the birth-chart requires great expenditure of energy; for it means building into the character qualities which have had no previous existence there.

Furthermore, the birth-chart, in mapping harmonies and discords, reveals whether or not the individual will attract fortune or misfortune if he engages in a certain occupation. Thus it is the function of the birth-chart to reveal not only the natural talents, but also under what surroundings the individual can use them to be of greatest benefit to himself, and to be able to contribute his utmost to the advantage of the world.

When, according to definite ratios, the planets in the sky move forward to make progressed aspects, these release energies within the astral body of man in such a manner that temporary lines are built across the astral body. These lines act as temporary stellar aerials which pick up in unusual volume the energy broadcast from the planets mapped by their terminals. Whether the new energy thus picked up, radio fashion, and added to the thought-cells of the astral body, are harmonious or discordant, and to what extent, is revealed by the particular aspect.

As such stellar lines, or aerials, leading across the astral body, terminate in certain compartments of the finer form, each of which contains the thought-cells relating to specific departments of endeavor, it can be known what phase of the life will be affected by this new energy, which gives unusual activity to certain thought-cells. This does not mean that the individual shall submit to foreshadowed misfortune in this department of life; but it does indicate that unless he does something about it things will happen in a certain way.

They will happen in the designated way because the four-dimensional cell-life within the compartment receiving the additional energy will start working from their four-dimensional plane to bring events to pass that correspond to the way they feel, and in relation to their department of life.

A progressed aspect thus indicates, not what will happen, but what will happen if nothing is done to prevent it; and it also indicates what should be done to prevent the event thus foreshadowed if the event is not desired, and what to do to get more benefit from the event if it is of a type which is beneficial.

Common Horse Sense, such as is pictured by the Horse Head, Equuleus, demands that the individual shall take advantage of all knowledge which will enable him to make a greater success of his life. The text therefore is: *Next to Love, Man's Most Useful Companion is Knowledge, and in Particular the Knowledge of the Manner in which the Planets Influence Human Life and Destiny.*

On the Wings of Pegasus

The next decanate to the one which relates to the employment of horse sense is also pictured by the fore parts of a horse. The head, which implies intellect, is pictured; and in addition the front legs. Unlike those horses of earth which keep their feet upon the ground, this one also is equipped with wings. The intelligence which it represents consequently must be such as soars to other than physical realms.

The travel-decanate of Aquarius, where the Sun may be found from January 30 to February 10 each year, is represented in the heavens by famed Pegasus, the Flying Horse.

When, according to the Greek story, Perseus had slain the Gorgon Medusa and cut off its head, he mounted on wings furnished him by Mercury, and sped homeward carrying the awful monster's head. It was blood which dripped from this symbol of the imagination falling into the ocean, that is, imagination vitalized by emotion, from which Pegasus sprang; a powerful steed whose other name is Inspiration.

All poets, it is said, before they can attract the Muse, first must drink at the fountain created by a blow from the hoofs of Pegasus. It seems that Pegasus in flying over Mount Helicon struck the ground sharply with his hoofs, and water instantly gushed forth; the sparkling clear spring of Hippocrene. Inspiration, which is the Key-word of the Gemini-decanate of Aquarius, pictured by the Flying Horse, does not flow without a definite contact with the earth. That which the unconscious mind perceives, before it can come into objective consciousness, must be touched, or associated with, something already in the objective mind. Only through such physical association can it be externalized on the physical plane.

Neptune is the planet which rules all forms of dramatic ability. It is related that Neptune tamed Pegasus and gave him to Bellerophon, son of the King of Ephyre, to aid him in conquering the Chimaera. This was a sea-monster composed of incongruous parts, the origin of the word chimera, which signifies foolish or wildly fantastic creations of the imagination.

If Neptune were to succeed in the production of high art, these incongruities of the imagination must first be slain. Pegasus, representing Inspiration, aided in overcoming such vain and discordant fancies, as he is said always to aid those whose work—poetry, painting, fiction, scenario or music—presents true dramatic worth.

Such drama does not appeal directly to the intellect, but to the emotions. And the source of the ability to produce it lies not so much with the intellect as with a more primitive method of thinking which employs feeling rather than ideas. It is the method of thinking which, because it has been so long in existence, is employed largely by the unconscious mind.

The use of well-defined concepts, such as commonly are expressed in words, is the last biological development of earth. It is confined to members of the human race. Such intellectual processes are not intimately associated with body states, but deal with relations through the use of special symbols that enable things to be examined and compared in the mind. These symbols permit of that type of mental activity called reasoning.

Life, however, existed on the earth hundreds of millions of years before this type of intellectual endeavor developed. And all that time it was face to face with the necessity of successfully adapting itself to its environment. New circumstances continually arose, calling for correct appraisal of conditions, and for appropriate actions, if it were to survive.

The protoplasmic cell coming into contact with something without itself which provided food or other advantage, experienced a feeling which in a more developed state we call pleasure. Coming into contact with an outside condition which tended to destroy it, there was experienced that which in a more developed state we call pain.

The pleasure or pain experienced under any special condition resulted in action, more or less appropriate, which gave an advantage or led away from danger. The feeling also conditioned the organism, so that under the same conditions again it would move in the same way with even greater alacrity. Pleasure and pain not only stimulate to initial action, but establish a habit of moving in the same manner when the feeling is again present.

The soul or character, which now occupies and functions through the body of a human being, has in its past organized and lived in association with, countless lower forms of life. Progressively it has learned to handle such forms, advancing from a simple organism to one more complex as it gained in experience, and therefore in ability. All of this knowledge, all of this ability, all of this mentality, which it has acquired through its entire progressive existence, is stored in the astral body, or unconscious mind.

Since entering human life this unconscious mind has been in contact with the special symbols used in modern language. It has been trained for only a few short years in the employment of concepts, and in the process of reasoning. Such use of the intellect is a very late thing, something which has had opportunity to impress it for a matter of a few years only. The language of feeling, however, especially that expressed through the sympathetic nervous system, is as old as its first appearance in any life-form on earth.

The vegetative functions of the body, the regulation of the ductless glands, and, in fact, all but a few of our actions, are directed by the unconscious mind not through the intellect, not through the brain, but through the process of feeling. This language of feeling is that to which the unconscious mind has been accustomed for ages, and it employs other symbols than those modern ones which we term words.

If, therefore, we are to tap the reservoir of the unconscious mind, instead of directing our attention to cerebral processes, we must learn to recognize and interpret the language of feeling. And the artist who, through any medium of expression, arouses appropriate response from others must be able to express himself in a manner not so much to intrigue the intellect as to appeal to the feelings, and this he must do by employing language which is recognized by the unconscious mind.

To analyze, in terms of the intellect, a beautiful sunset or a musical melody; to pick it to pieces to discern its ingredients; is to destroy it. Such things appeal to the unconscious mind and use a language which by its symbolism arouses feeling. We are moved by feeling because for millions of years it was the only language which organisms were able to recognize.

Therefore, if we are to make available what the unconscious mind recognizes, or what it may gain through its exploration of the unseen realms, we must not limit it to the language of intellect, to which as yet it is so unaccustomed, but must learn to recognize the language which it preferably uses. By all means, the critical function of the intellect should not be abandoned; for it is a necessary tool in clearcut discernment of reality. But in addition, we should cultivate the ability to recognize the feeling language of the unconscious mind and to interpret it.

To do this, attention must be paid to impressions, to feelings, and to symbols. When the unconscious mind is given to understand that dependence is being placed upon it to gather information, or to perform work, it will make an effort to do as required. It was accustomed for ages to being the exclusive agent for reporting to the organism conditions which were important to its welfare. But since it has organized a human form this function has been taken over almost exclusively by the intellect. It has formed the habit, therefore, of making no special effort to give reports or to gather information. But if this duty is turned over to it again in large degree, it will again become active, and can acquire knowledge to which intellect alone could never aspire.

Through practice, the nervous system can be made sensitive to vibrations, and to the impressions through which the unconscious communicates with the conscious mind. If such states of feeling are closely watched, and their reports later checked against actual events and conditions, as often as possible, the feeling method of thinking will again come into use to supplement the intellectual method of thinking. The unconscious mind will then find an avenue through which it can impart whatever information it possesses, or can acquire, to the objective consciousness.

Just how much Inspiration owes to what already is within the unconscious mind, how much to what it gains through astral travel, and how much to disembodied human beings on the inner plane, who communicate their thoughts, varies with the individual and with circumstances. Yet all three methods are open to the mind which habitually uses both intellect and feeling in its efforts.

Those who lecture, or give messages from a public platform, often rely very largely upon the Inspiration they receive from the audience. The unconscious minds of all those present constitute a reservoir of information which is widely varied and of considerable range. If the platform worker is sufficiently receptive, the thought-waves coming from the various members of his audience enable him to tune in rather fully on their unconscious minds. He thus has available for his use not only the information which they are aware of possessing, but vast funds of knowledge stored in the unconscious mind of each of which the individual possessing it has no objective knowledge.

In addition to such mundane sources of Inspiration, those who become intensely absorbed in some subject, in their sleep, or voluntarily without sleep when they know how, frequently travel to regions on the inner plane where others are interested in, and engaged in investigating, very much the same thing. In this astral travel they have the opportunity to exchange views with others more advanced, and the information thus gained is brought back either consciously, or stored in the unconscious mind to be drawn upon as their feelings and thoughts, while the attention is directed to the subject, permit.

The text is: *Under Special Conditions, while Still Maintaining Physical Life, it is Possible for Man to Free Himself from the Physical Body, to Visit the Homes of the Dead, to Enter the Halls of Learning, and to Bring Back in Full Consciousness the Knowledge Gained in Higher Spheres.*

The Sad Experience of Jonah

The legendary stories about giants such as Goliath, the Cyclopes and the Titans have their explanation in the zodiac in that point where the Sun reaches highest, the summer solstice; and their application to the life of man in reference to the ruthless use of reason and the development of selfish greed. These giants, however, are not pictured in the sky, but are known only through their relation to zodiacal position. They are destructive attributes which loom large upon the world's horizon. Yet there is another attribute which is even more far reaching, which is still more powerful for evil, and which is even more difficult to vanquish than these various types of selfishness. Its common name is Discord.

When the ancient wise men sought to picture in the heavens the force, or principle, which is most inimical to life, which attracts to man failure and disease, and which places the greatest obstacles in the way of progress, they looked about for some appropriate symbol. Because it is the emotional, or feeling, element which determines whether there is harmony or discord, and as water symbolizes the emotions, it was quite to be expected that they should select some creature living in the water. This denizen of the deep, as discord is a distortion of that which is pleasing and symmetrical, is required to be frightful and unnatural; and because it was to picture so vast an influence, it must be large as well as terrifying.

Cetus, the Sea-monster, is such a creature, the distortion of a whale; and commensurate with the importance of the influence it represents, it has been made the largest of all the constellations.

There are many sources of discord in human life. Planetary influence affords one important supply. Thus it is quite fitting that the universal symbol of Discord should picture one decanate of the sign which relates to astrological influences. The thoughts afford the initial supply of discordant energy to the finer form; and it is thus again appropriate that Discord be placed in association with the sign of the Man.

From the standpoint of prevalency and potency there is no source of Discord in human life that can compare with that generated in the nuptial relations. Hence, recognizing that unions not based on love afford the conditions most favorable to building Discords into the astral body, Cetus was placed in the sky where it would picture the marriage-decanate of the sign Aquarius, in which the Sun may be found each year from February 10 to February 20.

Not in relation to the close association of marriage, which permits the discordant thoughts of each most readily to reach and affect the finer body of the other, but as indicating the general effect of Discord, the story of Jonah is enlightening.

Jonah had been given certain work to accomplish which he feared to do. That he shirked doing it was bad enough, but in addition he also harbored the Discords of remorse. The emotional disturbance resulting is well symbolized by the sea which was whipped by a tempest; for Jonah had embarked on a ship in the endeavor to escape that which God had called upon him to do.

When Jonah had been cast into the sea, a voluntary sacrifice to save the other men on the ship, the waters immediately calmed. Yet he continued in Discord three days, as indicated by the three days during which he remained in the belly of the Seamonster. If Pisces, in which the Fish swim, be considered the sea wherein Jonah was thrown, the Sun must pass through its three decanates after the one pictured by Cetus before it reaches Aries, where the water comes to an end. When Jonah, after suffering from the Discord of a disturbed conscience, resolved his inner conflict by deciding to do that which he deemed to be his duty, he was released from the belly of the Sea-monster; that is, he was freed from Discord.

In the story of Andromeda, it was the boastful pride of her mother, Cassiopeia, that placed her in a position of distress. As so many in the world today are not responsible for the Discord which has overtaken them, so was Andromeda the victim of her mother's scheming ambition. The rock to which she was bound represents the materialism which demanded the sacrifice of her own spiritual aspirations to the false ideals of her associates.

Here we are concerned with Andromeda only to note that the Sea-monster, Cetus, who was sent by Neptune to devour her, is the type of monster which today destroys so many of our youths and maidens. It represents the Discords engendered, and fed from one person into the finer body of the other, when marriage is not a mutual love union, but a matter of material expediency. She was saved from this horrible death only by the arrival of her own Prince Charming, by Perseus, who loved her tenderly and made her his bride. That is, it was the harmony of true love and rightful marriage that saved her from the destruction of Discord.

On all planes of life Harmony is Life and Discord is Death. The health of the physical body is determined by the amount of harmony between the dynamic thought-structures of the astral body. The vibratory relations of the various thought organizations, one to the other, within the finer body reproduce themselves as functional and organic strength or weakness within the physical form. Thus it is in Stellar Diagnosis, to determine the predisposition to disease, the birth-chart is examined for its heaviest Discords. The most powerful Discord in the birth-chart is always the disease toward which there is the most pronounced predisposition.

That is, the most powerfully discordant aspect in the birth-chart maps the most pronounced discordant relation between the thought groups within the astral body. That such aspects thus reveal the diseases toward which there is a predisposition is not a matter of theory, but something which has been learned through the statistical study of thousands of birth-charts. The charts of 100 persons who have suffered from each disease are collected. Always there are similar pronounced discordant aspects in all the charts. These when tabulated in terms of percentage reveal the Birth-chart Constants of the particular disease.

This does not signify that any person in whose birth-chart these constants appear will inevitably suffer sooner or later from the given disease; but it does indicate that people who do not have these Birth-chart Constants in their charts will not have the disease; and that those who do have them will need to exercise precaution if they are to escape. Precautionary measures usually can be taken to prevent the development of the disease; but if its Birth-chart Constants are present, that person has weaknesses in his astral body which are reproduced in his physical body that will cause him to have the disease under conditions where another person not possessing these Discords would escape.

In such statistical work, in which the Discords within the finer body are determined which enable a given disease to manifest, the chart is also Progressed for the date when the disease first was noticed to be present. In this manner, using charts of 100 persons suffering from a particular disease, the temporary Discord that enables the disease to develop is also learned. This progressed aspect, which manifests as a temporary stellar aerial which picks up and adds additional discordant energy to the cells of the astral body that relate to the disease, when tabulated in terms of percentage, is called the Progressed Constant.

When the birth-chart contains the Birth-chart Constant of a particular disease and a time arrives when the Progressed Constant also is present, this warns the individual that he must use exceptional precaution to avoid conditions under which the disease commonly develops, and that he must use initiative to develop energies within himself, and conditions within his environment which will prevent the disease from getting a foothold.

It is one of the functions of astrology to indicate just what the danger is, when it will be most prominently present, and what should be done to prevent the affliction which the Birth-chart Constant and the Progressed Constant indicate is likely to develop.

Disease of the physical body is only one type of affliction to which man is subject. Yet all the other afflictions, such as financial loss. business failure, loss of loved ones, antagonisms from others, whatever misfortunes to which the individual may be heir, in a similar manner are mapped by Birth-chart Constants and Progressed Constants in his chart of birth.

These constants thus mapped. which show the nature of the misfortunes to which there is a predisposition, and the times when they are likely to develop, map specific Discords within the astral body. That is. whatever ill befalls the individual is always attracted by specific Discords within himself. And if he would free himself from them, even as Andromeda escaped, he must reorganize these discordant energies into harmonies.

These birth-chart aspects and progressed aspects merely map mental factors in the astral body; they are not the cause of the Discords. Furthermore, not only do the thoughts and feelings which originate with the individual have a power to build thought-structures such as attract good fortune or misfortune, but the thoughts and feelings of those with whom rapport is more or less completely established also feed similar energies into the finer form.

In the married state husband and wife are so closely associated that the thought energies and emotional energies of each find ready access to the astral body of the other. Thus they give each other mental treatments under the conditions of a close association which is most favorable for making the mental treatment effective. The avenues are open for the most ready exchange of finer energies.

Nor does the mere avoidance of marriage prevent the development of Discord. The basic urge for reproduction is so strong a factor in all normal life that the attempt to stifle it commonly leads to that form of Discord denoted by the Key-word of the decanate, which is Repression. Yet if marriage is to be beneficial the energy exchange must be harmonious. Hence the text is: *The Monster Which Demands the Sacrifice of the Fairest Youths of the Land is Discord in Marriage.*

Spiritual Astrology

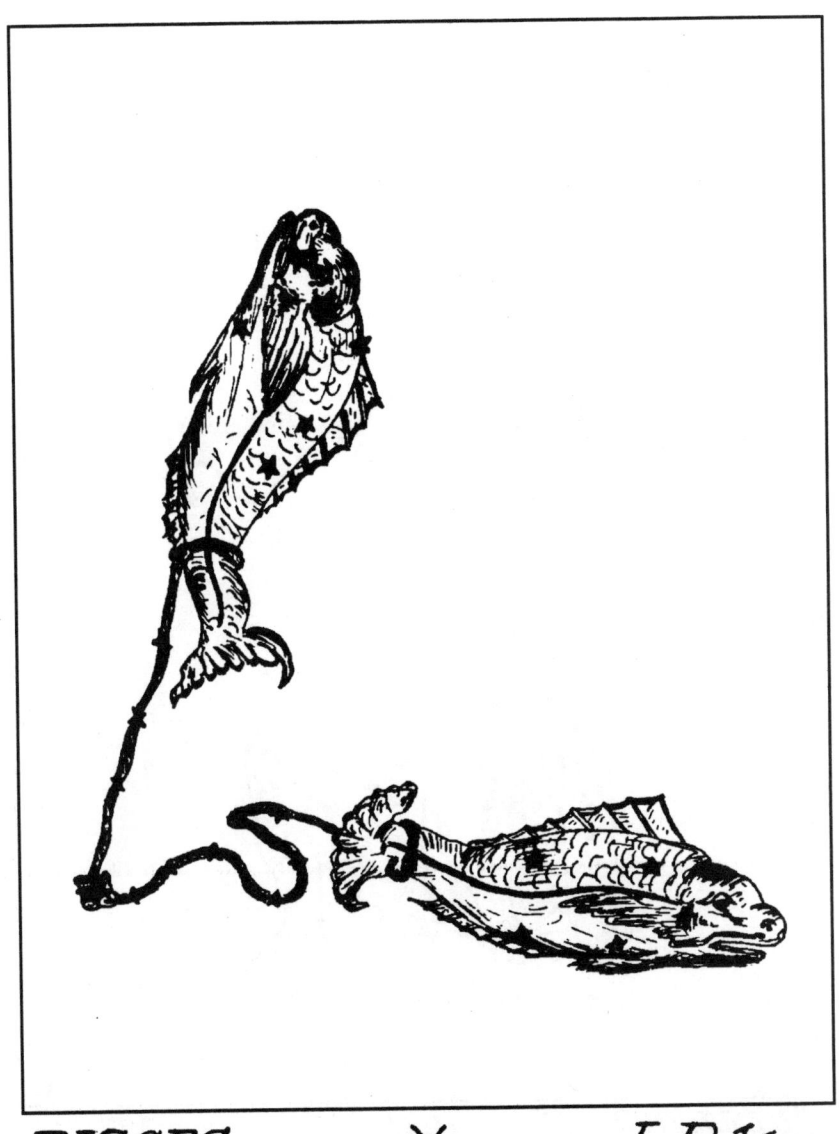

PISCES ♓ I Believe

ANDROMEDA ♓-♋ Self Sacrifice

CASSIOPEIA ♓-♏ Vicissitudes

Chapter 13

The Tree of Life

THE Eternal Tie That Binds.
Virgo represents the Garden of Eden. The exercise of the critical faculty, which is within its special province, is the way to the Tree of the Knowledge of Good and Evil. Yet information alone, no matter how comprehensive, is not sufficient to attain everlasting life, as the Bible clearly implies in Genesis 3:22:

> And the Lord God said, Behold, the man is become as one of us, to know good and evil: and now, lest he put forth his hand, and take also of the tree of life, and eat, and live forever.

The Bible then abruptly changes the subject. Having indicated that there is a Tree of Life, partaking of which man might live forever, it leaves man to his own ingenuity to find where it is located. Yet to anyone conversant with the ancient stellar doctrine that eternal progression depends upon both Love and Wisdom, and with the first principles of astrology which reveals that Polar Opposites, such as Love and Wisdom surely are, always occupy opposite stations in the zodiac, there could be no mystery where the Tree of Life must be located in the sky. It must lie across the zodiac from the Tree of Good and Evil.

Virgo holds a branch from the Tree of Good and Evil in one hand, and Hercules, picturing the middle decanate of the sign, holds another branch from that tree, on which the fruit yet hangs. The polar opposite of Virgo is Pisces. Pisces, because more appropriately it pictures the process by which eternal life is gained, and because a tree would not be a suitable emblem in the water where the Fishes swim, does not show a tree; but two of its decanates do. The Pisces-decanate of the sign presents a scepter made from the branch of a tree, held in a ruler's hand. That is, he is king over life and death. And the last decanate of the sign is pictured by a queen, who holds a branch of a palm tree in her hand, very much as does Virgo.

Furthermore, Pisces is the sign where the physical cycle of life ends. If there is to be still further life, such as indicated by the new cycle commenced in Aries, those processes which lead to revitalization should be commenced before the time of transition thus indicated. These are the processes so clearly indicated by the ribbon which binds the two Fishes of Pisces into an indissoluble union.

Specialization of parts—mechanics, statesmen, agriculturists, writers, artists, etc.—is familiar to us in that complex organization which we call our social system. And we also are familiar with the fact that two elements united often produce a chemical compound with possibilities tremendously more significant than the same two chemical elements possess when not so united.

We may be sure, therefore, that the ancient masters who traced the constellations in the sky did not unite the two Fishes of Pisces into a single system without having information of profound import to convey. They are not united rigidly, as are the cells of the physical body, but by a long ribbon which permits each Fish to move about without undue restriction from the other. Each thus seems to be permitted the exercise of its own initiative; but belongs to a system from which it can not separate.

Before attempting further to trace the significance of this universal symbol, let us see what the Greeks had to say about the constellation Pisces. It is related to a watery sign, and thus to the emotions. It is the exaltation of Venus, the goddess of love; that is, love finds its highest expression through Pisces. And it is ruled by Neptune, the upper-octave expression of Venus. Such expression, if it be true to the upper octave significance, relates to interior states which physical manifestations of love are unable to penetrate. They have their significance chiefly where the astral body is concerned.

The Greek legend is that Venus and her son Cupid one day were strolling along the bank of the river Euphrates, when quite unexpectedly Typhon put in an appearance. To escape this selfish monster, typical of Saturn, Cupid and Venus leaped into the water and transformed themselves into the two Fishes. To commemorate this event the Pisces Fishes were placed in the sky.

Venus and Cupid represent love. The Fishes into which they were transformed are denizens of the water, and thus signify emotions. While love has a binding power, the ribbon by which the two Fishes are united, to be true to the rulership of Neptune, must represent an actual invisible energy which unites them, but which does not greatly hamper the movements of either.

Love manifests on various planes or levels. But on the human plane, when there is natural harmony between the inner natures—that is, vibratory affinity between the finer bodies—and love has developed between the two persons of opposite sex, they easily and rather constantly tune in on each other's vibratory rates. Depending largely upon the activity of their inner forces and the state of their spiritual development, a circuit, or endless belt of energy forms between them. That is, there is a continuous current of astral energy circulating between them, much as there is a circulation of blood through the physical body of the individual.

This circuit is indeed a current of life, possessing amazing potentialities. These potentialities are commensurate to the height of the basic vibratory rates of the two between whom the circuit flows, and to the amount of energy generated by their love, each for the other. Not uncommonly those in love experience the blend of forces which if unbroken develops into this current. Some also are aware that such a current is in existence. But, as it belongs chiefly to the inner plane of life, mental discords tend to break it, and physical sensations tend to dissolve it.

It must be cultivated if it is to persist; and that cultivation must be along the line of developing and maintaining intense and tender love, each for the other. Grosser feelings and passion will effectually destroy this fine belt, or ribbon. It is sensitive to all lower expressions, and thrives on feelings which relate more to spiritual states than to those physical.

Selfishness, portrayed by the giant Typhon, is so restrictive in its influence that when it is present even in minor degree, and even when not related to the object of affection, it tends to destroy this endless belt of love. To maintain it those whose love has reached a plane where it can form such a ribbon of spiritual potentiality must expand their affections to embrace all creatures. The desire to destroy another, to deprive another of that which is justly his, or to in any way cause suffering to any living thing, tends to disrupt this fine ribbon by which the loving souls are joined.

The knot where the ribbons uniting the two Fishes are tied represents the Ego which is common to both souls, and which is the eternal spark of Deity by which they are energized. Thus the two souls and their Ego form a distinct system, which when so organized becomes a true spiritual cell in the cosmic body. Such a soul-mate system, or spiritual cell, has a distinctive form on the inner planes; and when made permanent is commonly referred to as an angel. It then no longer belongs to four dimensional existence, but by virtue of its new capabilities is typical of the truly spiritual, or five-dimensional plane.

The two souls comprising the angel do not lose their identity; no more so than Venus and Mars lose their identity because they both belong to the solar system. Liberty of action on the part of each soul is still retained; but before they are thus permanently united in a single five-dimensional form—as the two Fishes with their ribbon have a single form and yet each Fish has wide liberty of action—they must have come into a realization of their Cosmic work.

As an angel they perform the function in the cosmic scheme for which they have been specially educated by their experiences; and in this work they have complementary abilities. That is, each supplies certain talents, those of both together enabling them to do their Cosmic Work.

We may be sure, therefore, that those capable of uniting through the endless belt of finer energies that ultimately will provide the form of such an angel, will not have diverse or conflicting interests. Such divergent interests, through centering the mind strongly on different things, tends to disrupt or dissipate the endless belt of energy flowing between two people. Where the interests are, or an objective of attainment, in that direction the finer energies tend to flow. That is, the energies flow wherever the attention is directed. But when the interests of both are centered on the same things there is no dividing of the energy stream, and the forces of both flow along a single channel. This strengthens the bond between them.

The conditions which are most favorable, when the natural requirements are present, for strengthening the endless belt of finer energies between those who are deeply in love, are the desire to be as helpful and beneficial to all creatures as possible, having a common work by which this is chiefly accomplished, and the cultivation of tenderness and sympathy one for the other.

Neptune, the upper-octave planet ruling Pisces, is idealistic in his expression. Therefore, those who cultivate this highest expression of love on earth find it advantageous to idealize all they do. Whatever they do which they feel to be worthy, in the doing they keep the image of their loved one before them and feel that they are doing that thing, not because of duty, but for the sake of the other one. All that is accomplished is thus done for love. And the love motive becomes so powerful, under such cultivation, that hardships are not recognized as such, all life is filled with joy, and great accomplishment results.

The joy coincident with the establishment of the endless belt of love is only a small feature of its advantage; for its power to accomplish, working from the four-dimensional plane when loving and constructive thoughts are carried by it, is truly amazing. Herein lies a force which makes Faith, even of the size of a mustard seed, able to move mountains. The Sun is in the decanate pictured by the Fishes from February 20 to March 21. Its Key-phrase is, I Believe, and the text is: *Love is the Tree of Life, and its Fruit is Universal Brotherhood.*

The Two Keys of St. Peter

Cepheus signifies a rock, and the constellation in the sky designated by this name pictures the King of Ethiopia on his throne, with one foot upon the immovable Pole Star, representing Truth. Both Sagittarius and Pisces are dual signs, and both through Jupiter, which is the ruler of one and the co-ruler of the other, have some significance in matters of religion. Joseph, whose "Bow abode in strength," represents Sagittarius, the duality of which is symbolized by his coat of many colors. It is this coat which Cepheus, or Pharoah, whom Joseph served so well in the land of Egypt, still holds in one of his hands.

Pisces, the decanates of which are pictured by the king, queen and princess of Ethiopia, is the sign of imprisonment, deceit and secret enemies. It belongs to the dark half of the year. Joseph, representing the sign of dreams and prophecy, Sagittarius, told his dreams to his brethren, and these, in true 12th house fashion—for it is through its natural rule of the 12th house of a birth-chart that Pisces signifies these things—conspired secretly to destroy him. They took from him his coat of many colors, with which to deceive his father, and threw him into a pit, representing the sign Capricorn, lowest position of the Sun, into which this luminary moves immediately after it leaves Sagittarius.

Sagittarius is the sign of long journeys, hence Joseph when removed from the pit was taken to a far land. Pisces, through the 12th house, rules imprisonment and involuntary servitude; and not only was Joseph sold into slavery, but due to the perfidity and deception of Potiphar's wife, while in Egypt he was thrown into prison. And even, while still in Egypt, desiring to bestow a favor upon his brethren, he did it through deception. He concealed the money they paid him in the sacks of grain sold to them, and in addition concealed his cup in the sack of Benjamin, that he might have an excuse for detaining him.

The Pharoahs of Egypt were not only the rulers of this land of darkness, but they also were the religious potentates, some of whom had undergone initiation. It was the common thing for them to consult with their high priests, even as Pharoah called upon Joseph to give him council, in all important matters based upon conditions which would arise in the future. The priests who thus advised the ruler were versed in both astrology and in such divination as gained Joseph renown.

Peter, of New Testament mention, is a name which, like Cepheus, means rock. And it was upon a rock that Peter was commanded to found his church. In the sky this is, of course, the rock of ages, otherwise known as the Pole Star, which changeth not; the symbol of eternal Truth. Cepheus thus not only represents Pharoah, but in a later story pictures Peter, whose foot, or understanding—and Pisces rules the feet—must rest on Truth; and who holds the keys to hell and heaven.

These keys, by which Understanding of the Truth may be gained, are not pictured in Peter's hand, but adorn the crown placed on his head. They are shown as seven little spheres, representing the septenary of planets. They are placed on his head because the head is the region representing intellect; and it is the comprehension of the significance of these seven types of energy that opens the gate to an Understanding of Truth, which in turn permits entrance to the higher realms of being.

Peter, as shown in the sky, in addition to Joseph's coat of many colors which he grasps in one hand, also has an implement of power in the other. Understanding alone does not open the heavenly gates. That understanding must be applied in action. Therefore, he holds aloft a scepter, of a form symbolizing the virility and energy of the Sun, a symbol of the same import as the Common Gavel of Ancient Masonry.

Thus does this ruler of life and death, of the external world and the astral kingdoms which belong to the 12th house, indicate that he both knows the Truth, and that he applies that knowledge in appropriate action. The scepter of power indicates creative energy under control, and directed as the ruler wills. The control of energy such as the scepter represents indicates that scepter to be one symbol of the Tree of Life.

Joseph and Pharoah are not only linked, as types of Sagittarius and Pisces influences, in the Old Testament; but in addition to the Keys which Peter holds, the New Testament in Revelation mentions a Book of Seven Seals. Sagittarius, as natural ruler of the 9th house, the house of publishing, relates to books: and the seven seals are the impress which the seven planets make upon the Book of Nature. Yet this book, which rightfully belongs to Sagittarius and not to Pisces, when mentioned in Revelation is associated with the constellation Cepheus: "And I saw in the right hand of him that sat on the throne a book written within and on the backside, sealed with seven seals."

Cepheus, or Peter, pictures the Pisces-decanate of the sign which has rule over the astral plane and its denizens. Sagittarius is the sign of religion, seeing clearly and expressing benevolently. Pisces has a religious significance also; but it tends to rely on blind belief; for it is the sign of secret things and of self-undoing. It is because the denizens of the astral plane through the Pisces tendencies have been able to impress their ideas upon the human race, causing it to place Faith in those things which are to the advantage of these selfish astral entities, that the race during the Piscean Age was so bound and fettered by its religious misconceptions.

To state the matter in another way, the unseen enemies of mankind belong to the 12th house, ruled over by Pisces. Elementals and earth-bound discarnate human beings are close to the vibratory level of the earth, and are best able to contact it through the conditions represented by Pisces. Through the deception they are able to practice they can in some measure control the trend of human events, and themselves gain a satisfaction for their own desires. Obsession relates to this section of the zodiac, as do mystical manias and religious fanaticism; these being extreme expressions of the influence of such astral entities upon human life.

Pisces, however, is a dual sign; and in the higher expression of its attributes it founds its beliefs upon the very Rock of Truth. The astral plane holds entities which practice deception upon the people of the earth whenever they find those who are negative enough to be impressed. But it also, on its higher levels, provides a dwelling place for noble souls who have made extensive research on various planes of being. These, when opportunity offers, transmit facts they have learned to their neophytes upon the earth.

The knowledge and beliefs of those on earth are determined to a much greater extent than most realize by the influence of the invisible world. Not only do invisible entities impress their thoughts and desires upon those who unwittingly tune in upon their vibratory rates; but planetary energies stimulate thought-cells within the four-dimensional body of man, and these attract events and prompt to action. We can not say, as some Orientals do, that the physical world is maya, or illusion; for its energies also cause changes in the astral world; but we must acknowledge that most physical events and conditions trace their immediate cause to happenings on the astral plane.

We can not know the whole Truth if we ignore the physical world; but as the astral persists after the dissolution of the physical; as its sensations, experiences and scope are so much more vast than those of the physical; and as the immediate stimuli of physical movement are chiefly astral in origin; we can perceive the reason that prompted the ancients to place the constellation picturing Verity in that section of the zodiac which more than any other relates to the astral plane. The Sun is in this Pisces-decanate of Pisces from February 20 to March 1 each year.

Not only is the character of each life-form on the earth, that determines its destiny, embraced by the organization of its astral form; but the character so organized is that which persists beyond the dissolution of the physical. Man lives in his astral body, in fact, is chiefly an astral organization, while still in the flesh. And the same organization continues to live on the four-dimensional plane beyond the tomb. Real life and real death, therefore, such as Peter holds dominion over, relate to the four-dimensional plane which is more closely associated with Pisces than with any other sign.

Verity, which is the Key-word of the constellation, is an accurate comprehension of the facts and their relations to each other. Such recognition of Truth permits actions that make a successful adaption of the life-form to the conditions by which it finds itself surrounded. The keys which unlock the door of Truth also, therefore, unlock the doors of heaven and hell; for action based on falsehood and deception, such as one side of Pisces governs, leads to discord and destruction; while action based upon Verity, which the other side of Pisces governs, leads to harmony and eternal life.

Because all things in nature in their essential vibratory rates correspond to astrological influences, these astrological correspondences, such as are symbolized by the seven little globes in Peter's crown, are the Positive Key to that knowledge, which is essential to progress and to everlasting life. As a feminine complement to this positive key, to assist in unlocking the mysteries of the universe there is also a Receptive Key. This is embraced by the Tarot.

The golden key is the understanding of planetary law; for the character of each thing contacted is completely mapped by its astrological vibrations. The silver key is a duplicate of the one of gold, except that its action is feminine and passive, bearing the same relations to the latter that woman bears to man. In fact, the Tarot is to Astrology what the Moon is to the Sun. Astrology and the Tarot are known to initiates as the Two Keys. They are the Keys to Verity, the real keys for which Peter is renowned.

The text therefore is the Hermetic Axiom: *"As it is above so it is Below, and that which is Below is Like unto that which is Above."*

Prometheus Defies Convention

Paracelsus, according to all accounts, was the greatest physician of his day, performing cures where all the other doctors failed. Jesus offered harm to none except the cheating money-changers in the temple, healed the sick, and taught love and kindness. If one were less versed in the power of convention to bind all to old methods, and to persecute any who dare depart from what has been customary, it might be supposed that these great benefactors had been praised by their contemporaries. How Jesus fared need not be told; and Paracelsus was driven from place to place, his life constantly in danger from the members of his own profession, and was finally killed by ruffians believed to be in the pay of those whose outmoded methods of healing were less successful than his own.

On frequent occasions when machines have been introduced into some industry, those engaged in it have staged riots and broken the labor-saving devices. They believed that the machines would displace them; which was true if they were unwilling to learn how to handle the machines. A more successful method of healing also would take the livelihood from many members of the medical profession, as with less illness their services would no longer be needed; yet if they were progressive their energies could to advantage be turned into other equally valuable channels of human service.

It is almost impossible to advance any new method by which the human race can be benefited without this new method displacing the service, or at least affecting it, of some whose livelihoods depend upon it. And it is equally impossible to advance any new idea of importance by which the race can be benefited without it affecting the prestige of a large group of people who pose as authorities, or who hold some position of power which would be endangered if the new idea were to be generally accepted.

Progress is thus always gained only through conflict. In fact, progress consists of overcoming obstacles. And where human customs and human ideas are concerned the obstacles which cause the most acute conflict are prejudice and self-interest.

A thousand patents have been registered from successful models, and yet the labor-saving devices they represent, and the improvements in many lines which they could bring, lie dormant. These patents have been purchased by those who have money already invested in less useful things which would be displaced if better ones were placed upon the market. And to an even greater extent are ideals of high value to the human race suppressed by those with whose profits or prestige their adoption would interfere.

We need not think that the ridicule heaped upon Louis Pasteur when he advanced proof of the activities of bacteria in certain diseases, or the persecution of Galileo when he revealed the discoveries of his telescope, are new expressions of the antagonism of conservatives for those progressive. Even in a flock of birds, if one bird begins to act in an unprecedented manner the other birds become annoyed, and if the one departing from convention does not desist, the others birds set upon it, and either kill it or drive it from their midst.

Whether in that ancient time when the constellations first were given outline in the sky, or at the present day, if one were intrepid enough to break sharply with conventions, the least that could be expected was imprisonment. Throughout the ages those who have bestowed the greatest blessings on mankind have found themselves chained to the stone walls of dungeons. To depart too markedly from current practice or current belief, no matter how absurd it was, has always meant courting punishment.

Because such Self-Sacrifice has commonly been prompted by that sense of Universal Brotherhood which the higher side of Pisces promotes, and because Pisces, through its 12th house affinity relates to imprisonment and crime, the ancients placed Andromeda, the Chained Lady, in such a position as to picture the middle decanate of Pisces, where the Sun may be found each year from March 1 to March 11.

The Key-word of the decanate, Self-Sacrifice, is set forth in the universal symbolism not only of the story of Andromeda, but in that of Prometheus also. In the case of Andromeda the coast of her native land was being ravaged by the Sea-monster, Cetus. This was through no fault of the fair princess; but had been brought on by the arrogance of Cassiopeia, her mother.

Cassiopeia had incurred the wrath of Neptune, who was quite justified in resenting her claim to be more beautiful than the Nereides, nymphs of the sea; and Neptune, ruler of Pisces, had sent the Sea-monster to bring destruction to her land. Jupiter, planet of religion, was appealed to in an effort to save the country; and he decreed that only through offering her daughter as a sacrifice to the Sea-monster could Cassiopeia atone for her sin. Andromeda, therefore, not because she had transgressed, but to save her fellow countrymen from death, was chained to a wave-washed rock in the sea for Cetus to devour.

We who are interested in presenting The Religion of the Stars to the world, bringing, as it were, the fire from heaven that all may benefit thereby, find the story of Prometheus even more significant.

Prometheus, in the first place, was out of favor with the gods because he ridiculed some of their exaggerated pretensions. He was very much in the position of some of us who have actually traveled on the astral plane and had opportunity to observe the conditions there. He did not believe in the current ideas; no more than we believe the materialists who say that when the body disintegrates the soul exists no longer; nor the orthodox who say that a soul who transgresses must suffer eternal torment in hell and that heaven is devoid of useful occupation.

Those now who make actual demonstrations that the soul survives the dissolution of the physical body, and those who make actual demonstrations that the planets affect the life and destiny of man, are somewhat in peril of imprisonment. The materialist says the soul of man does not exist after the physical is gone, and can not come back. The orthodox says that it does exist somewhere. But if you stage a demonstration to prove that the so-called dead still persist and have recognizable personalities, you open yourself to persecution. A city ordinance—depending on the city—may demand that if you do, or if you help some unfortunate person through giving astrological advice, you must go to jail.

Prometheus, however, was not to be deterred through fear of gods or men from actions which he felt convinced would benefit the human race. Like the valiant souls of all ages who are responsible for the world's progress, he was willing to sacrifice his own interests if thereby mankind might be benefited. So, with the assistance of Minerva, he climbed the heavens and stole fire from the chariot of the Sun, and brought it down to earth, that man might have its use.

This so provoked Jupiter that he ordered Prometheus chained to a rock, even as Andromeda may now be seen chained, where a vulture was to feed on his liver. His liver thus consumed by day, grew again during the night, never entirely exhausted.

As the liver plays so significant a role in this story, it should be explained that the ancients as well as we moderns place this organ of the body under the rule of Jupiter, the planet which rules the 9th house in a natural birth-chart, and thus also religion and public expression. The liver of Prometheus, on which not the fearless eagle fed, but the carrion eating vultures who live from the profits of religious corruption, represents that priceless heritage which alone permits a healthy race; the freedom to publically express philosophical and religious convictions.

Both in ancient and in modern times the favorite method by which enemies of the public, such enemies as the 12th house rules, gain their ends and keep mankind in slavery to their own selfish advantage, has been to persecute the apostles of Truth, and to suppress the dissemination of correct information. It has been proclaimed that truth crushed to earth shall rise again. So also the liver of Prometheus, preyed upon by the human vultures who place a censorship on the dissemination of knowledge, and who purposely distort all information given to the public, grew again.

Those who attempt to enlighten the world always find it a painful process. Throughout the ages it has been the custom to imprison those who revealed the corruption of those in high places. The inquisition flourished to prevent facts being broadcast that would show the falsity of certain religious doctrines. Periodicals thrive chiefly upon their advertising, and an article or story which reveals some unpleasant truth about a product advertised in them can not get beyond the editorial desk. Radio stations commonly will not permit facts to be broadcast which tend to offend certain interests of power.

Yet Andromeda was not devoured by the Whale-monster. Instead she was rescued by Perseus, her Prince Charming, and had a happiness she could not have hoped for had she not endured Self-Sacrifice. And while Prometheus suffered for a time for gaining fire by which those of earth might live in greater comfort, he too eventually was released. Kind Chiron, representing the Higher Mind of Sagittarius, ruler of the 9th and of public expression, volunteered to take his place. And still later Hercules killed the vulture and he too was freed.

When the critical faculties of Hercules, picturing one decanate of Virgo, more widely are brought to bear upon the suppression and distortion of information, we may be sure that the vultures who misinform the public will no longer be tolerated. Furthermore, even while Andromeda and Prometheus were persecuted for their services to the public good they were being amply rewarded, as all who endure misfortune for the benefit of the human race are always rewarded, through building into themselves those qualities which ultimately would permit them far greater freedom in celestial realms than those could have who permitted injustice to thrive unmolested.

Thus does the text become: *He Who Sacrifices His Own Desires for the Welfare of Others Draws Down the Divine Fire from Heaven and With It Kindles the Highest Potencies of His Own Soul.*

The Cloak of Death or the Tree of Life

The last decanate of the zodiac, where the Sun may be found each year from March 11 to March 21, represents the end of the cycle of physical life. Among the constellations this point from which the transition is made to a new cycle is pictured by Cassiopeia, the Lady in the Chair, who with one hand removes the cloak which represents the physical body, and with the other holds aloft a branch from the Tree of Life.

Of all regions of the zodiac, the Scorpio-decanate of Pisces thus pictured has closest affinity with both the higher and the lower astral spheres in relation to the condition of existence immediately following physical death. It is here, as the soul leaves the physical body, symbolized by the removal of the cloak, that it experiences in full measure the effect of the astral circuit so well represented by the ribbon binding together the two Fishes of Pisces. This circuit, depending upon its quality and attachments, may become a shackle, such as that by which Andromeda is chained, or it may in truth become the Tree of Life, such as Cassiopeia holds.

The alternative revealed by this decanate, the Key-word of which is Vicissitudes, is well set forth in the stories relative to this woman. As one queen, her inordinate pride, selfish ambition and attachment to worldly honors caused her daughter, Andromeda, to be chained to the rock for Cetus to destroy. But in another story, she is the queen who furnished her two children, Helle and Phryxus, with the Ram of the Golden Fleece, which was to carry them from danger into safety.

The Bible also portrays this celestial constellation in alternate roles; in the Old Testament as Potiphar's wife, whose Scorpio desires, and secret enmity when her advances were repulsed, caused Joseph to be placed in prison; and in the New Testament by Mary Magdalene, out of whom went seven devils, and whom Jesus loved. John 11:5: "Now Jesus loved Martha, and her sister, and Lazarus."

When the Sun moves across the celestial equator at the time of the vernal equinox, at that moment it leaves the garment of winter darkness—that is, the longer nights than days—in the hands of Cassiopeia, marking the decanate from which it thus takes exit. This garment of winter symbolizes the physical body of man which is left behind when he passes to the next life. And this episode is still further explained by the cloak which Joseph left in the hands of Potiphar's wife when he fled her importunities.

As related in Genesis 38, Joseph had been given complete charge over Potiphar's affairs. He was in a position of trust and responsibility, and as nearly always happens to those who gain positions of power and influence, he was approached by one who used great pressure to influence him to betray that trust. Joseph might have lived now and had the same experience, so typical is it of present-day methods of disposing of one whose integrity becomes annoying to the corrupt who are in power; Genesis 12:

> And she caught him by his garment, saying, Lie with me: and he left his garment in her hand, and fled, and got him out. And it came to pass, when she saw that he had left his garment in her hand, and was fled forth, That she called unto the men of her house, and spake unto them, saying, See, he hath brought in an Hebrew unto us to mock us; he came in unto me to lie with me, and I cried with a loud voice: And it came to pass, when he heard that I lifted up my voice and cried, that he left his garment with me, and fled, and got him out.

When Joseph was placed in jail, due to the false charges of this woman of 12th house affinity it also suggests the circuit of energy pictured by Pisces by which those in love are bound into a single soul-mate system; and that if such a circuit is to result in greater freedom and power, rather than in greater bondage, it must have a vibratory rate which is uplifting and spiritual in quality, such as tender love and unselfish affection tend to generate. That is, if it is to provide the energy of the Tree of Life, rather than bind to lower astral regions, the circuit must raise the lovers to new heights of feeling, and stimulate new endeavors for the welfare of the race.

The circuit also can be formed between two people on a level that opens them to the influence of the lower astral plane. This results in the generation of great force; but the force so generated is confined in its effects to the things of a phenomenal nature, being unable to affect the finer substance of the higher astral spheres. That is, the ribbon of Pisces, unless generated by a fine and exalted type of love, tends toward imprisonment rather than to greater freedom. As is always true, that which can be used for good can also be used for evil. And this circuit, when built on a lower, coarser level, while giving great magical ability, tends in the direction of Death rather than in the direction of Life.

It then performs the same function as the circuit in a seance room when those present take hold of hands and sing. It generates a circuit of astral energy of great force, and also liberates etheric energy in volume. But the astral energy flow thus established, is of a vibratory rate corresponding to the elementals and other entities of the astral spheres closest to earth. These denizens of the realm signified by the house of self-undoing in a birth-chart, find such a circuit of energy of their own plane a stream that enables them to move into the astral bodies and in contact with the etheric energies, of those through whom the current flows. They are carried by the current wherever it goes, and as it goes through the bodies of those comprising the circle, they are able to bring their influence to bear directly upon the etheric energies and nervous systems of those thus contacted.

With a contact so fully established, either through a seance circle or through a circuit established between two lovers whose desires are on the level of those of Potiphar's wife, these 12th house astral entities are able to use both the etheric energies generated and the astral energies present, to bring things to pass on the physical plane. The energy may be used for healing, for influencing other persons to do as those on the circuit desire, for demonstrations of phenomena, or for the purpose of selfish magic.

On such a circuit, however, because it has affinity through its vibratory rate with lower astral entities, whenever the attention of those generating the energy is relaxed, this enables the denizens of the lower astral to take control and use the circuit for their own purposes, of which those from whom the energy is drawn have no knowledge.

Gradually, as the circuit continues, and gains strength, those who furnish the energy tend to lose control of it or even of its manufacture. The etheric component is felt by them racing through their nervous system. And its too great withdrawal from the vital reservoir of the body leaves them depleted and with an aching spleen. They still may direct it occasionally to some purpose of their own; but for the most part, even while they sleep, it is used by low astral entities to further their own ends in influencing the trend of thought and events on earth.

These 12th house entities, enemies of the human race, use the force thus placed at their command to impress upon sensitives wherever they can be contacted, ideas which tend to prevent an understanding of true spirituality, and which tend relentlessly to draw these sensitives into their power. And in time those who furnish the current, through having it constantly directed by the astral denizens to that end, lose all power to direct its flow, and are chained by it, and must do henceforth the bidding of their astral jailers.

Yet the same principle, a circuit of energy such as the ribbon of Pisces represents, when used upon a higher, unselfish plane, exalted by ecstatic feelings of tender love, instead of imprisoning, becomes the Tree of Life. It is true that on this more spiritual level it brings those on the circuit into contact with the intelligences of this higher region. But these are too wise and too unselfish to desire to use the energies thus made available to control either those on the circuit or to demonstrate amazing phenomena on the physical plane.

Thus it is that the circuit lifts or lowers those on it to the level of the after-life world corresponding to its vibratory rate. If that rate is low it brings intimate contact with low astral intelligences; but if that rate is high, it brings equally close contact with exalted intelligences of the higher astral planes. And these never take control. The information they impart is given merely as advice, with full liberty on the part of those receiving it to accept or reject.

Furthermore, when the energy of the circuit is that of an unselfish and spiritual love, in which all animal qualities and desires have been sublimated and true regeneration has taken place, it gives the ability not only here, but in the after life, to penetrate the higher spheres and to there enter upon the Cosmic Work.

It then becomes not such an influence as Mary Magdalene was under at first; for, according to St. Luke 8:22, she had at one time been possessed of seven devils; just such a condition as the lower circuit in connection with the 12th house influence tends to attract. But Mary Magdalene was loved by Jesus, who cast the devils out of her.

After this she became one of those who ministered to him at the cross, and who on going to the tomb which he had left, was told by the angel there to herald the resurrection to all the world. Instead of the devils which once she had had, having tuned in on a spiritual circuit in which unselfish love was dominant, she had partaken of the fruit of the Tree of Life.

Such a spiritual circuit, among other things, permits of passing to the next life in full consciousness. Thus the text with which the circle of constellations closes is: *Man May Pass from This Life to the Next, Even Through Death, With No Greater Break in His Affairs than Would be Occasioned by Leaving His Acquaintances in One City and Taking up His Activities in Another City Amid a Different Group of Friends.*

Study Questions

Chapter 1, **Our Spiritual Legacy**

1. What has enabled present-day man to possess mechanical contrivances superior to those of any people in the past?
2. What enabled certain peoples in the past to attain a spiritual wisdom superior to that which most people possess today?
3. What is the most ancient form of writing?
4. In what two ways can universal symbolism be employed to convey ideas?
5. For what purpose are pictures drawn and stories told by primitive people?
6. Why does the meaning conveyed by universal symbolism change but little with the passage of centuries?
7. From whence did the Stellar Wisdom probably reach the seven ancient centers of civilization?
8. Did the ancients use or commonly have need for, the minute precision which marks the work of the present-day laboratory scientists?
9. In what were the ancient wise men particularly interested?
10. Through what peoples did the constellated pictures reach us?
11. Did the ancients commonly recognize the earth to be round?
12. Why is the Vernal Equinox the best point to start both time and the east-west position of the heavenly bodies?
13. Are the constellations which picture the zodiacal signs each 30 degrees in extent?
14. How was it determined which pictured constellation portrayed the significance of a certain section of the zodiac?

15. What is a decanate, and how is its significance made known by a universal symbolism traced in the sky?
16. How many constellations do the old Greek sources show?
17. Why is the celestial longitude—the path of the sun—used to determine astrological positions rather than right ascension?
18. Do the outlines of the constellations suggest the pictures the ancients traced about them to portray the designated influence or spiritual teaching?
19. How is the correct succession of the ultra-zodiacal constellations ascertained?
20. In addition to indicating the influence of a particular section of the zodiac on human life, what other important idea did the ancients try to convey in the picture of each constellation?
21. Just what is the oral form of universal symbolism employed by primitive people to perpetuate ideas?
22. Where can this oral form of universal symbolism, for the purposes of studying the ideas of the ancients, now be found?
23. Why are moderns so ignorant of Stellar Wisdom?
24. What important factors were contained in the Aztec Swastika Calendar and the Aztec Triskelion Calendar?
25. Name some important features of the Arkansas Astrological Stone.

Chapter 2, **The Fountain of Youth**

1. The Sun is the source of what type of power?
2. Why were 7 full days allowed to pass before the Jewish boy was circumcised?
3. In what zodiacal sign are the cattle, Pharoah on his throne, and the captive in the dungeon, which are mentioned when the Lord smote the first-born in the Land of Egypt?
4. At the passover feast, why must the lamb be roasted?
5. When eaten at the passover feast, what do "bitter herbs" indicate?
6. Why was the feast of the passover to be attended with shoes on the feet, a staff in the hand, and why was it to be eaten in haste?
7. What was symbolized by the daubing of the blood of a lamb on the lintel and two side posts of the door to the house at the passover ceremony?
8. How does the passover have its counterpart in the precessional cycle?

Spiritual Astrology 285

9. What universal idea is suggested by the domestic triangle and represented by Triangulum?
10. What in modern science represents the heaven and the earth mentioned in the story of creation?
11. In terms of modern science, what did the Spirit of God moving on the waters represent?
12. In relation to food, why is light so important to human life?
13. In 1100 B.C., how did the Chinese determine the inclination of the earth to the ecliptic?
14. Why is triangulation so important?
15. What is the spiritual text for Triangulum?
16. What is the most characteristic factor common to enjoyment, love and the production and care of children?
17. The knowledge of what modern factor might have saved Ponce de Leon much travel in his search for the fountain of eternal youth?
18. What determines the plane or level to which the astral body moves after the dissolution of the physical?
19. What is signified by Phryxus reaching safety by being carried on the back of a ram?
20. What is signified by Helle becoming giddy and falling from the back of the Ram?
21. What does Goliath typify?
22. In reference to character building, what wisdom is represented by the dramatic legend of Medusa?
23. How can bad habits be cured?
24. What is the best way to escape an undesirable psychic influence?
25. How was Cassiopeia similar in character to many mothers of today?

Chapter 3, **Knights of King Arthur**

1. Why was it easy to interpret the significance of the kine and the ears of corn in Pharoah's dream?
2. Why were there two tablets of stone which Moses received, written with the finger of God, instead of one?
3. What is the significance of the Greek Tau and the English T?
4. Why was the golden calf which Aaron made a molten calf?
5. Why were the people called a stiffnecked people?

6. Why did divesting them of their earrings cause them to be naked?
7. What is meant by Moses causing the Israelites to drink of the ashes of the pulverized and burnt golden calf when he strewed these ashes on the water?
8. For what three things is a rabbit distinguished?
9. Why are eggs a persistent factor of the Easter celebration?
10. From what is the name Easter derived?
11. Why are Easter eggs colored in various hues?
12. Why are bunnies a persistent factor of the Easter celebration?
13. Why is a rabbit's foot used to ward off evil influences and bring luck?
14. What is probably the origin of having twelve jurymen in a panel, and why were there twelve knights in the story of King Arthur?
15. What are the three stars in Orion's belt called in the region of the Tigris and Euphrates; and by the Druids?
16. What two things did Orion, Sargon, Moses, Jason and King Arthur fight?
17. What caused the brawl at the yuletide feast of King Arthur?
18. In the King Arthur story, what is typified by the Bull pitching down upon him from the sky, and he ready with upraised club?
19. How did King Arthur solve the difficulty between his knights, and what psychological principle does this teach?
20. What does the story of Phaeton teach?
21. In the development of new forces, what is the one rule which is essential if Mastership is to be attained?
22. What was the feud between the 450 spurious prophets and Elijah?
23. Why was the altar which Elijah built composed of 12 stones?
24. How is true mastership shown?
25. By what token is a real Master known from a mere wonder-worker?

Chapter 4, Story of the Three Bears

1. How was the pence of the Good Samaritan marked?
2. What is the origin of the exclamation, "By Jiminy"?
3. Who were Damon and Pythias, and what was the bond between them?

4. How did they demonstrate the high moral quality of the Pythagorean order?
5. What did Pollux do when Castor was slain?
6. What is signified that only one of the two can be on earth at a time, the other remaining meanwhile confined in Pluto's dark realm?
7. In connection with the story of David and Jonathan what significance have the harp and the arrow held by one of the constellated twins?
8. Instead of three bears picturing the decanates of Gemini, what is used instead of the Middle-sized Bear?
9. What significance do the large feet of a bear have, and its habit of devouring everything presented that has possibilities as food?
10. What significance has the Indian legend of the spirit of the Pole Star?
11. Which of the three bears in the story represents Intuition, which represents Impulse and which represents Reason?
12. Why was the porridge of the Little Bear, in the Goldilocks story, just right?
13. When Goldilocks awakened in the Little Bear's bed, what was it that frightened her so that she jumped out of the window and ran home?
14. What star is the most brilliant of all the stars in the sky?
15. What are the amazing features of the companion star of Sirius?
16. Why was Sirius looked upon with such veneration by the Egyptians?
17. What marked the first of the month of Thoth, and how was it celebrated in ancient Egypt?
18. What is the origin of Dog Days?
19. What zodiacal position marks the place of the Titans and other giants?
20. What is the significance of the Tower of Babel, and of the mountains piled up by the Titans in their assault on heaven?
21. What is the significance of the confusion of tongues at Babel, and of the blood of the Titans giving rise to a race of ruthless men?
22. Who was Atlas, what was he compelled to do, and how many daughters did he have?
23. Why did Electra, of the Pleiades, wander to the Great Bear constellation to become the star Alcor?

24. What is signified by lighting of fires on pyramids, towers and eminences, in various parts of the ancient world?
25. What is the function of pleasure and pain?

Chapter 5, **The Ladder to Heaven**

1. What symbolizes the first of Cancer being the gate to heaven?
2. Where in the sky is Peter pictured, and what represents the gates to hell?
3. Astrologically, what was symbolized by the ladder in Jacob's dream?
4. What did the going up and coming down of the Sun each summer suggest?
5. What are the steps in soul progress revealed by Jacob's dream?
6. Toward what is every life form moving?
7. What is the spiritual text for the sign Cancer?
8. How can we see the power of the Sun start to diminish when it touches the Little Dog decanate?
9. In what way does Procyon, the Little Dog Star, announce the Savior of the Nile, Sirius?
10. Against what kind of transgressions did John, the great baptizer of Bible times, incessantly preach?
11. Through the influence of whom was Herod trapped into beheading John the Baptist?
12. What is the moral to the story of Old Dog Tray?
13. How does the Law of Affinity work in relation to ourselves?
14. Describe the apologetic person.
15. Describe the boastful person.
16. Describe the person who feels superior to others.
17. From what group of thought-cells do the above three maladjustments stem? And what planet maps them?
18. What is the spiritual text of the Hydra decanate of Cancer?
19. What evidence is there of a great inundation such as the sinking of Atlantis?
20. How many people, according to tradition, lost their lives in the sinking of Atlantis?
21. When reached by the equinoctial pointer, what two dividing lines in the zodiac relate to the times of greatest cataclysm?

Spiritual Astrology 289

22. How long is the precessional cycle?
23. In what year did the Equinox pass from Pisces back into Aquarius?
24. What occult conditions are reported to have occurred before both the flood of Noah and the sinking of Atlantis?
25. What lesson is imparted in the action of Noah when he first sent forth a raven and a dove to see if the earth was dry?

Chapter 6, **Is There A Santa Claus**

1. Why is the lion the universal symbol of desire?
2. What is signified by the young lion who roared against Samson?
3. What is the symbolical significance of honey?
4. What is signified by the conversion of the roaring lion into honey?
5. What is the astrological significance of the strength of Samson being in his hair?
6. What enabled Delilah to deprive Samson of his strength?
7. What is the spiritual text associated with Leo?
8. What is signified by those perishing who threw Shadrach Mesach and Abednego into the fiery furnace?
9. What is signified by these three walking about unhurt and with them a fourth, who appeared like the Son of God?
10. About how long ago was the equinox so situated as to indicate catastrophe to the earth by fire?
11. About when will the equinox again be so situated as to indicate catastrophe by fire?
12. How is it possible to like certain activities which in the past have been disagreeable?
13. What is the most successful way of defeating the pull of forbidden desire?
14. In what manner is the picture of the middle-decanate of Leo related to the picture of the sign Sagittarius?
15. What represents the chimney in the zodiac, and why?
16. Is there any mention of a Christmas tree or Santa Claus in the Bible?
17. Why does Santa Claus have whiskers?
18. Why is the traditional garb of Santa Claus red edged with white?
19. What is the significance of kissing under the mistletoe at yuletide?

20. What is the chief point about a crow which can be admired?
21. What is the significance of Corvus in the act of tearing a piece of flesh from the back of Hydra?
22. What was the nature of the news imparted by Corvus to Apollo; and did it bring benefit to anyone?
23. What is the unconscious motive of those who delight in gossip?
24. What is the effect of gossip on the character of the one who indulges in it?
25. For what purpose chiefly do people go to movies or read fiction?

Chapter 7, Why Eve Was Tempted

1. What sign represents the Garden of Eden, and why?
2. What is meant when Genesis relates that Adam and Eve heard the voice of the Lord God walking in the garden in the cool of the day?
3. Where in the sky is the Tree of Knowledge of Good and Evil located?
4. Why did Eve decide that the Tree of Knowledge was good for food?
5. What is the price that always must be paid for knowledge?
6. What is meant when the Bible states, "and the Lord God said, Behold the man is become as one of us, to know good and evil?"
7. What is the significance of the immaculate conception?
8. Why, in the light of modern astronomical knowledge, is Job's question, "Canst thou guide Arcturus with his sons?" so significant?
9. Why is it appropriate that servants and the marriage feast should be associated, as related in St. John's account of the first miracle?
10. What constellation pictures the decanate where water each autumn is converted into wine?
11. In what manner is the decanate thus pictured closely allied to stone?
12. Why were there six water pots of stone, in which water was converted into wine, instead of some other number?
13. What was the clew of thread furnished Theseus by Ariadne which enabled him to find his way from the labyrinth after slaying the Minotaur?
14. Why should Hercules have a constellation of so vast extent?

15. Just what was the nature of the work which Hercules undertook and accomplished in his twelve great labors?
16. What is the relation between the best quality and the worst quality of each sign, and how can this relation be turned to advantage?
17. Why is Monday the most appropriate day of the week on which to celebrate Labor Day?
18. Why is it appropriate that Labor Day should be celebrated when the Sun is in the Saturn-decanate of Virgo?
19. What is the significance of the paired foxes united by a firebrand, with which Samson destroyed the crops of the Philistines?
20. Why should the influence of tribulations be pictured in connection with the last decanate of Virgo?
21. Why are there twelve spikes on the Crown picturing tribulations?
22. Where does the Sun die each year, and how is this place related to the Northern Crown?
23. What was Job's attitude when his property and children were taken from him?
24. What is the psychological significance of the quotation from Job, "For the thing which I greatly feared is come upon me, and that which I was afraid of is come unto me"?
25. For what purpose, as Job learned, do people suffer affliction?

Chapter 8, **The Marriage in Heaven**

1. Why are the Scales a most fitting universal symbol of marriage?
2. What point in the zodiac marks the place where summer signs and winter signs are married?
3. What is the significance of Rosh-ha-Shannah, and when according to Leviticus 24, should it be observed?
4. In the most famous trial in the whole of human history what was the significance of the child of one woman being alive and the child of the other woman dead?
5. When Solomon called for a sword to decide the contention between the two women, in what way did he represent zodiacal relations to the sign of judgment?
6. Upon what universal doctrine did Solomon rely when deciding the true mother of the child?
7. In what way do the seven more days of light than of darkness

indicate the relation of good to evil?
What is symbolized by the following:
8. The spiral loop near the head of Serpens which lifts the head well above the body?
9. The loop near the tail of Serpens which gives the tail supremacy?
10. From whence did the doctrine of the serpent fire have its origin, and how are such practices related to the fiery serpents of the time of Moses?
11. What does the manna which fell from heaven, and on which the Israelites fed, symbolize?
12. What is represented by the brazen serpent which Moses raised upon a pole to cure those who had fallen into the serpent fire practices?
13. What is the significance of the feathered serpent of the Maya?
14. From the name of which planet is the word Satan derived?
15. What are the two points, or nodes, where the orbit of the Moon cuts the apparent orbit of the Sun, called?
16. What relation to these points, or nodes, have eclipses?
17. What is symbolized by the Dragon?
18. To symbolize what phenomenon in the sky does the Hopi snake dancer hold a snake in his mouth as he dances?
19. Why should Yom Kippur be observed when the Sun enters the Draco-decanate of Libra?
20. What qualities did the ancients wish to express when they traced a wolf in the sky?
21. What is the zodiacal significance of the Bible quotation: "Beware of false prophets, which come to you in sheep's clothing, but inwardly are ravening wolves"?
What is symbolized by the following:
22. The deep voice of Red Ridinghood's wolf?
23. The bright eyes of Red Ridinghood's wolf?
24. The big ears of Red Ridinghood's wolf?
25. The great teeth of Red Ridinghood's wolf?

Chapter 9, **The Scorpion and the Eagle**

1. Why does the scorpion so fittingly symbolize the intensity, power, cruelty and vileness of the destructive side of sex?

Spiritual Astrology

2. To what extent is all energy dependent upon that which broadly may be considered as expression of sex?
3. In what way are religion and art dependent upon the love impulse?
4. Why is the eagle considered as a symbol of highest spirituality?
5. How did the Mound Builders who left the Arkansas Astrological Stone symbolize the creative energy?
6. Why are the ceremonies of the Hopi Indians, in which the Thunderbird takes part, held in an underground kiva?
7. Upon what depends whether the creative energies of Scorpio will carry its user on the back of the Eagle into spiritual realms or will sink him in the mire of grossness and dissipation?
8. What is symbolized by the struggle between Ophiuchus and the serpent?
9. In what way does the thigh of Ophiuchus, which is out of joint, identify him with Jacob?
10. What relation is there between the thigh and the eagle pic-turing one decanate of the religious sign Sagittarius?
11. What is symbolized by the thigh being out of joint?
12. Why is the urge for reproduction so insistent a drive in every surviving form of life?
13. What is signified by the blessing received by Jacob when he was successful in his struggle?
14. Why is the Pisces-decanate of Scorpio the most fitting section of the zodiac to be pictured by the Altar?
15. What two regions of the invisible world does Pluto govern?
16. What is symbolized by the custom of hanging May Baskets?
17. For what kind of magic did Balak employ Balaam?
18. Indicate how the Aztec Priests of Darkness, when they gained supremacy, made human sacrifice popular?
19. Why was the sacrifice offered by Abel more acceptable than the one offered by Cain?
20. With what kind of a crown did the ancient Greeks mark the victor in the Pythian games?
21. Why, in Revelation 2:10, does it mention that before the crown of life is gained there will be tribulations 10 days?
22. What is the significance of Peter's admonition to feed the flock of God, and that as a result a crown of glory would be received?
23. What has the sublimation of the energies of Scorpio to do with

attaining the Universal Laurel Crown?
24. Why should one who seeks the Crown of Life make himself as familiar as possible with all the occult forces of nature?
25. What pattern of life must be held by anyone who is to be successful in attaining the Crown of Adeptship?

Chapter 10, **The Bow of Bright Promise**

1. Why is the Bow, as representing Sagittarius, a symbol of protection from danger?
2. Why is the horseshoe a symbol of good luck?
3. What is the distinction between the terms soul, mind and character?
4. Are there really two minds, as might be inferred from speaking of the Higher Mind and Lower Mind?
5. How did Chiron well express the Higher Mind which Sagittarius rules?
6. How did Eurytion, another Sagittarian, exemplify by his conduct the Animal Soul signified by the horse side of the dual sign?
7. How did Jezebel, when Jehu entered the city, exhibit the sporting side of Sagittarius; and how did the horseman, expressing the higher side of the sign, respond to her advances?
8. What zodiacal association is precedent for mentioning together streets of gold, the Great White Throne, and the harp on which angels play?
9. Pluto as ruler of the sign of sex, on the Eagle side relates to what kind of marriage?
10. What is the significance of Mercury furnishing the famous Harp on which Orpheus could play so sweetly?
11. What is implied through symbolism as the cause of Orpheus losing his beloved mate?
12. What was the power which enabled Orpheus to find Euridice in the realms of Pluto?
13. What is signified by the method applied by David to soothe the troubled spirit of Saul?
14. What is signified by the story that Aquila, when Jupiter was hiding from the fury of his father, brought him nectar to satisfy his hunger?

15. How does sex move from Scorpio in the house of death over into the house of religion?
16. What is symbolized by Jove's cup of wine and the goblet which carried the oriental soma juice?
17. In addition to Desire, what also is most essential to accomplishment?
18. Why is the image making power of the mind so important?
19. Why in sleep does the mind so commonly engage in fantasies rather than realities?
20. What does the arrow, Sagitta, symbolize?
21. What relation to the zodiac has Sagitta to the Giant Bear which also represents the Cyclops?
22. What do thunderbolts, which the Cyclops forged in Vulcan's workshop, symbolize?
23. What today represents the single eye of the Cyclopes?
24. What is the relation between Illumination and the arrow shot from Dan Cupid's bow?
25. What is illumination?

Chapter 11, **News From the Summerland**

1. Why are the days on which the solstices occur more easily ascertained than the days of the equinoxes?
2. How did Eratosthenes, from the top of the library building at Alexandria, determine the inclination of the ecliptic to the earth's equator?
3. What is the origin of the three golden balls displayed by pawnbrokers as the emblem of their trade?
4. From what event and what constellation is derived the word Panic?
5. What actions of Jacob identify him with the sign Capricorn when its worst quality is manifest?
6. What types of people at the present day represent the Jacobs and the Esaus, and how are they separated in the zodiac?
7. What is the prophecy regarding the ultimate fate of Esau?
8. What constellation pictures the decanate of the zodiac in which popular tradition holds Jesus was born?
9. Why, according to Luke, must John the Baptist have been born in

the sign Cancer?
10. What is signified astronomically by John's prophecy that; "He must increase, but I must decrease?
11. In what way are Swans related symbolically to those who dwell in the next life?
12. What manner of flight common to migrating swans suggests the Key-word of the first decanate of Capricorn?
13. In the after-life, if an individual's desires are higher than the plane on which he normally functions, in what way will he be affected?
14. What point in the zodiac represents the tomb, and why?
15. By what other name, and relating to the tomb, is the Dolphin Constellation in the sky called?
16. In the legends concerning it, what mission does the Dolphin always perform?
17. What is the moral of the Greek legend of the Dolphin and Hesiod?
18. What is the true way of repentance, either here or hereafter?
19. What is the symbolical significance of the Greek legend in which the Dolphin persuades the goddess who has taken a vow of perpetual celibacy to unite with Neptune?
20. What are the four Royal stars by which the ancient Sumerians plotted the sky as a great rectangle?
21. What is the teaching symbolically set forth in the story of Venus and Typhon as applying to escaping from selfishness?
22. What is the teaching thus set forth as to the most effective manner of counteracting the undesirable influence of any planet?
23. What were the three methods advocated by the ancients by which planetary energies could be brought under control?
24. What is the significance of Peter catching a fish which held a piece of money in its mouth of sufficent value to pay the taxes?
25. To bring things from the unconscious, what bond of association is necessary?

Chapter 12, **In the Reign of Aquarius**

1. What is the significance of the 24 hour gauge held in the left hand of Aquarius?
2. What is the significance of the water which Aquarius, with his right hand, pours down upon the earth?

Spiritual Astrology

3. How many major motions is the earth known to have?
4. Has the precession of the equinoxes, by which the equinox makes its Great Cycle in 25,868 years, anything to do with the movement of the Sun, along with other suns, around a center?
5. How many degrees of the zodiac are always covered by each sign, and in what way do the constellations picturing the signs differ from each other in this respect?
6. Close to what star does the First of Aries among the constellations probably lie?
7. Upon what astrological fact is based the belief that man must make tremendous advances in invention, psychology, electricity and the study of the stars early in the Aquarian Age?
8. What two things are immediately suggested by a horse?
9. What is the significance of Horse Sense?
10. Why is it so common to find educators believing astrology is an "exploded" science?
11. How does the Horse Sense of the layman tend to discredit the educator's claim that astrology is an "exploded science"?
12. How does the academic upholder of conventional tradition make use of the readings given by ten-cent advertisers as evidence that astrology is false?
13. Just what does a progressed aspect indicate?
14. What is signified by the wings with which Pegasus is equipped?
15. According to tradition, from what did Pegasus spring?
16. What is the significance of the spring of Hippocrene, from which all poets must drink if they are to attract the Muse?
17. What is the significance of Neptune giving Pegasus to Bellerophone to aid him in conquering the Chimaera?
18. Why does the unconscious mind commonly prefer to use the language of feeling?
19. Through what process can the unconscious mind be trained to impart whatever information it possesses, or can acquire, to the objective consciousness?
20. Why was a denizen of the water selected to symbolize the force or pinciple which is most inimical to life?
21. Which is the largest of the constellations, and what does it symbolize?
22. Why was Cetus placed in the sky where it would picture the marriage-decanate of the sign Aquarius?

23. What is symbolized by the ship on which Jonah embarked to escape that which God had called upon him to do?
24. What is represented by the three days during which Jonah remained within the belly of the Sea-monster?
25. What is represented by Andromeda being saved by her own Prince Charming, Perseus, from the destructive influence of Cetus?

Chapter 13, **The Tree of Life**

1. Is information alone, no matter how comprehensive, sufficient to attain everlasting life?
2. In what sign, according to the first principles of astrology which reveal that Polar Opposites always occupy opposite stations in the zodiac, must the Tree of Life be located?
3. What is represented by the ribbon which binds the two Fishes of Pisces into an indissoluble union?
4. What is the significance of the legend that Venus and Cupid, to escape Saturn, leaped into the water and transformed themselves into the two fishes of Pisces?
5. To maintain the ribbon of spiritual potentiality how must the affections of those thus united expand?
6. What is represented by the knot where the ribbons uniting the two Fishes are tied?
7. In what way do those who cultivate the highest expression of love on earth find it advantageous to idealize all they do?
8. What does the name Cepheus signify?
9. To whom does the coat which Cepheus, or Pharoah, holds in his hand belong?
10. What is the astrological significance of Joseph, even when benefiting his brethren, doing it through deception?
11. Where are the keys of Peter to heaven and hell pictured in the sky?
12. In addition to understanding, the symbol of what is held aloft in the hand of Cepheus to indicate his ability to open the heavenly gates?
13. What is meant by the Book of Seven Seals mentioned in Revelation, and why is it associated with Cepheus?

Spiritual Astrology

14. Why is it so difficult to get any new method by which the human race can be benefited accepted?
15. What commonly has happened, in all ages, to those who broke too sharply with conventions?
16. Why was it most appropriate to place the constellation picturing a heroic effort to benefit humanity so it would represent one of the decanates of Pisces?
17. Why was Prometheus, even before he stole the fire, out of favor with the gods, and how does this represent some who now make actual demonstrations of unpopular truths?
18. What is represented by the vulture which daily fed upon the liver of Prometheus while he was chained to the rock?
19. What is signified by the vulture finally being killed by Hercules?
20. By what constellation is pictured the last decanate of the zodiac from which the Sun annually passes to commence a new cycle of life?
21. What two Greek stories indicate the alternative— the shackle which binds, or the Tree of Life— associated with the last decanate of Pisces?
22. What two stories from the Bible relate to the alternatives associated with the last decanate of Pisces?
23. If the circuit between two people who are in love is to provide the energy of the Tree of Life, rather than to bind to lower astral regions, what must be its nature?
24. How do the 12th house entities, enemies of the human race, use such energies as they can contact to prevent people from acquiring an understanding of true spirituality?
25. Do the exalted intelligences of the higher astral plane ever take control or make demands?

Index

Aaron, molten calf and, 47
Abednego, 115
Abel, altar of, 186-190
Achilles, Chiron and, 201
Actaeon, 97
Action
   desires and, 228
   stimulants for, 253
Adam and Eve, 133, 134, 135, 146
Adeptship, crown of, 190-194, 205
Aerials, 251
Aesculapius, Chiron and, 201
Affections
   marriage and, 233
   transfer of, 232
Ahab, 96
Akhenaten, 14
Alcor, 81
Alcyone, 81
Aldebaren, 234
Alexandrian Library, 14, 221, 222
Alpha Arietis, 245
Amphitrite, 231
Andromeda, 25, 34, 39, 167, 201, 259, 276, 278
   Cetus and, 257
   illustration of, 263
   Perseus and, 277
   Pisces and, 275
   Self-Sacrifice and, 275
Animal Soul, 201
Antares, 234
Anu Enlil Series, 9
Apis, 45
Apollo, 185, 213
   raven and, 125-126
Aquarian Age, 26-27, 244, 245, 246
   Knowledge and, 247

Aquarius, 18, 26, 103, 104, 116, 118, 139, 243, 244, 252
   illustration of, 239
   influence of, 246, 247
   Knowledge of, 246
   urn of, 234, 238
Aquila, 208, 212
   illustration of, 197
Ara, 186, 189
   illustration of, 175
Arcturus, 137-138
Arges, 212
Argo, 106
   illustration of, 88
Ariadne, thread from, 137-141
Aries, 7, 8, 10, 11, 24-25, 27, 32, 34-37, 47, 50, 158, 180, 188, 257, 266
   First of, 244-245
   illustration of, 19
Arion, Dolphins and, 233
Aristotle, scholasticism and, 7
Arkansas Astrological Stone, 14, 15, 178, 179
Arrow, Cyclopes and, 212-216
Arthur, King: knights of, 53-57
Assurbanipal, library of, 51
Astarte, 49
Asterope, 81
Astral body, 34, 194, 228, 233, 253-254, 258
   discords within, 259
   energies within, 250-251
   map of, 249
   senses of, 215
   thought-cells and, 193
Astral energy, 235, 267, 280
Astral plane, 38, 194, 227, 229, 233
Astral travel, 210, 255

Astrolabe, 31
Astrological Lore of All Ages (Benjamine), 14
Astrology
　Aztec, 15
　condemnation of, 248-249
　knowledge of, 247
　natal, 12
　popularity of, 248-249
　practical, 35
　Tarot and, 273
Astrology of the Aztecs, 14
Astronomy, 6, 8
Atlantis, 4, 5, 45, 52, 103, 105, 106, 162
　sinking of, 50, 51, 104
Atlas, 81, 83
Atonement, 167
Auriga, 58, 59, 61
　illustration of, 44
Autumnal Equinox, 146, 156, 158
Avesta, 45
Aztec Calendar Stone, 15
Aztecs, 222
　summer solstice and, 82

Bacchus, orgies of, 205
Balaam, Balak and, 187
Bel, temples of, 82-83
Bellerophon, 252
Benjamine, Elbert, 14
Big Bear, 71, 73
Birth-chart, 93, 94, 114, 248, 249-250, 280
　Constants, 258, 259
　fraudulent, 249
　map of, 250
　rectifying, 245
Book of Nature, 271
Book of Seven Seals, 271
Bootes, 137, 138, 139, 141
　illustration of, 130
Bow, 199-200
Bowman. *See* Sagittarius
Braggarts, 98
Brahma, Vishnu and Siva, 31
British Museum, 116
Brontes, 212
Bull of Marathon, 139

Cain, altar of, 186-190
Cancer, 89-91, 93, 94, 101, 103, 116, 118, 121, 122, 125, 202, 212, 225, 244
　illustration of, 85

Ship in, 104
　tropic of, 31
Canis Major, 78
　illustration of, 65
Canis Minor, 94
　illustration of, 86
Capricorn, 11, 25, 61, 103, 116, 118, 121, 122, 202, 224, 225, 229, 234, 270
　deceitfulness of, 223
　diplomacy and, 222-223
　ideals of, 237-238
　illustration of, 217
　tropic of, 31
Cassiopeia, 11, 25, 34, 39, 257, 278, 279
　illustration of, 264
　Neptune and, 275
Castor, 69, 70, 71, 200
Celibacy, 231, 232
Centaurs, 121, 202
Centaurus, 119, 120, 122, 123, 171
　illustration of, 109
Century of Progress Exposition (Chicago), 137-138
Cepheus, 25, 89, 269, 270, 271
　illustration of, 262
Cetus (Sea-monster), 39, 256, 275, 278
　Andromeda and, 257
　discord and, 257
　illustration of, 242
Chaldeans, 49
　Anu Enlil Series of, 9
　constellations and, 6, 7, 8-9
Character, 75-76, 238
Charon, 32
Chimaera, 252
Chiron, 201, 277
Christmas, Santa Claus and, 121
Church of Light Quarterly, The, 14
Clairaudience/Clairvoyance, 75, 215
Clavigero, Triskelion Calendar and, 15
Cleaeno, 81
Cloak of Life, 278-282
Coelus, 212
Colchis, 34
Colure, 158, 202
Common Gavel of Ancient Masonry, 271
Common good, serving, 194, 227-228
Companionship, types of, 125
Consciousness, 91, 137
　higher states of, 193
　leaving, 233

objective/subjective, 200, 237, 255
    See also Unconscious mind
Constellations, 30, 119
    chart, ix (figure)
    development of, 6-9
    relationships of, 9-12
Conversion, using, 236
Copernicus, scholasticism and, 7
Corona, Ischys and, 126
Corona Australis, 190
    illustration of, 176
Corona Borealis, 147, 148
    illustration of, 132
Coronis, Apollo and, 125
Corvus, 124, 125
    illustration of, 110
Cosmic rays, 29
Cosmic Work, 268, 281
    contributing to, 191-192
Crater, 104, 118, 121, 122, 208
    illustration of, 108
Creation, trinity and, 31
Creative energy, 160, 178-179, 184-185, 189
Critas, 103
Criticism, constructive/destructive, 144, 145
Cro-Magnon Man, 4, 5
Cromlechs, 18, 60
Crow, 126
    carrion for, 127-128
    habits/characters of, 123-124
Crown of Adeptship, 190-194, 205
Crown of Life, 193
Cupid, 214
    Pisces Fishes and, 267
    Typhon and, 266-267
Cyclopes, 256
    Arrow and, 212-216
Cygnus, 226
    illustration of, 218

Damon, Pythias and, 67-71
Daniel, 111, 115, 116
Darkness, 159
    symbolism of, 155
Dates, setting, 117-118
David, 36, 37, 70, 71
    Harp and, 206, 207
    Jonathan and, 68
Death, 189, 193, 280
    Discord and, 258
    house of, 208
    Pluto and, 188

sign of, 190
Thunderbird and, 180
Delilah, Samson and, 114
Delphinus, 234
    illustration of, 219
De Montufar, Alonso: Aztec Astrology Stone and, 15
Desire, 181, 208
    action and, 228
Devotional exercises, value of, 207
Diana, 97
Dionysius, 68, 69
Discord, 257
    Death and, 258
    determining, 256
    mapping, 250, 259
    mental, 267
    preventing, 260
    universal symbol of, 256
Divine Plan, 191, 203
    understanding, 192-193
Dolphin
    Neptune and, 232-233
    rescue by, 229-234
Domestic triangle, 28, 34
Donelly, Ignatius, 4
Draco, 163-164, 167
    illustration of, 153
Dragon
    battle with, 163-168
    death of, 166
    symbolism of, 167
Dragon's Head/Tail, 164, 165, 166
Duran, Diego, 15

Eagle, 181, 186, 189
    heaven trip of, 207-212
    Sagittarius and, 208
    Scorpio and, 178-179
    sex influence and, 209, 210
    symbolism of, 178
Earth, movement of, 243-244
Easter, 46, 50
Ego, 268
    Soul and, 167
Einstein, Albert, 1
Electra, 81-82
Elijah, 70, 125
    mantle of, 58-62
Elisha, 214
Elysian gates, 48, 91
Emotional expressions, 181, 232
    marriage and, 260
Endocrinology, 33

Eoster, 49
Ephraimites, 35
Equinox, 23, 104
   movement of, 243, 244
   See also Autumnal Equinox; Vernal Equinox
Equuleus, 25, 247, 251
   illustration of, 240
Eratosthenes, 7, 221, 222
Eridanus, 32, 34, 35, 36, 45, 51, 58
   illustration of, 21
Esau
   Jacob and, 221-225
   Sagittarius and, 223
Etesian winds, 77-78
Etheric energies, 34, 59, 280
Euclid, 2
Euridice, 203
   Orpheus and, 204, 205
Eurytion, 202
Evidence, geological/biological/ethnological, 4
Evolutionary progress, parenthood and, 90
Exodus, 25, 46

Father, Son and Holy Ghost, 31
Feathered serpent, 162, 163
Feelings, 91
   attention for, 254-255
Folsom people, 5
Foot, symbolism of, 52-53
Formalhaut, 234
Fountain of Eternal Youth, 31-36
Four-dimensional plane, 227-229, 250, 251, 269, 272, 273
Furies, Harp and, 204

Galileo, criticism of, 274
Ganymede, 208
Garden of Eden, 133-137
Gemini, 67, 71, 75, 80, 89, 91, 200-202, 212
   illustration of, 63
Genesis, 80, 89, 104, 133, 134, 182, 188, 190, 223, 265, 279
George, 163, 165
Giant Bear, 80, 81, 93, 212
Gileadites, 35
Gilgamesh, 51, 59
Goat, 222-223, 224
Golden Calf, 45-49, 54
Golden Fleece, 53, 105, 278
Goldilocks, 73, 74

Goliath, 36, 37, 256
Gomorrah, 51, 52, 116
Good Samaritan, pence of, 67
Gorgon Medusa, 36, 38, 39, 252
Grave Digger of Caravans, 180
Great Bear, 73, 74, 81, 82, 84, 137
Great Cycle, 104, 243
Great Dog Star, 94, 212
Great Initiate of the Maya, 14
Great Pyramid of Egypt, cosmic knowledge and, 5
Great Spirit, 72, 199
Great White Throne, 203

Halloween, 13, 50
Harmony
   determining, 256
   domestic, 93
   Life and, 258
   mapping, 250
Harp, 203-207
Helle, 34, 35, 278
Hercules, 27, 101, 111, 122, 148, 243, 277
   Chiron and, 201
   illustration of, 131
   Tree of Good and Evil and, 265
   twelve labors of, 141-146
Herod, 95, 96, 135, 136
Herodias, 95, 97
Hesiod, Dolphins and, 230
Heye Foundation, 117
Higher Mind, 200, 202, 204
   Divine Plan and, 203
   dominance of, 201
   Eagle and, 209
   sign of, 199
Hipparchus, 7, 10, 30
History of Atlantis, The (Spence), 4
"History of the Indians of New Spain" (Duran), 15
Hitler, Adolf, 16
Holy Ghost, 136
Hopi Indians
   ceremonies of, 179
   Dragon and, 166
   lightning and, 179
   passover and, 23
   snake dance of, 166
   Sun ceremony of, 214
Horse Head, 247, 251
Horse Sense, 247-251
Horseshoe, luck of, 199-203
Hydra, 93, 98-99, 101, 125

Spiritual Astrology

illustration of, 87
Hydrophobia, 78-79

Illumination, 212, 215, 216
Imagination, using, 210
Impressions, attention for, 254-255
Impulse, 73-75
Inca, 116
Individuality, importance of, 101
Inner plane, 227, 233, 237, 238, 268
Insanity, 55
Inspiration, 252, 255-256
Intellect, 80
    language of, 254
Intuition, 73, 74, 75, 83
Invisible energies, gauging/
    determining, 193
Iolaus, 101
Isaac, Jacob and, 224
Ischys, Corona and, 126
Ishtar, 49, 51
Isis, 31, 136
Ixion, 205
    Harp and, 204

Jacob, 89, 90, 187, 204
    Capricorn and, 223
    dream of, 92
    Esau and, 221-225
    Ophiuchus and, 181-185
Jamieson, Alexander: atlas by, 10-11
Jason, 54, 105
    Chiron and, 201
Jaw of the Ox, 45
Jealousy, 189
Jehu, 202
Jesus, 147, 158, 222, 225, 226, 278
    Mary Magdalene and, 281
    persecution of, 273-274
    spiritual teaching by, 138-139
Jewish Encyclopedia, quotation
    from, 156
Jews, 25
    Autumnal Equinox and, 156
    passover and, 23
    Stellar Wisdom and, 24
Jezebel, 59, 96, 202
Joash, Syrians and, 214
Job, 137
    Satan and, 148-149
    travails of, 256-260
    triumph of, 146-150
Job's Coffin, 230
John, 138, 147, 226, 278

John the Baptist, 94-95, 225
Jonah, Discord and, 257
Jonathan, 68, 70, 71
Joseph, 45, 269, 270, 271, 278
    Potiphar's wife and, 279
Jove, 58, 69, 80, 208, 209
    Eagle and, 207
Judges, 35
Judgment day, 155-159
Juno, 39, 180
Jupiter, 120, 121, 190, 199, 208
    colure and, 224
    discords and, 236
    Prometheus and, 276

Keys to Verity, 273
King of Ephyre, 252
King of Ethiopia, 269
Kings, 202, 214
    First, 59, 125
    Second, 96
Knowledge, 193
    ancient, 1
    Aquarian religion and, 247
    astronomical, 1, 2-3, 5-6
    spiritual, 5
Krishna, 163
Kundalini, 35, 59

Labor-saving devices, breaking, 274
Lamb, 25
    passover and, 26
Laocoon, 185
Laurel Crown, 190-194
    attaining, 191-192, 205
Law of Affinity, 33, 97
Law of Correspondences, 6
Legacy
    recording, 2-4
    source of, 4-5
Legions of Darkness, 192
Lemuria. *See* Mu
Leo, 17, 32, 103, 112, 113, 115-116, 118-
    120, 122-124, 208
    Crater in, 104
    illustration of, 107
Lepus, 50, 51
    illustration of, 42
Leucippus, 69
Levites, 48
Leviticus, 156
Libra, 50, 75, 133, 138, 146, 147, 158,
    159, 164, 166, 181
    scales of, 156

Life, 280
    Harmony and, 258
Light, 30
    symbolism of, 155
Lion, 111-112
Little Bear, 71-75, 81
Little Dipper, 72
Little Dog Star, 94
Little Red Ridinghood, 168-172
Liver, role of, 276-277
Lost Pleiad, 81
Lot, 52, 53, 116, 118
    wife of, 205
Love, 206, 213, 265, 267, 281
    acquiring, 235, 269
    honest, 127
    importance of, 159
    religion and, 178
    Wisdom and, 214
Love life, evolutionary stages of, 232-233
Lower Mind, 200, 201, 212
Luke, 225, 281
Lunar Eclipse, 165
Lupus, 168, 171
    illustration of, 154
Lyra, 203, 212, 243
    illustration of, 196

Machines, breaking, 274
Maia, 81
Marriage, 160, 162, 163, 231
    affectional expression and, 233
    regenerate, 232, 233
    universal symbol of, 155
Mars, 268
Mary Magdalene, 278, 281
Mathematics, development of, 6
Matthew, 89, 168, 237
Maya, 57, 116
    books by, 102-103
    love principle and, 162
    summer solstice and, 82
Maypole, 13, 57, 58
Mazzaroth, 137
Medeus, Chiron and, 201
Mediumship, irresponsible, 194
Medusa, 37, 38, 39
Melville, Henry, 11
Mental Antidotes, using, 236
Mental images, building, 211
Mercury, 36, 49
    antidote for, 236
    Harp and, 204
    as mental antidote, 236
Merope, 81
Mesach, 115
Mexican National Museum, Aztec Calendar Stone at, 15
Michal, 70
Middle Sized Bear, 73
Milky Way System, movement of, 243-244
Minerva, 37, 276
Minos, 139, 140
Minotaur, 138, 139, 140
Mitchell-Hedges, M. A., 116, 117
Mithra, 222
Montezuma, 136
Moon, 143
    Domestic Urges and, 169
    Father/Mother principle and, 160
    Full, 160, 165
    Inconstant, 93
    movement of, 244
    New, 160, 165, 167
    Nodes of, 164
    orbit of, 164
Moon goddess, 165, 166
Moral cowardice, 113-115
Moses, 46, 47, 48, 54, 113, 162
    serpent fire and, 161
Mother Bear, 74
Mother Earth, 136
Mound Builders, 17, 82, 179
Mu, 4, 5, 45, 103, 162
Muse, Pegasus and, 252
Museum of the American Indian, 116, 117
Mystical manias, 272
Myths, 3, 13

Narcissus stage, 232
Natural selection, energy production and, 209
Nautical Almanac, 9, 10
Neanderthal Man, 4
Nebuchadnezzar, 115, 116
Nectar, Venus and, 209
Neptune, 39, 231-232, 266, 267
    Cassiopeia and, 275
    Cetus and, 257
    Dolphin and, 232-233
    dramatic ability and, 252
    as mental antidote, 236
    Pisces and, 269
    sacrifice to, 185
Nereides, 39, 275

Newcomb, Simon, 137
Newton, Isaac, 1
Noah, 50, 51, 104, 105, 116, 199
   dove and, 124
Northern Crown, 148
North Star, 81
Numbers, 161, 187

Objective Mind, 73
Obsession, 272
Occult laws, 194
Oedipus stage, 232
Old Dog Tray, 96
Old Testament, Sagittarius/Pisces
   influences in, 271
Ophiuchus, 50, 204
   illustration of, 174
   Jacob and, 181-185
Orion, 46, 54-58, 180
   illustration of, 43
Orisis, Isis and Horus, 31
Orpheus, 203, 206
   Euridice and, 204, 205
   Harp and, 204-205

Pain, action and, 253
Pan, legend of, 223
Panic, 223
Paracelsus, persecution of, 273-274
Parenthood
   benefits of, 92-93
   evolutionary progress and, 90
Passover, ancient/modern, 23-27
Pasteur, Louis: criticism of, 274
Paul, 183, 184
Pawnbrokers, 222
Pegasus, 25, 251-256
   illustration of, 241
Periander, 233
Periodicals, persecution by, 277
Perseus, 27, 36-40, 49, 158, 258
   Andromeda and, 277
   Gorgon Medusa and, 252
   illustration of, 22
Peter, 89, 236, 237
   First, 191
   keys of, 269-273
Phaethon, 58, 59, 62, 180
Pharoah, 45, 271
Philip, 95
Philistines, 144
Phoebus, 58
Phryxus, 34, 278
Physical environment, impact of, 211

Pictographs, 3, 4, 8, 11, 24, 28-29, 58
   interpretation of, 12
Piscean Age, 39, 246
Pisces, 25, 26, 34, 104, 118, 122, 186,
   201, 244, 245, 270, 271-273, 279,
   280
   Andromeda and, 275
   Belief of, 246
   Fishes of, 266-269, 278
   illustration of, 261
   Jonah and, 257
   Jupiter and, 269
   Neptune and, 269
   in Old Testament, 271
   ribbon of, 281
   Rock of Truth and, 272
   Universal Brotherhood and, 275
   Virgo and, 265, 266
Pisces Australis, 234, 238
   illustration of, 220
Planetary influences, 246-247
   counteracting, 235-236
Plato, Timaeus and Critas of, 103
Pleasure
   action and, 253
   forbidden, 119
Pleiades, 50, 81, 82, 103, 104, 118
   blindness and, 52
Pleione, 81
Pluto, 38, 39, 70, 179, 189-191, 194,
   203, 209, 210
   Death and, 188
   Harp and, 204
   influence of, 188
   Orpheus and, 205
   Saul and, 206
   Semites and, 187
   wickedness and, 186
Poets, 190
   Pegasus and, 252
Polar Opposites, 265
Pole of the Ecliptic, 10
Pole Star, 7, 10, 72, 73, 75, 89, 101,
   164, 269, 270
Pollux, 69, 70, 71, 200
Ponce de Leon, Juan: fountain of
   youth and, 33
Posidonius and Chaldea, 14
Positive Key, 273
Potentialities, spiritual, 267
Potiphar's wife, 270, 278, 280
   Joseph and, 279
Power Urges, 99, 100
Prayer, value of, 207

Precessional cycle, 104, 243
Priests of Darkness, 190
    human sacrifice and, 188
Priests of the Shadow, 187-188
Prime Meridian, 7, 9, 10
Problem of Lemuria, The (Spence), 4
Procyon, 94
Progress
    conflict and, 274
    evolutionary, 90
Progressed Constant, 259
Prometheus, 201, 273-274
    Jupiter and, 276
    persecution of, 275-277
    Self-Sacrifice and, 275
Psychometry, 215
Ptolemy, 10, 14, 52
Pythagorean sect, 69
    Stellar Wisdom and, 68
Pythias, Damon and, 67-71

Queen of Spades, 136
Quetzalcoatl, 136

Rabbit's foot, luck from, 49-53
Radio stations, persecution by, 277
Rainbow Bridge, 199
Rally Forces, using, 236
Ram, 168, 190
Raven, 125-126
    carrion for, 127-128
    habits/characters of, 123-124
Reason, 73-75, 80-83, 212-215, 253
Rebekah, Jacob/Esau and, 224
Receptive Key, 273
Regulus, 234
Religion, 20
    Eagle and, 209
    house of, 208
    love and, 178
    significance of, 246
Religion of the Stars, 247, 275
    Constellation Chart, x (figure)
    stone monuments for, 16-18
Repentance, true way of, 231
Reproduction, urge for, 183-184, 260
Research, 105
Restitution, making, 230-231
Revelation, 71, 146-147, 164, 180, 191
Rig-Veda, Eagle and, 208
Rock of Truth, 272
Romulus and Remus, 67
Rosh-ha-Shanah, 156, 167
Royal Stars, 234

Sacrifices, 185, 188, 190
Sagitta, 213
    Illumination and, 212
    illustration of, 198
    Wisdom and, 214
Sagittarius, 36, 119-122, 178, 186, 190, 202, 203, 206, 214, 223, 244, 270
    as dual sign, 210
    Eagle and, 208
    Higher Mind and, 201, 212, 277
    illustration of, 195
    Jupiter and, 269
    luck with, 200
    in Old Testament, 271
    Religion and, 183, 199, 212
    sex energy and, 182
Samson, 143
    Delilah and, 114
    foxes and, 144, 145
    moral weakness of, 113-114
    riddle of, 113
    troubles of, 111-112
    Virgo and, 142
Samuel, 206
    Second, 71-72
Santa Claus, 119-123
Sargon, 46, 53, 54
Satan
    Job and, 148-149
    Saturn and, 164
Saturn, 120, 141, 208, 223, 229, 266
    colure and, 224
    Egyptian portrayal of, 234
    influence of, 235, 236
    as mental antidote, 236
    planetary vibrations of, 235
    Satan and, 164
    self-seeking influence of, 209
    thought-vibrations of, 235
    Venus and, 235
    vibratory rate of, 236
Saul, 70
    obsessions of, 206, 207
Scales, 155-158
    symbolism of, 159
Science, 29
    material, 1
    significance of, 246
    symbolism of, 138
Scorpio, 18, 50, 180, 181, 190, 192, 194, 203
    Eagle and, 178-179
    energy, 209
    as Great Deceiver, 186

illustration of, 173
jealousy and, 189
sacrifice and, 188
Scorpion, 59, 203
   Pluto and, 205
   Sagittarius and, 199
   wings for, 177-181
Seance circle, 280
Self-criticism, destructive, 145
Self-culture, 145
Self-esteem, 182, 184
Selfishness, 246, 256, 267-268
   escaping, 235
Self-Sacrifice, 275, 277
Semites, Pluto and, 187
Serpens, 159, 163, 181
   illustration of, 152
Serpent, 160-161
   feathered, 162, 163
   symbolism of, 160-161, 162
Serpent fire, wisdom and, 159-163
Seven Sisters, 81-82
Sex influence, 180-182, 184, 209
   diverting, 185
   maladjustment in, 183
   spiritual, 210
Shadrach, 115, 116, 118
Sheep, 168
   symbolism of, 189
Sirius, 77-78, 94
Snake. See Serpent
Snake dance, 166
Sodom, 50, 51, 52, 116
Solar Eclipse, 165
Solar-Lunar energies, 160
Solomon
   judgment by, 157
   Scales and, 158
Solon, 103
Soma juice, 208
Sothic period, 77
Soul
   awareness of, 135
   Ego and, 167
   evolutionary ladder of, 90
   knowledge of, 2
   unaware, 135
Soul-mates, 210, 268, 279
Southern Crown, 190, 191
Southern Fish, 235-238
Spence, Lewis: books by, 4
Spherical geometry, science of, 30
Spirit of God, 30, 32
Spiritual Alchemy, 149

Spiritual attributes, 48, 163
Spiritual channels, 209, 282
Spiritual development, 47, 61, 90-91,
   159, 163, 201, 267
Spiritual doctrines, 15, 17
Spiritual form, 79, 93
Spirituality, 188, 207
   attaining, 61, 178, 190, 192
Spiritual nutrition, 161, 162
Spiritual powers, 162
Spiritual teaching, 27, 138-139
   perpetuating, 12-13
Stellar lines, 251
Stellar Religion, 14, 17
   love principle and, 162
Stellar Wisdom, 133
   ignorance of, 13-16
   Jews and, 24
   Pythagorean sect and, 68
   spread of, 5-6
Steropes, 212
Stone monuments, 16-18
Suicide, 205
Summerland, news from, 225-229
Summer solstice, 82, 222, 256
Sun
   Father/Mother principle and, 160
   journey of, 120-121
   movement of, 243, 244
   symbolism of, 185
Sun ceremony, 214
Sun god, triumph of, 166
Superiority, 98, 99-101
Swan, 225, 226, 229
Swastika, 15, 17
Symbols
   attention for, 254-255
   language of, 35
Sysyphus, Harp and, 204

Tantalus, Harp and, 204
Tarot, astrology and, 273
Taucross, 46
Taurus, 8, 17, 45-47, 49-51, 53, 54, 57,
   58, 60, 61, 70, 139
   golden calf and, 48
   illustration of, 41
Taygeta, 81
Terra, 212
Theseus, thread for, 137-141
Thinking, 91
   understanding, 254
Thoth (Mercury), 77
Thought-cells, 33, 56, 71, 91, 92, 96,

97, 100, 137, 227, 228, 235, 236, 250, 251, 272
  formation of, 193
Thought-energy, 144, 145, 227
  marriage and, 260
Thought-structures, 149, 259
Thunderbird, 179, 208, 209, 212, 214
  Death and, 180
Thunderbolts, 207, 212, 213
Timaeus, 103
Titans, 79-81, 256
Tower of Babel, 82
Tree of Life, 265, 271, 278-282
Tree of the Knowledge of Good and Evil, 265
Triangle, drama of, 27-31
Triangulum, 31, 36
  illustration of, 20
Trigonometry, science of, 30
Trinity, importance of, 31
Triskelion Calendar, 15-16
Tro-Cortesianus, 102
True Mastership, 60-61
Truth, 83, 89, 101, 164, 269, 273, 277
Twins, 67-71, 206
Typhon
  encountering, 223, 266-267
  escaping, 235
  selfishness and, 267
  Venus and, 234-238

Unconscious Mind, 73, 74, 75, 101, 127, 144, 145, 182, 184, 253-254
  communication with, 255
  language of, 254
  symbolism and, 254
  tapping, 254-255
  See also Consciousness
Understanding, 270, 271
Universal Brotherhood, 275
Universal symbolism, 3, 4, 12, 13, 15, 24-28, 32, 39, 47-48, 120, 141, 142, 155, 161, 164, 178, 266
Uranus
  astrology and, 247
  as mental antidote, 236
Ursa Major, illustration of, 66
Ursa Minor, illustration of, 64

Vedas, 45

Venus, 47-48, 112, 158, 161, 162, 231, 268
  love life and, 232
  Nectar and, 209
  Pisces Fishes and, 267
  Saturn and, 235
  Typhon and, 234-238, 266-267
  vibratory rate of, 236
Veritas (Melville), 11
Verity, 272, 273
Vernal Equinox, 7, 10, 24-26, 30, 103, 104, 116, 118, 158, 279
  movement of, 244, 245
Veytia, 15
Vibratory rates, 33, 34, 39, 162, 178, 193, 207, 215, 231, 272, 273, 281
Virgin Mother, 122, 135
Virgo, 34, 45, 122, 133, 134, 136, 139-142, 144, 146, 157-159, 244, 277
  Garden of Eden and, 265
  illustration of, 129
  Pisces and, 265, 266
  scientific progress and, 138
  Tree of Good and Evil and, 265
Virility, symbolism of, 185
Visual images, building, 211
Vitality, symbolism of, 185

Water-holes, depicting, 3
Waterman, 103
Winter solstice, 222, 223
Wisdom, 213, 265
  Love and, 214
  serpent fire and, 159-163
  See also Stellar Wisdom
Wise Men of the East, 54
Wolf, 169-172
  universal symbol of, 168

Yom Kippur, 156, 167

Zodiac, 120
  chart, ix (figure)
  constellations and, 9-12
  development of, 8-9
  Knight Errant of, 36-40
  pictograph of, 8
  signs of, 55, 142-143
  stellar wisdom and, 13
Zodiacal Longitude, 10, 11-12

Other Brotherhood of Light Books _____

The following pages present brief descriptions of the 21 Brotherhood of Light courses, written by C. C. Zain. The information contained therein represents the ancient wisdom of the Hermetic Tradition, transmitted orally in earlier ages only to initiates of The Brotherhood of Light. It was the life's work of Elbert Benjamine, under the pen name of C. C. Zain, to present this complete system of esoteric knowledge in an organized format, available for the first time to the public.

CS. 1, Laws of Occultism
Inner Plane Theory and the Fundamentals of Psychic Phenomena

$16.95   6x9   192pp

The word "occult" means hidden or unseen. *The Laws of Occultism* is the study of unseen energies and the subjugation of these energies, insofar as we are able, to human control. There are in existence undeviating natural laws that are yet unexplained by physical science. In this course various types of psychic phenomena are examined and explained. The nature of the inner plane and how it affects human life and activities is revealed.

1. Occult Data **2.** Astral Substance **3.** Astral Vibrations **4.** Doctrine of Nativities **5.** Doctrine of Mediumship **6.** Spiritism **7.** Phenomenal Spiritism

---

CS. 2, Astrological Signatures
Evolution of the Soul and the Nature of Astrological Energies

$16.95   6x9   256pp

This is our best book for those beginning their study of astrology. The Signs of the Zodiac, the Planets, the Mundane Houses and the Aspects are all discussed in detail. The philosophy of "The Religion of the Stars" concerning the nature of the soul, how it makes progress and why the experiences of life are necessary to prepare it for a higher destiny is presented. Of special interest are the chapters concerning the facts and fancies of reincarnation and the ancient ritual of Egyptian Initiation.

1. The Two Keys **2.** The Zodiac **3.** Mundane Houses **4.** The Mission of the Soul **5.** Physiology and Correspondence **6.** Doctrine of Signatures **7.** Facts and Fancies About Reincarnation I **8.** Facts and Fancies About Reincarnation II **9.** The Ritual of Egyptian Initiation

---

CS. 3, Spiritual Alchemy
The Hermetic Art of Spiritual Transformation

$16.95   6x9   128pp

The ancient alchemist sought transmutation and immortality. For the soul to be immortal it must build for itself an imperishable spiritual body in which it can function after the dissolution of both the physical and astral forms. The experiences of life are symbolized by the metals of alchemy. Through proper mental attitude we purify the metals, develop our character and create our destiny. The various states of consciousness available to man are set forth and analyzed.

1. Doctrine of Spiritual Alchemy **2.** Seven Spiritual Metals **3.** Purifying the Metals **4.** Transmutation **5.** Higher Consciousness

CS. 4, Ancient Masonry

The Spiritual Meaning of Masonic Degrees, Rituals and Symbols

$16.95   6x9   336pp

In this course the rituals and symbols of Ancient Masonry are revealed. For the modern Freemason this is an unprecedented work enabling him to perceive the esoteric and spiritual significance of the symbols and all things done in the lodge room. The astrological significance of the symbols and their relationship to soul-development are thoroughly discussed.

    1. Ancient Masonry Introduction **2.** Entered Apprentice and the Planets **3.** Entered Apprentice and the Signs **4.** Numbers and Opening the Lodge **5.** Initiating a Member **6.** Fellowcraft **7.** Lodge Emblems **8.** Master Mason **9.** Mark Master Mason **10.** Royal Arch **11.** Degrees of the Cross **12.** Ineffable Degrees **13.** Historical Degrees

---

CS. 5, Esoteric Psychology

Success Through Directed Thinking and Induced Emotion

$16.95   6x9   320pp

Of all the energies that influence man none have a more powerful effect than his own thoughts. Directing one's thinking is the most potent of all forces to control one's life and destiny. Commonly, our efforts to exercise control are hindered due to faulty conceptions or repressions that result from environmental conditioning. Whether this conditioning expresses in a subtle way or in one that is more obvious, the consequence is a thwart to progress. Esoteric Psychology contains information which will assist in identifying and eliminating these obstacles to progress.

    1. Doctrine of Esoteric Psychology **2.** Reason and Intuition **3.** Language and the Value of Dreams **4.** Desire and How to Use It **5.** Why Repression is Not Morality **6.** How to Rule the Stars **7.** How to Apply Suggestion **8.** Correct Use of Affirmations **9.** How to Think Constructively **10.** How to Cultivate Subliminal Thinking **11.** How to Develop Creative Imagination **12.** How to Demonstrate Success

---

CS. 6, Sacred Tarot

The Art of Card Reading and the Underlying Spiritual Science

$16.95   6x9   336pp

The Sacred Tarot is a favorite of metaphysical students everywhere and companion to the *Brotherhood of Light Egyptian Tarot Cards*. With this book, the student can readily determine the astrological correspondence of any number, name, color, gem or other object. In this course the "Religion of the Stars" system of numerology is set forth and divination by means of numbers is explained. It is also considered to be one of the most complete, detailed syntheses of the Tarot archetypes as they manifest spiritual truths in different areas of occult science. Each of the 78 cards is explained and 11 tarot card spreads are illustrated.

    1. Doctrine of Kabalism **2.** Foundation of the Science **3.** Scope and Use of Tarot **4.** Involution and Evolution of Numbers **5.** Reading the Meaning of Numbers **6.** Making an Astrological Chart of a Name **7.** Influence of Changing the Name **8.** Reading Names in Detail **9.** The Color of a Name **10.** Natural Talismans and Artificial Charms **11.** Chronology of the Tarot **12.** Solution of Ancient Cycles **13.** How to Read the Tarot

CS. 7, Spiritual Astrology
The Origins of Astro-Mythology and Stellar Religion

$16.95   6x9   352pp

This course describes the outstanding attributes of those born under the influence of each of the 48 ancient constellations. Also revealed are the specific spiritual doctrines associated with each of the constellations. These spiritual doctrines, formulated by the most wise of prehistoric times, later found their way into ancient mythology, the Bible and other sacred writings. Course VII sets forth the most significant of these stories associated with these doctrines and reveals their true meaning.

1. Our Spiritual Legacy 2. The Fountain of Youth 3. Knights of King Arthur 4. Story of the Three Bears 5. The Ladder to Heaven 6. Is There a Santa Claus 7. Why Eve Was Tempted 8. The Marriage in Heaven 9. The Scorpion and the Eagle 10. The Bow of Bright Promise 11. News From the Summerland 12. In the Reign of Aquarius 13. The Tree of Life

---

CS. 8, Horary Astrology
How to Erect and Judge a Horoscope

$16.95   6x9   224pp

This course is often chosen by beginning students of astrology for its technical lesson, "How to Erect a Horoscope", as well as for its clearly organized system for judging any horoscope. More advanced students refer to this volume for horary chart interpretation. The section on horary astrology is of special interest for its explanation of how and why this branch of astrology can solve a problem relating to events past, present and future. Also included for beginning students are CC Zain's chart erection short-cuts, for which he designed the Church of Light #2 Chartpad.

1. How to Erect a Horoscope 2. Strength and Aspects of the Planets 3. First Seven Steps in Judging Any Horoscope 4. The Doctrine of Horary Astrology 5. Questions Relating to First Six Houses 6. Questions Relating to Last Six Houses 7. How to Select the Best Time for any Undertaking 8. Chart Erection Short Cuts and Examples

---

CS. 9, Mental Alchemy
How Thoughts and Feelings Shape Our Lives

$16.95   6x9   224pp

The astrological energies mapped by a birthchart are not the cause of the conditions and events that come into one's life. It is the character of the individual that determines our destiny. Character is composed of thought cells built and organized on the inner plane. Course IX explains how these thought cell groups, which constitute man's unconscious mind, have been formed before his birth, and how they are modified after birth by experience. Of importance is an explanation of how these thought cells can and should be reconditioned to work for the things the individual desires.

1. The Inner Nature of Poverty, Failure and Disease 2. Just How to Find the Thought-Cause of Any Condition 3. How to Find a Mental Antidote 4. How to Apply a Mental Antidote 5. Just How to Heal Yourself 6. Just How to Attain Realization 7. Just How to Give Absent Treatments

CS. 10-1, Natal Astrology, Part One

Delineating the Horoscope

$16.95   6x9   224pp

As the Lessons on astrology emphasize, much is to be gained through a diligent application of the rules when interpreting a horoscope. In a step-by-step fashion, Delineating the Horoscope presents the Hermetic system of natal astrology along with the unsurpassed "Outline of a Complete Astrological Reading." Beginning and advanced students will enjoy the explanations of the 36 decanates, illustrated with examples of renowned persons having Sun, Moon or Ascendant in that decanate.

1. First Eighteen Decanates Analyzed **2.** Last Eighteen Decanates Analyzed **3.** Stature, Temperament, Disposition and Mental Ability **4.** Vitality, Health and Disease **5.** Business, Finances and Vocational Selection **6.** Friends, Enemies and Associates **7.** Love, Marriage and Partnership **8.** How to Delineate a Horoscope

---

CS. 10-2, Natal Astrology, Part Two

Progressing the Horoscope

$16.95   6x9   224pp

A technical manual on the Hermetic system of major and minor progressions. The progressed aspects of natal astrology reveal probable future events through indicating the manner in which an individual's thought-cells will work to attract events. With this information the individual can learn to take precautionary actions by reconditioning the energy so that a more desirable outcome can be achieved. To round out the study of natal astrology, a lesson on the Hermetic system of rectifying the horoscope is included for use in erecting a birthchart when the exact birth time is unknown.

1. Hermetic System of Progressions **2.** Major Progressions of Sun and Angles **3.** Major Progressions of the Moon **4.** Major Progressions of the Planets **5.** Minor Progressions of the Sun and Angles **6.** Minor Progressions of the Moon and Planets **7.** Transits, Revolutions and Cycles **8.** Rectifying the Horoscope

---

CS. 11, Divination & Character Reading

Tools and Techniques for Enhancing ESP

$16.95   6x9   192pp

Divination is a means for assisting extension of consciousness on the inner plane to acquire the information desired. It is then brought up into the region of objective consciousness. Clairvoyance, precognition, telepathy, the divining rod, teacup and coffee cup methods, among others, are discussed in detail. The last four lessons are devoted to learning to read character based on physical characteristics.

1. Doctrine of Divination **2.** Tea-cup and Coffee-cup Divination **3.** Divining Rod and Other Divination **4.** Instantaneous Character Reading **5.** Significance of Body and Head **6.** Instantaneous Reading from Profile **7.** Instantaneous Vocational Analysis

CS. 12-1, Natural Alchemy, Part One
Evolution of Life

$16.95   6x9   224pp

We live in kinship with all life forms, animate and inanimate. For man to understand his place in nature, and thus what his relation should be to other life-forms, to other people, and to God, he needs to know how the various life-forms, including man, have developed to the state they now occupy. Cs. XII-1 offers the unique interpretation of the Religion of the Stars on how natural selection and adaptation is influenced by psychokinesis, ESP and inner-plane influence.

1. Origin of the Earth **2.** Origin and Development of Plants **3.** Progress of Invertebrate Life **4.** Fishes and Amphibians **5.** Reptiles and Birds **6.** Development Among Mammals **7.** Development of Man **8.** Development of Knowledge

---

CS. 12-2, Natural Alchemy, Part Two
Evolution of Religion

$16.95   6x9   224pp

This course deals with the evolution of those ideas which constitute man's various religions. Cs. XII-2 begins with the most primitive religions and shows how these, and the cultures coincident with them, gradually developed into the more complex systems of belief of today. The tenets of each important present day religion are explained, and finally there is set forth the basic tenets of the Religion of the Stars.

1. The Foundations of Religion **2.** Early Religions of the World **3.** Religion in Historic Times **4.** Tao, Confucianism, Zoroastrianism and Mohammedanism **5.** Hinduism and Buddhism **6.** Judaism and Christianity **7.** The Stellarian Religion **8.** Astrology is Religion's Road Map

---

CS. 13, Mundane Astrology
Interpreting Astrological Phenomena for Cities, Nations and Groups

$16.95   5X7   272pp

Astrological energies influence the trend of world events. When a natal chart isn't available, these influences can be determined through the mundane cycle charts of nations, cities, groups, etc. This course is one of the few technical manuals on the erection of mundane cycle charts and their delineation. Such information is valuable because it enables one to take precautionary actions and arrange personal affairs to take most advantage of city, national or world conditions. It also helps one to foresee conditions and thus exert political influence in support of those measures which insure peace and give people freedom from want, freedom from fear, freedom of expression and freedom of religion.

1. Doctrine of Mundane Astrology **2.** Cycles of Pluto and Neptune **3.** Cycles of Uranus **4.** Cycles of Saturn **5.** Cycles of Jupiter **6.** Cycles of Mars **7.** Major Conjunctions of the Planets **8.** Cycles of the Sun **9.** Cycles of the Moon **10.** Precise Predicting: Eclipses

CS. 14, Occultism Applied

How to Increase Your Happiness, Usefulness and Spirituality

$16.95   6x9   320pp

Just how to use occult knowledge and occult energies in everyday life is considered in detail in Course XIV. It shows us that each soul is being trained for its own cosmic work and has its own kind of job to do in God's Great Evolutionary Plan, pointing out the advantage of living the completely constructive life. To gain the things we desire from life usually requires that some of our habit systems be changed. Changing habits is not easy, but the three fundamental principles given in Cs. XIV will give the quickest and surest success.

1. Finding One's Cosmic Work **2.** Living the Completely Constructive Life **3.** Diet and Breathing **4.** How to Keep Young **5.** How to Be Attractive **6.** How to Have Friends **7.** How to Get Employment **8.** How to Make Money **9.** How to Achieve Honors **10.** How to Be Successful in Marriage **11.** How to Have a Pleasant Home **12.** How to Be Happy

---

CS. 15, Weather Predicting

The Hermetic System of Astrological Weather Analysis

$16.95   6x9   192pp

Astrological energies have a profound influence over the weather conditions of earth. They indicate changes from the normal of a given locality in temperature, moisture and wind, quite precisely. This is particularly useful information for those involved in agriculture, aviation, travel or planning a social event. It is an aspect of the science that should not be neglected by anyone seeking a complete, working knowledge of astrology. *Weather Predicting* is a complete treatment of the subject and the only text available entirely devoted to astrological influences on the weather.

1. Astrological Weather Predicting **2.** Reading Astrological Weather Charts **3.** Astrological Temperature Charts **4.** Astrological Air Movement Charts **5.** Astrological Moisture Charts **6.** Unusual Weather **7.** Tornadoes and Hurricanes

---

CS. 16, Stellar Healing

Astrological Predisposition, Diagnosis and Treatment of Disease

$16.95   6x9   320pp

Health is a valuable asset. The positions of the planets in the birthchart indicate the diseases toward which an individual is predisposed. *Stellar Healing* gives the birthchart and progressed constants of 160 diseases. It also sets forth what is probably the most effective of all methods of drugless healing, and indicates the specific Stellar Treatment. In addition, it shows how to calculate in terms of ASTRODYNES, HARMODYNES and DISCORDYNES the precise power and harmony of any planet, aspect, sign or house. ASTRODYNES are the unsurpassed mathematical formula for the measurement of astrological power.

1. Stellar Anatomy **2.** Basis of Stellar Diagnosis **3.** Principles of Stellar Healing **4.** Technique of Stellar Healing **5.** Stellar Healing in Practice **6.** Diagnosis and Treatment **7.** Abdominal Troubles - Bleeding **8.** Blindness - Coronary Thrombosis **9.** Cyst - Hay Fever **10.** Headache - Mumps **11.** Nervous Breakdown - Scarlet Fever **12.** Sciatica - Yellow Fever

CS. 17, Cosmic Alchemy

The Spiritual Guide to Universal Progression

$16.95   6x9   256pp

Man is not an isolated unit. Instead he is a member of world society, and should be an energetic worker in the realization of God's Great Evolutionary Plan. This course indicates how each person can become active in achieving the realization of this plan. In this progress there will be no more wars, poverty will be abolished, educational facilities and the widest access to information should be available to all. Cs. XVII shows exactly what spirituality is and the three general methods of gaining it; 1. viewing events from the standpoint of spiritual alchemy, 2. cultivating thoughts, feelings and actions that arise from the desire to benefit others, and 3. raising the vibratory rate through a heightened intellectual and emotional appreciation.

1. Conquest of War 2. Abolition of Poverty 3. Cosmic Politics 4. Heredity and Environment 5. How to Be Spiritual 6. Spiritual Value of Education 7. How to Appraise Spiritual Values 8. Minor Aids to Spiritual Advancements 9. Major Aids to Spiritual Advancements

CS. 18, Imponderable Forces

The Wholesome Pathway

$16.95   6x9   192pp

Cs. XVIII explains how much reliance should be placed on transits, minor progressed aspects, major progressed aspects and other astrological conditions, and the proper attitude toward such astrological weather. It indicates how sympathies and antipathies work and how much importance to attribute to birthstones, numbers, names and environmental vibrations. Since the greatest enemy of fear and superstition is thorough understanding, this course explains in detail ceremonial magic, sorcery and witchcraft, and how to protect oneself against black magic of any kind. It shows how to avoid the influence of suggestion and inversive propaganda. *Imponderable Forces* gives a comprehensive survey of the wholesome pathway, and how to follow it.

1. How to Act Under Adverse Progressed Aspects 2. Sympathies and Antipathies 3. Ceremonial Magic 4. Sorcery and Witchcraft 5. Ritual and Religion 6. Press, Radio and Billboard 7. The Wholesome Pathway.

CS. 19, Organic Alchemy

The Universal Law of Soul Progression

$16.95   6x9   192pp

To live in harmony with nature's laws we must understand them. Humans are not set apart from other living things, but all life forms come under one uniform, universal law. This course explains how soul progress occurs; its original polarity, as indicated by its astrological signature, is energized by its ego and conditioned through pleasure and pain. Nature uses pleasure and pain, not as reward or punishment, but to inform the organism whether is it successfully adapting to its environment. Cs. XIX gives information about the problems and habits of other life forms, why there is no unpardonable sin, how the cosmos is managed and an outline of the general cosmic plan.

1. The Ceaseless Surge of Life 2. Every Life Form Manifests a Soul 3. The Universal Law of Soul Progression 4. The Uses of Pleasure and Pain 5. The Universal Law of Compensation 6. The Universal Moral Code 7. Discerning God's Great Plan

CS. 20, The Next Life

A Guide to Living Conditions on the Inner Plane

$16.95   6x9   272pp

Life on earth is but one phase of existence. Physical life constitutes necessary schooling so that the soul can function effectively on a higher plane where it will be less restricted. By understanding the nature of the life to come, the individual is better prepared to live this life and the next. Course XX gives a great deal of information about the conditions to be met and the activities of life after physical death. It tells about the various levels of the inner plane world, about the three methods of birth into the next life, about the influence of desires there, of the effect of sorrowing for those who have passed to the next life and how they may be helped, of the work to be done there and how education is handled. *The Next Life* is not only interesting, but the information it contains will be a highly valuable guide to anyone when they pass from the physical.

1. Turning the Dial to Inner Planes **2.** Properties of Life on The Inner Plane **3.** Birth Into the Next Life **4.** Astrological Influences in the Next Life **5.** Occupations of the Next Life **6.** Education and Progress in the Next Life **7.** Earth Bound Souls and the Astral Hells **8.** Domestic Relations of the Next Life **9.** Social Contacts and Amusements in the Next Life **10.** Through Astral and Spiritual to Celestial

---

CS. 21, Personal Alchemy

The Neophyte's Path to Spiritual Attainment

$16.95   6x9   272pp

The student who has gained the knowledge contained in the first 20 Brotherhood of Light courses is apt to decide to develop himself and his powers to the very best advantage. Consequently, *Personal Alchemy* gives precise instructions on the steps such an individual should take, and the order in which he should take them.

1. Three Things Every Neophyte Should Know **2.** The First Three Habits a Neophyte Should Adopt **3.** Avenues to Illumination **4.** Spiritual Hindrance by Family and Friends **5.** Spiritual Trends in Personal Conduct **6.** How to Keep Mentally and Physically Fit **7.** What to Eat When Mercury or Uranus is Afflicted **8.** What to Eat When Sun, Moon or Pluto is Afflicted **9.** What to Eat When Saturn, Jupiter or Neptune is Afflicted **10.** What to Eat When Venus or Mars is Afflicted.

To Order Brotherhood of Light Books:

Qty	#	Item	Price	Amt

Please include shipping & handling charges: $6.00 first item, $1.00 for each additional item.

Subtotal	
Shipping	
TOTAL	

YES ! Please send me a free catalog.

Ship To: _____

Address _____

City _____

State & Zip Code _____

Telephone _____

For ☐ **MasterCard** ☐ **Visa** Orders Only:

Card No. _____ Exp Date _____

Card Holder Signature _____

Send your check or money order to:
The Church of Light,
2341 Coral Street, Los Angeles, CA 90031-2916
(213)226-0453